Th

B

N

The Treasury of BABY NAMES

Compiled by Katie Martin-Doyle

Worth Press
Cambridge

This edition published in 2006 by
Advance Marketing (UK) Ltd
Bicester
Oxfordshire

ISBN 1 903025 28 1

First published 1999
by Ashwell Editions

Reprinted 2000, 2001, 2002, 2003, 2004, 2005

CIP catalogue records for this book are available from the British Library and the Library of Congress.

Compiled by Katie Martin-Doyle

Designed by
Playne Books Limited
Pembrokeshire

Editors
Janice Douglas
Gill Davies

Typeset in Times Roman

Printed in Finland by WS Bookwell

For Jane and Kit,
who named me.

It would be impossible to acknowledge personally all those who have contributed to this collection; the work of thousands lies behind the reference works and books that were consulted in its making, and I most sincerely thank them all.

CONTENTS

INTRODUCTION

Every society has its own systems and conventions of naming, and it is not the aim of this book or of this introduction to attempt to expound them all. However, what is perhaps most surprising about the world's naming systems is the number of similarities they have with each other. Most citizens of the world have bestowed upon them – at birth or shortly afterwards – both a name indicating the family into which they were born, and a name that is their own and by which they will be known throughout their lives.

Names confer identity, history, character, and a society's store of names reflects its history, religion, literature and culture. This book aims to explore the stock of names used in the English-speaking world. This has always been influenced by – in fact, it consists almost entirely of – names from other societies and cultures. The earliest of these imports were those brought by military invaders, including those from within Britain. During the Dark Ages attacks by warriors from the areas known today as Wales and Scotland introduced many of the ancient Celtic names still in use in Britain today. Similarly, the first truly 'English' names were those brought to Britain by the Anglo-Saxons, who used the German tradition of name formation consisting generally of two elements, each with a distinct meaning. These do not always appear to make sense; Edgar, for example, derives from two elements meaning 'prosperous' and 'spear'.

A previous occupation, by the Roman armies of Julius Caesar, had not left any specific names behind, although the advanced Roman system of naming did leave its mark. By the time of their invasion of Britain the Romans had developed a three-name system. The first was a personal name, of which there were very few to choose from. The second name was the family name and usually ended -ius or, for women, with the feminine ending -a. The third part was a cognomen, or nickname, often first given to an ancestor. So, taking the great Roman emperor Gaius Julius Caesar as an example, Gaius was his own name, Julius his family name and Caesar his cognomen, in this case derived from his rank. Although this system eventually broke down in Rome, it influenced naming systems around the world because of the large extent of the Roman empire, and it remains the basic pattern for many societies today.

Names derived from the mythologies of Greece and Rome first appeared in Britain in various altered forms, usually as the names of early saints. For example, St Denis's name derived ultimately from Dionysius. The original Greek and Roman forms became increasingly popular as the classical myths became more widely known.

With the advent of Christianity to Britain biblical names also became popular. These usually had Roman Catholic connections and included the names of early Christian martyrs and saints. They were mostly Hebrew in origin, but occasionally had Aramaic, Etruscan, Egyptian or, in the case of New Testament names, Greek roots. After the establishment of the Church of England during the Reformation, Catholic names fell out of favour, especially in Puritan England, and other names were taken from the Bible, especially from the Old Testament. The first British settlers of America, who were strongly Puritan, had a notable preference for these.

One of the most significant influxes of names into the English-speaking world came as a result of the Norman invaders who arrived from Gaul in 1066. Most of these were themselves largely of Germanic origin, being descended from the Franks, a Germanic tribe that migrated to Gaul in the 4th century. Within a century of their arrival in Britain, William, the name borne by their commander, William the Conqueror, had become the most popular masculine name in Britain. A successful colonisation indeed. A glance through this book will reveal just how many names in common use today date from this time.

The trend of adopting the names of admired historical or public figures has survived from the success of William in 1066 into our own times, when an actress in an Australian soap opera made Kylie one of the most popular girl's names in the English-speaking world.

Fascinating fashions in names can be traced. At the end of the 19th century, for instance, there was a craze for naming girls after flowers. A glance at the tables of popular names included in this book shows the popularity of Lily, Violet, Rose, Ivy and Daisy. Over the years flower names – and associated ones such as Fleur and Flora – have never faded entirely from favour, and recently new ones including Fern and Poppy have sprung into vogue.

Today naming has taken a fanciful turn. Although the old and traditional names are still widely used throughout the English-speaking world and, indeed, have undergone a revival in recent years, there is an ever-greater tendency to invent names, or respell existing names. The increasing dominance of the international media and the extensive merging of cultures can lead to a swift adoption of a name around the world. We have almost reached a time when a name can no longer be said to 'belong' to any one society. In Norway and Sweden the authorities have become so alarmed at the erosion of the traditional northern European names and at the eccentricity of certain modern imports that their Ministries of Ecclesiastical Affairs have drawn up a list of acceptable names, from which all parents are required to choose their child's name. Any name not listed, or any variant in spelling not included, requires permission from the Ministry, or the parents face a stiff fine.

This runs counter to the prevalent trend in the United States, and to a lesser extent in Britain, where the more fanciful a spelling, the more original a combination of elements, the better. Naming has always been, and no doubt will remain, a fluid art, partly concerned with continuing ancient traditions and partly with striking out in new territory. Often prospective parents invest a tremendous amount of time and thought in the naming of their imminent arrival. Even if they finally agree on a name, they may change their minds once the baby is born, feeling that he or she just does not suit the name they had picked.

There are so many factors to take into account before bestowing on a child a name that he or she will bear for the rest of their lives. Is a much-loved parent, grandparent, relative or friend to be honoured by choosing their name? Might the name be shortened in the playground to a form the parents dislike? If a sweet or playful choice, will it grow with the child, suiting a fifty year-old as much as a toddler? Some children may rejoice in an unconventional name – such as Dakota, Ireland or Panda – that marks them out in the world of Emmas or Andrews, but others can feel it more as a bane than a blessing. Perhaps the safest course in such cases is to provide a second, plainer name, which can be used if the child prefers.

Whereas traditional names are timeless, giving no clues to the bearer's age, certain names are so closely associated with a celebrity, television series or song that they identify the owner very closely as a child of a specific era. A significant number of Jolyons and Fleurs, for example, were born during or just after the television screening of *The Forsyte Saga*, while Beatles hits gave rise to a flood of Michelles and Judes. Similarly, some names are more prevalent in certain social groups then in others, thus revealing the bearer's social background – or sometimes the parents' social aspirations. Indeed, a child's name often says more about the parents than about the child itself. Nevertheless, while there are all sorts of considerations to bear in mind when selecting a name, it would be a pity if they came to cloud what is above all a joyful, miraculous and momentous event.

No reference book of the stock of names can hope to be comprehensive: it can only hope to serve as a useful, enlightening guide. This book seeks to explore the origin and meaning of each name listed, and where relevant any information about its history and associations. While focusing on the treasury of names used within the English-speaking world, it also includes the most popular Hindu and Arabic names, and other names from around the world that are now in regular use in the Western world. In assembling such a wide and inspiring selection, its intention is to enhance the fun and enjoyment in deciding on a baby's name, and to add to the sense of excitement that builds as the long-awaited day draws near.

Calendar of Feast Days

This calendar includes saints regarded by both the eastern and western churches.

January

1
Justin, Basil, Martina

2
Caspar, Stephanie, Abel

3
Frances, Daniel, Genevieve

4
Gregory, Christiana, Benedicta, Roger

5
Edward, Simon, Emily (Amelia), Paula

6
Andrew, Balthasar, Raphaela

7
Felix, Lucian, Crispin

8
Laurence, Lucien

9
Adrian, Julian, Peter

10
Dermot, Gregory, William

11
Honorata (Honora), Brandan

12
Benedict, Tatiana, Tania

13
Mungo, Veronica, Yvette, Godfrey

14
Malachi, Mungo, Felix, Hilary

15
Paul, Isidore, Micah

16
Mark (Marcellus), Henry, Priscilla, Otto

17
Antony, Rosaline

18
Susanna, Peter, Christine, Margaret, Priscilla, Dermot

19
Henry, Marius, Martha, Gerontius, Pia

20
Fabian, Sebastian

21
Alban, Agnes

22
Dominic, Vincent

23
John, Raymond, Gladys, Bernard

24
Timothy, Vera

25
Paul, Joel

26
Aubrey, Conan, Paula

27
John, Angela, Julian, Marius, Theodoric

28
Cyril, Peter

29
Francis

30
Sebastian, Hyacinth, Martina, Matthias

31
Julius, Aidan, John, Mark, Louisa, Marcella,

February

1
Henry, Ignatius, Brigid

2
Laurence, Catherine, Joan (Jane), Mary

3
Blaise, Oscar, Oliver, Laurence, Margaret

4
Andrew, Gilbert, Joseph, Joan, Nicholas, Isidore

5
Paul, Agatha, Adelaide, Joachim, Matthias, Caius

6
Titus, Dorothy, Luke, Gerald

7
Richard, Theodore, Juliana, Moses, Luke

8
John, Stephen, Sebastian, Isaiah

9
Cyril, Apollonia

10
William, Hyacinth

11
Benedict, Lucius, Mary, Gregory, Victoria

12
Antony, Eulalia, Marina, Alexis, Julian

13
Stephen, Beatrice, Katherine

14
Abraham, Cyril, Valentine

15
Claud, Georgia, Sigfrid, Jordan

16
Gilbert, Juliana, Philippa, Samuel, Jeremy

17
Finan, Fintan, Julian, Reginald

18
Flavian, Simeon

19
Conrad, Boniface

20
Peter, Amy, Mildred

21
Noel, Robert, George

22
Peter, Margaret

23
Peter, Martha, Lazarus, Milo

24
Matthias (Matthew), Lucius, Adela

25
Claud, Ethelbert, Walburga

26
Leo, Victor, Isabel, Alexander

27
Augustus, Gabriel, Leander, Ann

28
Oswald, Antonia, Louisa

29
Hilary (Hilarus), Roman

March

1
Christopher, David, Antonia, Roger, Felix

2
Chad, Henry, Agnes

3
Aelred, Camilla, Marcia, Owen, Anselm

4
Casimir, Christopher, Adrian, Peter, Lucius, Humbert

5
Kieran, Teophilus, Virgil

6
Cyril, Colette, Felicity, Perpetua

7
Jermyn, Thomas, Paul

8
Felix, John, Julian, Beata, Humphrey, Stephen

9
Dominic, Gregory, Catherine, Frances

10
John, Anastasia, Caius

11
Angus, John, Teresa, Constantine

12
Gregory, Maximilian, Paul, Simon, Seraphina, Bernard, Fina

13
Gerald, Roderick, Euphrasia, Sanchia, Patricia, Solomon

14
Arnold, Matilda, Eustace

15
Clement, William, Louisa, Zachary

16
Gabriel, Herbert, Isaac, Julian, Paul, Abraham

17
Joseph, Patrick, Gertrude

18
Christian, Cyril, Edward, Alexander, Narcissus

19
Andrew, Joseph

20
Baptist, Cuthbert, Herbert, Martin, Alexandra, Claudia, Sebastian

21
Benedict, Nicholas, Cornelia

22
Basil, Nicholas, Zachary, Catherine, Leah

23
Joseph, Sibyl, Aquila

24
Gabriel, Bertha, Katherine, Simon

25
James, Lucy, Mary, Richard, Harold

26
Basil, Felix, William, Emmanuel

27
John, Rupert, Augusta, Lydia

28
John, Gwendolen

29
Jonah, Mark, Jane

30
John, Peter

31
Benjamin, Guy, Jane, Aldo, Amos

April

1
Gilbert, Ludovic, Hugh, Catherine,

2
Francis, John, Margaret, Mary, Theodosia, Constantine

3
Pancras, Richard, Irene

4
Ambrose, Benedict, Isidore, Tierney

5
Gillian, Gerald, Vincent,

6
William, Catherine, Marcia

7
Alexander, Ashley, Herman, Ralph, Ursula, George, Llewellyn

8
Walter, Julia

9
Hugh, Mary, Monica

10
Mark, Terence, Michael, Ezekiel

11
Leo, Philip, Gemma, Isaac

12
Angelo, Zeno, Damian

13
Edmund, John, Ida

14
Caradoc, Justin, Lydwina, Bernard, Eustace

15
Anastasia, Sylvester

16
Benedict, Magnus, Bernadette

17
Robert, Stephen, Clare, Elias

18
Mary, Andrew, James

19
James, Leo

20
Robert, Simon, Agnes

21
Anselm, Conrad, Theodore
Simeon

22
Bartholomew, Theodore

23
George, Giles, Helen, Gerard

24
Egbert, Euphrasia, Ives

25
Mark, Robert, William

26
Clarence, Peter, Stephen

27
Anthony, Peter, Zita

28
Louis, Paul, Theodora, Patrick

29
Hugh, Joseph, Peter, Wilfrid,
Robert

30
Benedict, James, Miles, Catherine,
Marian, Rosamund, Sophia

May

1
James, Peregrine, Philip, Isidora,
Patience, Bertha, Joseph
Sigismund, Walburga

2
Zoe

3
Alexander, Aylwin, Maura, Viola,
Philip, Timothy

4
Walter, Antonia, Monica, Ethelred,
Florian, Silvanus

5
Hilary, Judith, Angelo

6
Antony, Benedicta, Prudence

7
John, Flavia, Augustus, Giselle

8
Michael, Peter, Victor, Benedict,
Boniface

9
Gregory, Nicholas, Gerontius

10
Isidore, Beatrice, Job

11
Francis, Walter, Aloysius, James

12
Ignatius, John, Flavia, Jane, Dominic,
Gemma

13
Andrew, Robert, Imelda

14
Giles, Michael, Petronilla, Mary

15
Nicholas, Magdalen, Bertha, Hilary, Rupert, Dionysia

16
Brendan, Simon, Maxima, Peregrine

17
Bruno, Pascal, Basilla

18
Eric, Felix, Claudia, Julitta, Alexandra, Camilla

19
Dunstan, Ivor, Celestine

20
Bernadine, Orlando, Ethelbert

21
Andrew, Daphne, Theobald, Theophilus

22
John, Peter, Julia, Rita

23
William, Ivo

24
David, Philip, Simeon, Vincent, Susanna (Susan), Patrick, Joanna

25
Gregory, Madeleine, Mary, Sophie, Urban, Dionysius

26
Augustine (Austin), Philip, Eve, Mariana, Lambert, Zachary

27
Bede, Julius, Frederick

28
Bernard, Margaret, Augustine (Austin)

29
Richard, Mary, Theodosia, William

30
Ferdinand, Laurence, Joan, Felix, Hubert, Isaac

31
Angela, Camilla, Petronilla

June

1
Conrad, John, Angela, Simon, Theobald

2
Nicholas, Stephen, Blandina, Eugene, Elmo (Erasmus)

3
Cecil, Charles, Claudius, Kevin, Clotilda, Olive, Isaac, Matthias, Paula

4
Francis, Cornelius, Walter, Vincentia

5
Boniface, Ferdinand, Niall, Marcia, Franco, Valeria

6
Bertrand, Norbert, Pauline, Valeria, Claud (Claudius), Felicia, Philip

7
Robert, Ann

8
John, William, Calliope, Melania

9
Columba, Vincent, Ann, Diana, Amata, Cecilia, Richard

10
John, Margaret, Olive, Zachary

11
Barnabas, Peter, Flora, Paula, Fortunatus

12
John, Stephen, Antonia, Christian, Leo, Humphrey

13
Antony, Aquilina, Lucien

14
Basil, Valerius

15
Vitus (or Guy), Germaine, Alice, Yolanda

16
John, Justina, Julitta, Aurelian

17
Adolph, Botolph, Harvey, Teresa, Emily, Manuel, Sanchia

18
Elizabeth, Marina, Guy, Fortunatus, Mark

19
Gervase, Humphrey, Gillian (Juliana), Bruno, Odo

20
Francis, Thomas, Michelina (Michelle), John, Alban

21
Aloysius, Demetria, Lazarus, Ralph, Terence

22
Alban, Innocent, John

23
Thomas, Etheldreda (Audrey)

24
John, Ivan, Bartholomew

25
Guy, William, Febronia, Lucy, Solomon

26
John, Paul

27
Samson, Madeleine, Ferdinand

28
John, Irene, Marcella, Paul

29
Paul, Peter, Emma, Judith, Salome

30
Bertram, Godwin, Paul, Theobald, Lucina

July

1
Derek, Theobald, Aaron, Simeon, Theodoric

2
Otto, Mary, Reginald, Marcia

3
Aaron, Anatole, Julius, Leo, Bernardine

4
Andrew, Henry, Martin, Bertha, Aurelia, Odo, Ulric

5
Antony, Michael, Edna, Philomena, Grace, Gwen (or Blanche), Zoe

6
Romulus, Dominica, Isiah

7
Cyril, Peter, Prosper, Ralph, Hedda

8
Eugene, Isabel (Elizabeth), Veronica, Adrian, Aquila, Arnold, Edgar, Morwenna, Priscilla, Raymond

9
Adrian, Godfrey, Thomas, Jane, Alberic, Barnabas, Cornelius, Everild, Jerome, Nicholas, Veronica

10
Amelia, Rufina, Emmanuel, Maurice

11
Oliver, Olga

12
David, John, Veronica, Fortunatus, Jason, Monica

13
James, Silas, Thomas, Eugene, Joel, Mildred

14
Bonaventure, Humbert, Ulric

15
Donald, Henry, Swithin, Angelina, Edith, Baldwin, David

16
Mary, Eustace, Milo, Valentine

17
Alexis, Kenelm, Antoinette, Leo, Nahum

18
Emlyn, Frederick, Bruno, Camillus, Edith, Marina

19
Ambrose, Vincent, Justa, Rufina, Aurea, Jerome

20
Elias, Jerome, Margaret, Paula, Elijah, Marina, Silas, Silvanus

21
Laurence, Victor, Julia, Angelina, Constantine, Daniel

22
Mary Magdalene, Theophilus, Joseph

23
John, Joan, Romola, Susanna (Anna), Balthasar, Caspar (Gaspar)

24
Boris, Francis, Antoinette, Charlotte, Christina, Christiana, Declan, Felicia

25
Christopher, James, Rudolph, Valentina, Thea

26
William, Anne

27
Joyce, Lucy, Berthold, Celestine, Natalia, Rudolph, Theobald

28
Antony, Samson, Victor

29
Olaf, Martha, Beatrice, Felix, Flora, Lucilla, Urban

30
Everard, Julitta

31
Ignatius, Helen

August

1
Peter, Charity, Faith, Hope, Justin, Kenneth, Eiluned

2
Basil, Stephen, Alfreda, Alphonsus

3
Augustine, Peter, Stephen, Lydia, Nicodemus, Gamaliel

4
Dominic, Perpetua

5
Thomas, Mary, Afra (Aphra), Oswald

6
Peter, Octavian

7
Albert, Claudia

8
John, Joan, Myron

9
Oswald, Samuel

10
Laurence, Asteria, Gerontius (or Geraint), Philomena

11
Alexander, Peter, Philomena, Susanna (Susan), Lelia

12
Clare (Clara), Murtagh

13
William, Gertrude, Hippolytus

14
Antony, Athanasia, Marcellus

15
Stephen, Mary, Napoleon, Stanislaus

16
Joachim, Serena, Titus

17
Clare, Hyacinth, Benedicta, Cecilia, Myron, Septimus

18
Beatrice, Helen, Milo, Evan

19
John, Louis, Emily, Sarah, Magnus, Timothy, Thecla

20
Bernard, Oswin, Herbert, Philibert, Ronald, Samuel

21
Abraham, Bernard, Jane

22
John, William, Andrew, Hippolytus, Sigfrid, Timothy

23
Eugene, Philip, Claudius, Eleazar, Zacchaeus

24
Bartholomew, Nathaniel, Owen, Emily, Alice, Joan (Jane)

25
Gregory, Louis, Joan, Patricia, Lucilla

26
Adrian, Thomas, Elizabeth, Elias

27
Amyas, David, Joseph, Margaret, Gabriel, Hugh, Rufus

28
Augustine, Julian, Moses, Adelina, Alexander, Vivian

29
John, Richard, Candida, Sabina, Basilla, Medericus (Merry)

30
Felix, Rose

31
Aidan, Raymond

September

1
Giles, Michael, Joan, Verena, Anna, Augustus, Gideon, Joshua

2
Stephen, William, Adeline, Margaret, René

3
Anthony, Phoebe, Dorothy, Euphemia, Gabriel, Gregory, Simeon

4
Boniface, Hermione, Rebecca, Rose, Rosalia, Candida, Ida, Marcellus, Moses

5
Laurence, Urban, Vitus

6
Bertrand, Beata, Magnus, Zacharia

7
Ralph, Regina, Eustace

8
Adrian, Mary, Natalia, Sergius

9
Isaac, Kieran, Peter, Wilfrida, Louise, Seraphina

10
Ambrose, Charles, Nicholas, Dominica, Aubert, Candida, Isabel

11
Daniel, John, Hyacinth, Theodora

12
Guy, Mary

13
Philip, Roland, Amatus

14
John, Louis, Cormac

15
John, Catherine, Mary, Roland, Albinus

16
Cornelius, Cyprian, Edith, Eugenia, Euphemia, Ludmilla, Ninian, Lucy, Victor

17
Francis, Lambert, Hildegard, Ariadne, Columba, Narcissus, Justin

18
Joseph, Irene, Sophia

19
Theodore, Emily, Mary, Constantia, Susanna

20
Eustace, Vincent, Philippa, Candida

21
Laurence, Matthew, Agatha, Maura, Jonah

22
Felix, Maurice, Thomas, Jonas

23
Adam, Linus, Helen, Thekla

24
Gerard, Robert, Mary

25
Finbar, Vincent, Aurelia, Herman, Albert, Sergius

26
Cornelius, Noel, Cyprian, Justina, René

27
Cosmo, Damian, Delphine, Adolphus, Caius, Cosmas, Terence

28
Laurence, Wenceslas, Bernadine, Solomon

29
Michael, René

30
Francis, Gregory, Jerome, Otto, Sophia, Simon

October

1
Christopher, Julia, Francis, Nicholas

2
Angela, Theophilus

3
Thomas, Teresa, Gerard

4
Francis, Aurea, Berenice

5
Placid, Felicia, Flora

6
Bruno, Faith, Mary, Magnus, Aurea

7
Matthew, Justina, Mary, Augustus, Julia, Mark

8
Bridget, Laurentia, Margaret, Sergius, Simeon

9
Denis, John, Louis, Abraham, Dionysius, Gunther

10
Daniel, Francis, Samuel

11
Alexander, John, Kenneth, Mary, Bruno, Juliana, Canice

12
Edwin, Maximilian, Wilfred, Cyprian

13
Edward, Gerald, Magdalen, Maurice, Theophilus

14
Dominic

15
Leonard, Aurelia, Teresa, Willa

16
Bertrand, Gerard, Baldwin, Hedwig

17
Richard, Margaret, Rudolph

18
Luke, Gwendoline (Gwen), Candida, Blanche

19
Peter, Philip, Cleopatra, Lucius, Laura

20
Andrew, John, Irene, Adelina, Martha

21
Peter, Celine, Ursula

22
Philip, Mary

23
Ignatius, John, Josephine, Bartholomew

24
Martin, Raphael, Antony, Septimus

25
Crispin, Isidore, Thaddeus, Balthasar, Dorcas (or Tabitha), George, Theodoric

26
Lucian, Albinus, Cuthbert, Damian

27
Caleb, Vincent, Sabina, Antonia

28
Jude, Simon, Anastasia, Eunice, Godwin

29
Maximilian, Valentine, Narcissus, Terence

30
Jermyn, John, Dorothy, Alphonsus, Artemas, Marcellus, Zenobia

31
Quentin

November

1
Julian, Mary, Cledwyn

2
Ambrose, John, Maura, Tobias

3
Hubert, Ida, Silvia, Winifred, Malachy, Valentine

4
Charles, Emery, Frances

5
Martin, Zachary, Bertilla, Elizabeth, Cosmo

6
Leonard, Helen Margaret

7
Engelbert, Ernest, Peter, Carina, Florentius, Gertrude, Rufus

8
Geoffrey, Godrey

9
George, Theodore

10
Andrew, Florence, Tryphena

11
Bartholomew, Joseph, Martin, Theodore

12
Gabriel, Martin, Matthew, René

13
Nicholas, Eugene, Stanislaus

14
John, Laurence

15
Albert, Leopold, Roger

16
Edmund, Lewis, Agnes, Gertrude, Margaret

17
Denis, Gregory, Hugh, Hilda, Theodora, Victoria, Zacchaeus, Dionysius

18
Paul, Peter, Constant, Odo

19
Crispin, Elizabeth

20
Edmund, Felix, Octavius, Silvester

21
Albert, Mary, Rufus

22
Cecily (Cecilia), Philemon

23
Clement, Gregory, Felicity, Lucretia, Margaret

24
Flora, Mary, John, Thaddeus

25
Catherine, Elizabeth, Joyce, Moses

26
Conrad, John, Leonard, Silvester, Peter

27
Fergus, Leonard, Virgil, Bernadine, James

28
James, Stephen

29
Cuthbert, Frederick, Blaise, Brendan

30
Andrew, Justina, Maura

December

1
Alexander, Edmund, Hugh, Natalie, Nahum, Ralph

2
Adam, Vivienne, Aurelia, Bibiana (Viviana)

3
Edward, Francis, Claudius, Xavier, Jason, Lucius

4
Osmund, Peter, Ada, Barbara, Bernard, Osmond

5
John, Nicholas, Bartholomew

6
Nicholas, Denise, Abraham, Dionysia, Gertrude, Tertius

7
Ambrose, Martin, Urban, Josepha

8
Lucina, Mary

9
Cyprian, Julian, Delphine, Valeria, Peter

10
Brian, Sidney, Eulalia, Gregory,Julia

11
Daniel, Jerome,, Franco

12
Antony, Denise, Agatha, Cormac, Dionysia

13
John, Jane, Lucy, Odile, Ottilie, Aubert, Judoc (Judocus, Josse), Lucia, Ottillia (Odilia)

14
Conrad, John

15
Paul, Christiana, Mary

16
Sebastian, Adelaide, Mary, Adelaide, Albina, Azaria

17
Ignatius, John, Florian, Lazarus, Olympias

18
Rufus

19
Timothy, Urban, Fausta, Thea

20
Dominic, Ignatius

21
Peter, Thomas, Esther

22
Judith, Adam

23
Nicholas, Victoria

24
Gregory, Adele, Irmina, Adam, Adela, Eve

25
Emmanuel, Noel, Anastasia, Eugenia

26
Denis, Stephen, Christina, Dionysius, Vincentia

27
John, Fabriola, Theodore

28
Antony, Francis, Theophila

29
David, Thomas, William, Marcellus

30
Eugene, Rayner, Margaret, Sabinus

31
Silvester, Catherine, Melania, Columba, Cornelius, Fabian, Sextus

UK
Top 50
Boys' Names

Top 50 first names for boys in the British Isles

UK Boys	1	2
1900	William	John
1925	John	William
1950	David	John
1975	Stephen	Mark
1993	Daniel	Matthew
1998	Jack	Thomas
2000	Jack	Thomas
2001	Jack	Thomas
2002	Jack	Joshua
2003	Jack	Joshua
2004	Jack	Joshua

New names and fun combinations that celebrities in the British Isles have used for their sons include:
Brooklyn and Romeo
(David and Victoria Beckham),
Elijah Bob Patricius Guggi Q (Bono),
Lennon (Liam Gallagher and Patsy Kensit),
Rolan (Marc Bolan) and
Zowie Bowie (David Bowie).

US
Top 50
Boys' Names

Top 50 first names for boys in America

US Boys	1	2
1900	John	William
1925	Robert	John
1950	Robert	Michael
1975	Michael	Jason
1993	Michael	Christopher
1998	Michael	Jacob
2000	Jacob	Michael
2001	Jacob	Michael
2002	Ethan	Caleb
2003	Jacob	Michael
2004	Jacob	Aidan

New names and fun combinations that celebrities in the USA have used for their sons include:
Dylan Jagger and **Brandon Thomas**
(Pamela Anderson and Tommy Lee),
Prince Jackson, **Prince Michael** plus
Prince Michael II (Michael Jackson),
Rocco (Madonna),
River Jude (Demi Moore and Bruce Willis)
and **Sage Moon Blood** (Sylvester Stallone).

UK Boys	3	4	5	6	7	8
1900	George	Thomas	Charles	Frederick	Arthur	James
1925	George	James	Ronald	Robert	Kenneth	Frederick
1950	Peter	Michael	Alan	Robert	Stephen	Paul
1975	Paul	Andrew	David	Richard	Matthew	Daniel
1993	James	Christopher	Thomas	Joshua	Adam	Michael
1998	James	Daniel	Joshua	Matthew	Samuel	Callum
2000	James	Joshua	Daniel	Harry	Samuel	Joseph
2001	Joshua	James	Daniel	Harry	Samuel	Joseph
2002	Thomas	Daniel	James	Matthew	Lewis	Luke
2003	Thomas	James	Daniel	Oliver	Benjamin	Samuel
2004	Thomas	James	Daniel	Samuel	Oliver	William

US Boys	3	4	5	6	7	8
1900	Charles	Robert	Joseph	James	George	Samuel
1925	William	James	Charles	Richard	George	Donald
1950	James	John	David	William	Thomas	Richard
1975	Matthew	Brian	Christopher	David	John	James
1993	Matthew	Joshua	Andrew	James	John	Nicholas
1998	Matthew	Nicholas	Joshua	Christopher	Brandon	Austin
2000	Matthew	Joshua	Christopher	Nicholas	Andrew	Joseph
2001	Matthew	Joshua	Christopher	Nicholas	Andrew	Joseph
2002	Aidan	Jacob	Dylan	Tyler	Andrew	Ryan
2003	Joshua	Matthew	Ethan	Joseph	Andrew	Christopher
2004	Ethan	Ryan	Matthew	Michael	Tyler	Joshua

UK Boys	9	10	11	12	13	14
1900	Albert	Ernest	Robert	Henry	Alfred	Sidney
1925	Thomas	Albert	Eric	Edward	Arthur	Charles
1950	Brian	Graham	Philip	Anthony	Colin	Christopher
1975	Christopher	Darren	Michael	James	Robert	Simon
1993	Luke	Andrew	Benjamin	Samuel	Stephen	Robert
1998	Joseph	Jordan	Connor	Ryan	Luke	William
2000	Matthew	Callum	Luke	William	Lewis	Oliver
2001	Matthew	Lewis	Luke	Oliver	William	Benjamin
2002	Ryan	Ben	Joseph	Samuel	Adam	Callum
2003	William	Joseph	Harry	Matthew	Lewis	Luke
2004	Benjamin	Joseph	Harry	Matthew	Lewis	Ethan

US Boys	9	10	11	12	13	14
1900	Thomas	Arthur	Harry	Edward	Henry	Walter
1925	Joseph	Edward	Thomas	David	Frank	Harold
1950	Gary	Charles	Ronald	Dennis	Steven	Kenneth
1975	Jeffrey	Daniel	Steven	Eric	Robert	Scott
1993	Justin	David	Daniel	Ryan	Steven	Robert
1998	Tyler	Zachary	Andrew	Joseph	Daniel	Jonathan
2000	Daniel	Tyler	William	Ryan	Brandon	John
2001	Daniel	William	Anthony	David	Tyler	John
2002	Logan	Austin	Aaron	Joshua	Matthew	Zachary
2003	Daniel	Nicholas	William	Anthony	David	Tyler
2004	Nicholas	Connor	Zachary	Andrew	Dylan	Jack

UK Boys	15	16	17	18	19	20
1900	Joseph	Harold	Harry	Frank	Walter	Herbert
1925	Leslie	Sidney	Frank	Peter	Dennis	Joseph
1950	Geoffrey	William	James	Keith	Terence	Barry
1975§	Jason	Stuart	Neil	Lee	Jonathan	Ian
1993	Jamie	Aaron	Jonathan	Alexander	Joseph	Ryan
1998	Harr	Benjamin	Lewis	George	Alexander	Oliver
2000	Ryan	Benjamin	George	Liam	Jordan	Adam
2001	Callum	George	Adam	Ryan	Jake	Alexander
2002	Harry	Oliver	William	Liam	Benjamin	Jordan
2003	Ethan	George	Adam	Alfie	Callum	Alexander
2004	Luke	Charlie	George	Callum	Alexander	Mohammed

US Boys	15	16	17	18	19	20
1900	Louis	Paul	Ralph	Carl	Frank	Raymond
1925	Arthur	Jack	Paul	Kenneth	Walter	Raymond
1950	Joseph	Mark	Daniel	Paul	Donald	Gregory
1975	Andrew	Mark	Aaron	Benjamin	Kevin	Sean
1993	Joseph	Zachary	Jonathan	William	Kyle	Tyler
1998	John	William	David	Ryan	Anthony	James
2000	Zachary	David	Anthony	James	Justin	Alexander
2001	Ryan	Zachary	Ethan	Brandon	James	Alexander
2002	Blake	Nicholas	Noah	Hayden	Brayden	Gabriel
2003	Alexander	Ryan	John	James	Zachary	Brandon
2004	Jayden	Logan	Caden	Caleb	Alexander	Nathan

UK Boys	21	22	23	24	25	26
1900	Edward	Percy	Richard	Samuel	Leonard	Stanley
1925	Alan	Stanley	Ernest	Harold	Norman	Raymond
1950	Malcolm	Richard	Ian	Derek	Roger	Raymond
1975	Nicholas	Gary	Craig	Martin	John	Carl
1993	David	Liam	Jack	Richard	William	Jordan
1998	Adam	Jake	Liam	Michael	Nathan	Kieran
2000	Alexander	Jake	Connor	Cameron	Nathan	Kieran
2001	Ethan	Liam	Cameron	Connor	Jordan	Mohammed
2002	George	Connor	Nathan	Jake	Jamie	Cameron
2003	Ryan	Mohammed	Cameron	Connor	Charlie	Ben
2004	Ryan	Dylan	Jacob	Adam	Ben	Jake

US Boys	21	22	23	24	25	26
1900	Francis	Frederick	Albert	Benjamin	David	Harold
1925	Carl	Albert	Henry	Harry	Francis	Ralph
1950	Larry	Lawrence	Timothy	Alan	Edward	Gerald
1975	Jonathan	Timothy	Ryan	Joseph	Adam	Richard
1993	Jacob	Brian	Brandon	Eric	Sean	Cody
1998	Justin	Dylan	Alexander	Kyle	Jordan	Robert
2000	Jonathan	Christian	Austin	Dylan	Ethan	Benjamin
2001	Dylan	Justin	Jonathan	Christian	Austin	Samuel
2002	Elijah	Justin	Alexander	Benjamin	Cole	Addison
2003	Jonathan	Justin	Christian	Dylan	Samuel	Austin
2004	Noah	William	Jackson	Joseph	Christopher	James

UK Boys	27	28	29	30	31	32
1900	Reginald	Francis	Fred	Cecil	Wilfred	Horace
1925	Leonard	Alfred	Harry	Donald	Reginald	Roy
1950	Kenneth	Andrew	Trevor	Martin	Kevin	Ronald
1975	Philip	Kevin	Benjamin	Peter	Wayne	Adam
1993	Craig	Mark	Nicholas	Ashley	Nathan	Lee
1998	Jacob	Ben	Cameron	Aaron	Bradley	Christopher
2000	Mohammed	Jamie	Jacob	Michael	Ben	Ethan
2001	Jamie	Dylan	Nathan	Jacob	Ben	Charlie
2002	Charlie	Ethan	Michael	Alexander	Kieran	Aaron
2003	Jacob	Dylan	Liam	Nathan	Jake	Jamie
2004	Alfie	Connor	Cameron	Liam	Nathan	Harvey

US Boys	27	28	29	30	31	32
1900	Howard	Fred	Richard	Clarence	Herbert	Jacob
1925	Eugene	Howard	Lawrence	Louis	Alan	Norman
1950	Douglas	George	Frank	Patrick	Anthony	Philip
1975	Paul	Jeremy	Thomas	Charles	Joshua	William
1993	Anthony	Thomas	Kevin	Alexander	Jordan	Timothy
1998	Christian	Brian	Eric	Samuel	Jose	Steven
2000	Noah	Samuel	Robert	Jose	Kevin	Nathan
2001	Benjamin	Noah	Kevin	Jose	Logan	Robert
2002	Connor	Christian	Nathan	Tristan	Evan	Ian
2003	Jose	Benjamin	Nathan	Logan	Kevin	Gabriel
2004	Daniel	Benjamin	Anthony	Cameron	Austin	Evan

UK Boys	33	34	35	36	37	38
1900	Cyril	David	Norman	Eric	Victor	Edgar
1925	Derek	Henry	Geoffrey	David	Gordon	Herbert
1950	Leslie	Charles	George	Thomas	Nigel	Stuart
1975	Anthony	Alan	Graham	Adrian	Colin	Scott
1993	Oliver	Shaun	Scott	Callum	Lewis	Paul
1998	Charlie	Mohammed	Jamie	Brandon	Robert	Kyle
2000	Charlie	Bradley	Brandon	Aaron	Max	Dylan
2001	Michael	Keiron	Max	Bradley	Brandon	Owen
2002	Dylan	Jacob	Alex	Kyle	Owen	Christopher
2003	Owen	Max	Tyler	Harvey	Kieran	Michael
2004	Jamie	Owen	Tyler	Max	Louis	Kyle

US Boys	33	34	35	36	37	38
1900	Ernest	Jack	Herman	Philip	Stanley	Donald
1925	Gerald	Herbert	Fred	Earl	Philip	Stanley
1950	Raymond	Bruce	Jeffrey	Brian	Peter	Frederick
1975	Peter	Nathan	Todd	Douglas	Gregory	Patrick
1993	Benjamin	Corey	Adam	Jeffrey	Aaron	Richard
1998	Kevin	Noah	Thomas	Benjamin	Cameron	Nathan
2000	Cameron	Thomas	Hunter	Jordan	Kyle	Caleb
2001	Nathan	Thomas	Cameron	Hunter	Gabriel	Caleb
2002	Gavin	Brandon	Ashton	Jared	Mason	Adam
2003	Robert	Noah	Caleb	Thomas	Jordan	Hunter
2004	Luke	Gavin	Brayden	Brandon	Christian	John

UK Boys	**39**	**40**	**41**	**42**	**43**	**44**
1900	Leslie	Bertie	Edwin	Donald	Benjamin	Hector
1925	Walter	Cyril	Jack	Richard	Douglas	Maurice
1950	Edward	Gordon	Roy	Dennis	Neil	Laurence
1975	Timothy	Barry	William	Dean	Jamie	Nathan
1993	Ben	John	Edward	Anthony	Jake	Charles
1998	David	Andrew	Charles	Reece	Edward	Owen
2000	Kyle	Reece	Robert	Christopher	David	Edward
2001	Louis	Aaron	Tyler	Kyle	Reece	Edward
2002	Sam	David	Brandon	Bradley	Reece	Max
2003	Kyle	Brandon	Alex	Louis	Aaron	Bradley
2004	Michael	Kieran	Aaron	Bradley	Edward	Brandon

US Boys	**39**	**40**	**41**	**42**	**43**	**44**
1900	Earl	Elmer	Leon	Nathan	Eugene	Floyd
1925	Daniel	Leonard	Marvin	Frederick	Anthony	Samuel
1950	Roger	Carl	Dale	Walter	Christopher	Martin
1975	Shane	Kenneth	Edward	Nicholas	Chad	Anthony
1993	Nathan	Travis	Charles	Derek	Patrick	Mark
1998	Sean	Hunter	Caleb	Connor	Aaron	Ethan
2000	Jason	Logan	Aaron	Eric	Gabriel	Brian
2001	Jordan	Kyle	Jason	Aaron	Eric	Luis
2002	Christopher	Seth	Bailey	Kyle	Nathaniel	Michael
2003	Cameron	Kyle	Elijah	Jason	Jack	Aaron
2004	David	Sean	Gabriel	Jonathan	Samuel	Elijah

UK Boys	**45**	**46**	**47**	**48**	**49**	**50**
1900	Jack	Percival	Clifford	Alexander	Baden	Bernard Redvers
1925	Bernard	Gerald	Brian	Victor	Wilfred	Francis
1950	Clive	Eric	Frederick	Patrick	Robin	Donald Joseph
1975	Justin	Damian	Thomas	Joseph	Alexander	Alistair
1993	Martin	Philip	Carl	Bradley	Kieran	Simon
1998	Alex	Dylan	Ethan	Jonathan	Sam	Max
2000	Charles	Owen	Louis	Alex	Joe	Rhys
2001	Alex	David	Robert	Harrison	Christopher	Joe
2002	Andrew	Tyler	Scott	Robert	Joe	Louis
2003	Edward	Reece	Harrison	Charles	David	Archie
2004	Alex	Archie	Harrison	Henry	Charles	Toby

US Boys	**45**	**46**	**47**	**48**	**49**	**50**
1900	Ray	Roy	Sydney	Abraham	Edwin	Laurence
1925	Bernard	Edwin	Alfred	Russell	Warren	Ernest
1950	Craig	Arthur	Andrew	Jerome	Leonard	Henry
1975	Justin	Keith	Bradley	Donald	George	Dennis
1993	Jeremy	Jason	Jesse	Samuel	Jared	Dustin
1998	Luis	Jared	Cody	Jason	Logan	Adam
2000	Luis	Adam	Jack	Juan	Isaiah	Connor
2001	Isaiah	Brian	Elijah	Isaac	Jack	Connor
2002	Cody	Anthony	Carson	Daniel	Isaac	Brian
2003	Isaiah	Angel	Luke	Connor	Luis	Isaac
2004	Colin	Justin	Alex	Mason	Jordan	Thomas

UK TOP 50 GIRLS' NAMES

Top 50 first names for girls in the British Isles

New names and fun combinations that celebrities in the British Isles have used for their daughters include:
Apple (Gwyneth Paltrow and Chris Martin),
Daisy Boo and **Poppy Honey** (Jamie Oliver), **Dandelion** (Keith Richard)
Fifi Trixi Belle, **Little Pixie**, **Peaches Honeyblossom** and **Heavenly Hiraani Tigerlily** (Bob Geldof)
and **Nell Marmalade** (Helen Baxendale).

UK Girls	**1**	**2**
1900	Florence	Mary
1925	Joan	Mary
1950	Susan	Linda
1975	Claire	Sarah
1993	Rebecca	Charlotte
1998	Chloe	Emily
2000	Chloe	Emily
2001	Chloe	Emily
2002	Chloe	Emily
2003	Emily	Ellie
2004	Emily	Ellie

US TOP 50 GIRLS' NAMES

Top 50 first names for girls in America

New names and fun combinations that celebrities in the USA have used for their daughters include:
Puma (Erykah Badu),
Rainbow Joan of Arc (known as Rain) plus
Summer Joy (Arlyn and John Phoenix),
Sonnet (Forest Whitaker)
and **Tallulah Belle**
(Demi Moore and Bruce Willis).

US Girls	**1**	**2**
1900	Mary	Ruth
1925	Mary	Barbara
1950	Linda	Mary
1975	Jennifer	Amy
1993	Brittany	Ashley
1998	Kaitlyn	Emily
2000	Emily	Hannah
2001	Emily	Madison
2002	Madison	Hannah
2003	Emily	Madison
2004	Emma	Madison

UK Girls	3	4	5	6	7	8
1900	Alice	Annie	Elsie	Edith	Elizabeth	Doris
1925	Joyce	Margaret	Dorothy	Doris	Kathleen	Irene
1950	Christine	Margaret	Carol	Jennifer	Janet	Patricia
1975	Nicola	Emma	Joanne	Helen	Rachel	Lisa
1993	Laura	Amy	Emma	Jessica	Lauren	Sarah
1998	Megan	Jessica	Sophie	Charlotte	Hannah	Lauren
2000	Megan	Charlotte	Jessica	Lauran	Sophie	Olivia
2001	Megan	Jessica	Sophie	Lauran	Charlotte	Hannah
2002	Jessica	Megan	Sophie	Lauren	Charlotte	Hannah
2003	Chloe	Jessica	Sophie	Megan	Lucy	Olivia
2004	Jessica	Sophie	Chloe	Lucy	Olivia	Charlotte

US Girls	3	4	5	6	7	8
1900	Helen	Margaret	Elizabeth	Dorothy	Catherine	Mildred
1925	Dorothy	Bett	Ruth	Margaret	Helen	Elizabeth
1950	Patricia	Susan	Deborah	Kathleen	Barbara	Nancy
1975	Sarah	Michelle	Kimberly	Heather	Rebecca	Catherine
1993	Jessica	Amanda	Sarah	Megan	Caitlan	Samantha
1998	Sarah	Hannah	Ashley	Brianna	Alexis	Samantha
2000	Madison	Ashley	Sarah	Alexis	Samantha	Jessica
2001	Hannah	Ashley	Alexis	Samantha	Sarah	Abigail
2002	Alexis	Jordan	Chloe	Taylor	Emma	Abigail
2003	Hannah	Emma	Alexis	Ashley	Abigail	Sarah
2004	Emily	Kaitlyn	Hailey	Olivia	Isabella	Hannah

UK Girls	**9**	**10**	**11**	**12**	**13**	**14**
1900	Dorothy	Ethel	Gladys	Lilian	Hilda	Margaret
1925	Betty	Eileen	Doreen	Lilian	Vera	Jean
1950	Barbara	Ann(e)	Sandra	Pamela	Pauline	Jean
1975	Rebecca	Karen	Michelle	Victoria	Catherine	Amanda
1993	Rachel	Catherine	Hannah	Katie	Emily	Sophie
1998	Rebecca	Lucy	Amy	Georgia	Katie	Bethany
2000	Hannah	Lucy	Georgia	Rebecca	Bethany	Amy
2001	Olivia	Lucy	Ellie	Amy	Katie	Georgia
2002	Ellie	Amy	Rebecca	Lucy	Katie	Olivia
2003	Charlotte	Hannah	Katie	Ella	Grace	Mia
2004	Katie	Megan	Grace	Hannah	Amy	Ella

US Girls	**9**	**10**	**11**	**12**	**13**	**14**
1900	Frances	Alice	Marion	Anna	Sarah	Gladys
1925	Jean	Ann(e)	Patricia	Shirley	Virginia	Nancy
1950	Sharon	Karen	Carol(e)	Sandra	Diane	Catherine
1975	Kelly	Elizabeth	Julie	Lisa	Melissa	Angela
1993	Stephanie	Katherine	Emily	Lauren	Kayla	Rachel
1998	Taylor	Madison	Hayley	Jessica	Megan	Alyssa
2000	Taylor	Elizabeth	Lauren	Alyssa	Kayla	Abigail
2001	Elizabeth	Jessica	Olivia	Taylor	Emma	Alyssa
2002	Isabella	Paige	Haley	Faith	Mackenzie	Emily
2003	Samantha	Olivia	Elizabeth	Alyssa	Lauren	Isabella
2004	Sarah	Abigail	Sophia	Kaylee	Alyssa	Madeline

UK Girls	15	16	17	18	19	20
1900	Winifred	Lily	Ellen	Ada	Emily	Violet
1925	Marjorie	Barbara	Edna	Gladys	Audrey	Elsie
1950	Jacqueline	Kathleen	Sheila	Valerie	Maureen	Gillian
1975	Trac(e)y	Samantha	Kelly	Deborah	Julie	Louise
1993	Victoria	Stacey	Natalie	Jade	Stephanie	Lucy
1998	Emma	Olivia	Courtney	Shannon	Eleanor	Jade
2000	Ellie	Katie	Emma	Abigail	Molly	Grace
2001	Rebecca	Molly	Bethany	Emma	Holly	Ella
2002	Bethany	Emma	Jade	Holly	Molly	Georgia
2003	Amy	Holly	Lauren	Emma	Molly	Abigail
2004	Mia	Lily	Abigail	Emma	Amelia	Molly

US Girls	15	16	17	18	19	20
1900	Grace	Lilian	Florence	Virginia	Edith	Lucy
1925	Joan	Martha	Marion	Doris	Frances	Marjorie
1950	Christine	Cynthia	Donna	Judith	Margaret	Janice
1975	Kristen	Carrie	Stephanie	Jessica	Christine	Erin
1993	Nicole	Jennifer	Elizabeth	Chelsea	Courtney	Rebecca
1998	Katherine	Elizabeth	Jasmine	Makayla	Kayla	Rachel
2000	Brianna	Olivia	Emma	Megan	Grace	Victoria
2001	Lauren	Grace	Kayla	Brianna	Anna	Megan
2002	Olivia	Alyssa	Morgan	Brianna	Grace	Dakota
2003	Grace	Jessica	Brianna	Taylor	Kayla	Anna
2004	Brianna	Grace	Alexis	Sydney	Samantha	Riley

UK Girls	**21**	**22**	**23**	**24**	**25**	**26**
1900	Rose	Sarah	Nellie	May	Beatrice	Gertrude
1925	Florence	Hilda	Winifred	Olive	Violet	Elizabeth
1950	Marilyn	Mary	Elizabeth	Lesley	Catherine	Brenda
1975	Sharon	Donna	Kerry	Zoe	Melanie	Alison
1993	Danielle	Kirsty	Samantha	Gemma	Abigail	Chloe
1998	Abigail	Ellie	Molly	Laura	Alice	Sarah
2000	Courtney	Shannon	Caitlan	Eleanor	Jade	Ella
2001	Caitlan	Abigail	Grace	Jade	Mia	Shannon
2002	Shannon	Caitlan	Abigail	Laura	Leah	Sarah
2003	Caitlin	Amelia	Bethany	Lily	Rebecca	Georgia
2004	Lauren	Millie	Holly	Leah	Caitlin	Rebecca

US Girls	**21**	**22**	**23**	**24**	**25**	**26**
1900	Clara	Doris	Marjorie	Annie	Louise	Martha
1925	Marilyn	Alice	Eleanor	Catherine	Lois	Jane
1950	Janet	Pamela	Gail	Cheryl	Suzanne	Marilyn
1975	Laura	Nicole	Stacy	Tracy	Andrea	Ann(e)
1993	Amber	Christina	Kristen	Heather	Lindsey	Danielle
1998	Lauren	Brittany	Allison	Victoria	Abigail	Courtney
2000	Rachel	Anna	Sydney	Destiny	Morgan	Jennifer
2001	Victoria	Destiny	Sydney	Rachel	Jennifer	Jasmine
2002	Adriana	Kaitlyn	Ashley	Kayla	Jaden	Brooke
2003	Victoria	Megan	Sydney	Chloe	Rachel	Jamine
2004	Lauren	Taylor	Chloe	Ella	Ava	Elizabeth

UK Girls	**27**	**28**	**29**	**30**	**31**	**32**
1900	Ivy	Mabel	Jessie	Maud	Eva	Agnes
1925	Edith	Ivy	Peggy	Phyllis	Evelyn	Iris
1950	Wendy	Angela	Rosemary	Shirley	Diane	Joan
1975	Caroline	Lin(d)say	Jennifer	Angela	Susan	Hayley
1993	Holly	Claire	Hayley	Zoe	Jodie	Elizabeth
1998	Holly	Caitlan	Rachel	Elizabeth	Amber	Paige
2000	Leah	Alice	Holly	Laura	Anna	Jasmin
2001	Eleanor	Alice	Jasmin	Courtney	Leah	Amelia
2002	Ella	Grace	Courtney	Rachel	Eleanor	Mia
2003	Leah	Millie	Eleanor	Jasmine	Daisy	Elizabeth
2004	Georgia	Bethany	Eleanor	Isabelle	Ruby	Daisy

US Girls	**27**	**28**	**29**	**30**	**31**	**32**
1900	Ann(e)	Blanche	Eleanor	Emma	Hazel	Esther
1925	Phyllis	Florence	Mildred	Carol(e)	Carolyn	Marie
1950	Brenda	Beverly	Carolyn	Ann(e)	Shirley	Jacqueline
1975	Rachel	Karen	Wendy	Christina	Amanda	Mary
1993	Melissa	Tiffany	Kelsey	Kelly	Michelle	Alyssa
1998	Amanda	Sydney	Nicole	Jennifer	Anna	Rebecca
2000	Haley	Jasmine	Nicole	Julia	Kaitlyn	Amanda
2001	Julia	Isabella	Morgan	Chloe	Kaitlyn	Natalie
2002	Lauren	Alexia	Gabrielle	Samantha	Sydney	Megan
2003	Sophia	Jennifer	Morgan	Natalie	Julia	Kaitlyn
2004	Ashley	Makayla	Lily	Anna	Kayla	Megan

UK Girls	**33**	**34**	**35**	**36**	**37**	**38**
1900	Jane	Evelyn	Frances	Kathleen	Clara	Olive
1925	Annie	Rose	Beryl	Lily	Muriel	Sheila
1950	Jane	Lynne	Irene	Janice	Elaine	Heather
1975	Dawn	Joanna	Lucy	Natalie	Charlotte	Andrea
1993	Kelly	Kimberley	Natasha	Alexandra	Nicola	Kerry
1998	Georgina	Danielle	Nicole	Grace	Natasha	Ella
2000	Sarah	Elizabeth	Amelia	Rachel	Amber	Phoebe
2001	Elizabeth	Anna	Amber	Lily	Laura	Sarah
2002	Nicole	Jasmine	Natasha	Danielle	Zoe	Amelia
2003	Alice	Courtney	Shannon	Erin	Isabella	Abbie
2004	Freya	Isabella	Elizabeth	Jasmine	Erin	Alice

US Girls	**33**	**34**	**35**	**36**	**37**	**38**
1900	Ethel	Laura	Marie	Julia	Beatrice	Gertrude
1925	Norma	Anna	Louise	Beverly	Janet	Sarah
1950	Joanne	Lynn(e)	Marcia	Denise	Gloria	Joyce
1975	Christy	Danielle	Jodi	Shannon	Tanya	Alison
1993	Hannah	Allison	Erica	Alicia	Amy	Crystal
1998	Emma	Olivia	Morgan	Destiny	Madeline	Stephanie
2000	Natalie	Katherine	Hailey	Alexandra	Stephanie	Maria
2001	Nicole	Hailey	Haley	Katherine	Alexandra	Sophia
2002	Cade	Caitlyn	Jackson	Alana	Savannah	Avery
2003	Hailey	Destiny	Haley	Katherine	Nicole	Alexandra
2004	Zoe	Mackenzie	Kylie	Natalie	Allison	Maya

UK Girls	**39**	**40**	**41**	**42**	**43**	**44**
1900	Amy	Catherine	Grace	Emma	Nora(h)	Louisa
1925	Ethel	Alice	Constance	Ellen	Gwendoline	Patricia
1950	Marion	June	Eileen	Denise	Doreen	Judith
1975	Laura	Paula	Mari	Teresa	Elizabeth	Suzanne
1993	Chelsea	Eleanor	Jennifer	Leanne	Melissa	Alice
1998	Chelsea	Leah	Anna	Victoria	Phoebe	Zoe
2000	Natasha	Niamh	Zoe	Paige	Nichole	Abbie
2001	Rachel	Phoebe	Erin	Millie	Zoe	Abbie
2002	Alice	Erin	Abbie	Louise	Amber	Elizabeth
2003	Anna	Amber	Freya	Isabelle	Poppy	Paige
2004	Evie	Amber	Paige / Abbie		Madison	Phoebe

US Girls	**39**	**40**	**41**	**42**	**43**	**44**
1900	Alma	Mabel	Minnie	Pauline	Rose	Fanny
1925	Evelyn	Edith	Jacqueline	Lorraine	Grace	Ethel
1950	Kathy	Elizabeth	Laura	Darlene	Theresa	Joan
1975	Lori	Robin	Theresa	Emily	Susan	Tara
1993	Jamie	Kimberly	Laura	Erin	Alexandra	Mary
1998	Sierra	Jordan	Alexandra	Mackenzie	Natalie	Savannah
2000	Savannah	Chloe	Rebecca	Sophia	Mackenzie	Allison
2001	Amanda	Maria	Mackenzie	Stephanie	Savannah	Allison
2002	Kailey	Madeline	Jasmine	Elizabeth	Ariana	Sarah
2003	Maria	Savannah	Stephanie	Mia	Mackenzie	Allison
2004	Katherine	Morgan	Mia	Jasmine	Isabel	Jordan

UK Girls	45	46	47	48	49	50
1900	Minnie	Lucy	Daisy	Eliza	Phyllis	Ann(e)
1925	Sylvia	Nora(h)	Pamela	Grace	Jessie	Mabel
1950	Sylvia	Helen	Yvonne	Hilary	Dorothy	Joyce
1975	Kirsty	Sally	Tina	Jane	Ann(e)	Jacqueline
1993	Louise	Harriet	Lisa	Kayleigh	Megan	Naomi
1998	Samantha	Alexandra	Jasmine	Amelia	Louise	Lydia
2000	Mia	Imogen	Lily	Alexandra	Chelsea	Erin
2001	Nicole	Paige	Niamh	Daisy	Natasha	Alexandra
2002	Anna	Millie	Samantha	Chelsea	Paige	Lily
2003	Phoebe	Sarah	Isabel	Rachel	Aimee	Ruby
2004	Poppy	Aimee / Courtney		Niamh	Anna	Isabel

US Girls	45	46	47	48	49	50
1900	Agnes	Carrie	Edna	Evelyn	Harriet	Ida
1925	Gloria	Laura	Audrey	Esther	Joanne	Sally
1950	Elaine	Michelle	Judy	Diana	Frances	Maureen
1975	Heidi	Jill	Tonya	Tammy	Kathleen	Erica
1993	Katie	Cassandra	Anna	Casey	Victoria	Tayler
1998	Julia	Amber	Bailey	Danielle	Kelsey	Erica
2000	Isabella	Amber	Mary	Danielle	Gabrielle	Andrea
2001	Jenna	Andrea	Rebecca	Jordan	Mary	Gabrielle
2002	Alexandra	Audrey	Alexa	Isabelle	Zoe	Natalie
2003	Amanda	Jordan	Jenna	Faith	Paige	Makayla
2004	Rachel	Julia	Jessica	Savannah	Ariana	Victoria

A to Z
GIRLS' NAMES

A

Abbey, Abbie, Abby, Abi
Diminutives of Abigail.

Abigail
From Hebrew *avigail*, meaning 'father's rejoicing'. A biblical name; borne in the Old Testament by the wife of King David (1 Samuel). Abigail refers to herself so often as David's handmaiden, that the name came to be synonymous with 'maid'. Diminutives: Abbey, Abbie, Abby, Abi, Gail, Gale, Gayle.

Ada
Origin uncertain; possibly from the Old German names Eda or Etta, or a diminutive of Adah, Adela, Adelaide or Adeline. The name was borne by a 7th-century abbess of Saint-Julien-des-Prés at Le Mans. It was first introduced to Britain from Germany in the 18th century.

Adah
Hebrew, meaning 'ornament'. A biblical name; borne in the Old Testament by the wives of Lamech and Esau. A Puritan adoption, the name has been in occasional use since the 16th century.

Adela
Old German, from athal, 'noble'. First introduced to Britain by the Norman invaders, it was borne by one of the daughters of William I. It was particularly popular in the 18th century. Diminutives: Addie, Addy, Della. Variations: Adele, Adeline. See also: Ethel.

Adelaide
Norman French version of Adelheid, an Old German name derived from *athal*, 'noble', and *heid*, 'state of'. It was borne in the 10th century by the wife of Otto the Great, Holy Roman Emperor, who ruled as regent after his death. The name was popularised in Britain by the wife of William IV, after whom the capital city of South Australia was named. Diminutives: Addie, Addy. See also: Alice, Heidi.

Adele
French form of Adela.

Adeline
Origin disputed; possibly a diminutive of Adelaide, a diminutive of Adele or a name in its own right. It certainly comes from the same roots as these, being from Old German *athal*, meaning 'noble'. First seen in the Domesday Book, it was popular in the Middle Ages and revived in the 19th century. Diminutives: Alina, Aline.

Adrienne
French feminine form of Adrian. Variations: Adrianne, Adriana, Adrianna.

Afra
Origin uncertain; either a Latin term for a woman from 'Africa' (in Roman times this meant the area around Carthage), or a variation of Aphra.

Africa
Actually ancient Irish Gaelic, a version of Aifric (meaning 'pleasant'). It is now more often connected with the continent and is sometimes given to Afro-American women in recognition of their ancestral homeland.

Agatha
Greek, from *agathos*, 'good'. Borne by a 3rd-century martyr who was tortured and murdered at Catania in Sicily. She is sometimes depicted in paintings holding a salver containing her severed breasts. Her feast day is 5th February. The name underwent a popular revival in the 19th

century, but is rarely found in modern times. Diminutives: Aggie, Aggy.

Aggie, Aggy
Diminutives of Agatha.

Agnes
Greek, from *hagnos*, 'chaste, holy'. Borne by a young Roman girl who was martyred on the orders of Diocletian at the age of just thirteen, in c. 304. She had refused several offers of marriage, declaring herself to be devoted to Christ, and is regarded as the patron saint of virgins. Her feast day is 21st January. There is a custom that if young girls follow an elaborate routine on St Agnes' Eve they will dream of their future husband. John Keats wove the superstition into his poem *The Eve of St Agnes* (1820). Diminutives: Aggie, Aggy, Ness, Nessa, Nesta. Variations: Angeta (Northern European), Anis, Annes, Annice, Annis, Inez, Senga.

Aileen
Scottish form of Eileen.

Ailie
Diminutive of Aileen, Ailsa and Alison, among others, particularly in Scotland.

Ailsa
Modern Scottish, originating from Ailsa Craig, an island in the Firth of Clyde. Diminutive: Ailie.

Aimée
French, the past participle form of *aimer*, 'to love', meaning 'beloved'. In use since the Middle Ages, it is occasionally found in the English-speaking world.

Aisha
Arabic, meaning 'alive', 'thriving' or 'prospering'. Borne by the third and favourite wife of Muhammad, daughter of Abubekr, the name is hugely popular in the Arab world. It is also fairly popular in the English-speaking world in a variety of forms, including Ayesha, first brought to attention outside the Arab world when H Rider Haggard used it in his novel *She* (1887) in which he gave the meaning as 'she who must be obeyed'.

Aisling
(*ash-ling*) Irish Gaelic word meaning 'vision' or 'dream'. Only adopted as a first name in the 1960s, it has since become popular, along with many Irish names and all things Irish. Variation: Aislinn. It is also in use as a boy's name.

Aithne
(*eth-nee*) Irish Gaelic, from *aod*, meaning 'fire'. It is the feminine form of Aidan. Variations: Eithne, Ethna (*et-na*), Ethne (*en-ya*), Ethnea. See also: Edina.

Alana, Alanna
Feminine forms of Alan, of modern coinage, or variations of Alannah.

Alannah
Irish Gaelic, from Oleanbh, an endearment meaning 'O my child'. Variations: Alana, Alanna.

Albany
A modern adoption, probably from an ancient source. Albany is an ancient name for the northern part of Scotland, probably derived from the Celtic *alp*, meaning 'rock' or 'crag'. The same area was named Caledonia by the Romans. It could also be a feminine version of Alban. Variations: Albina, Albinia.

Alberta
Feminine form of Albert. The Canadian province was named for Princess Louise Alberta, daughter of Queen Victoria and

Prince Albert, and wife of a governor general of Canada. Variations: Albertina, Albertine.

Albreda
Old German name meaning 'elf counsel'. Variation: Elvira

Aldith
From Old English eald 'old' and gyth 'battle' rarely used nowadays.

Alethea
Greek, from *aletheia*, 'truth'. Probably first adopted in Britain by the Puritans because of its meaning, it was further popularised by the Spanish Infanta, Maria Alethea, who was briefly courted by Charles I. Variation: Althea.

Alex
Diminutive of Alexa, Alexia, Alexandra, Alexandria or Alexandrina (all feminine forms of Alexander).

Alexa
Variation of either Alexia or Alexis.

Alexandra
Feminine form of Alexander. Variations: Alexa, Alexia, Alexandria, Alexandrina. Diminutives: Alex, Alexa, Alix, Lex, Lexie, Lexy, Sandie, Sandra, Sandy, Tiggy, Zandra.

Alexia
Feminine form of Alexander. Variation: Alexa.

Alexis
Greek, from *alexios*, 'to defend' or 'to ward off'. Originally a masculine name, it was borne by a 13th-century saint of the Russian Orthodox church, the patron saint of hermits and beggars. His feast day is 17th July. The name is now in regular use throughout the English-speaking world, for both boys and girls. Variations: Alexa, Alexia.

Alfreda
Variation of Elfreda or the feminine form of Alfred

Ali
Diminutive of Alice, Alicia, Alina, Aline or Alison.

Alice
Old French, originally a common adaptation of Adelaide, but recognised as a name in its own right by the time of its 19th-century revival. It was widely popularised by Lewis Carroll's *Alice's Adventures in Wonderland* (1865). Variation: Alys.

Alicia
Latin form of Alice. Variations: Alisa, Alissa, Alyssa.

Alina, Aline
Medieval diminutives of Adeline.

Alisa
Variation of Alicia.

Alison, Allison, Allyson, Alyson
Old French, originally a medieval pet form of Alice. It has been consistently popular in Scotland, thus acquiring an erroneous reputation as a Scottish name. Allison is the most usual spelling in the US.

Alissa
Variation of Alicia.

Allegra
Italian, meaning 'lively'; probably influenced by the musical term *allegro*. It was apparently first used by Lord Byron for

his illegitimate daughter (1817-22) by Claire Claremont. It has subsequently been used in the English-speaking world, but not in Italy as a rule.

Allie, Ally
Diminutives of Alice, Alicia, Alina, Aline or Alison.

Alma
Origin disputed; contenders are: from Latin *almus*, meaning 'caring' or 'bountiful' (source of the phrase *alma mater* for an educational establishment); from *alma*, Italian, meaning 'soul' or 'spirit'; or after the 1854 Battle of Alma, during the Crimean War. In Matthew Prior's poem *Alma, or The Progress of the Mind* (1718), Alma is the queen of Body Castle and intended to personify the mind. In Edmund Spenser's *The Faerie Queene* (1590-6), Alma typifies the soul.

Almira
Arabic, from *amira*, 'princess'.

Aloysia
(*al-oo-ish-a*) Feminine form of Aloysius.

Althea
Greek, from *althainein*, 'to heal'. In classical legend Althea was the daughter of Thestius, king of Aetolia, and mother of the hero Meleager. When Meleager was born Althea was told that her son would live for as long as a log of wood then burning on the fire remained unburnt. She snatched it from the fire and kept it safe until years later when, her brothers having been killed by Meleager, she wrought her revenge by throwing the log on the fire. Her son died as the log burned. The name was popularised in the 17th century by the poet Richard Lovelace (1618-58), who used it for his beloved Lucy Sacheverall, in his poem *To Althea, from Prison* (1649).

Alys
Welsh form of Alice.

Alyssa
Variation of Alissa.

Amabel
Latin, from *amabilis*, 'lovable'. Diminutives: Bel, Bell, Bella, Belle, Mabel, Mabella, Mabelle, Mable. Variations: Anabel, Annabel, Annabella, Annabelle, Arabella.

Amalia
Variation of Amelia.

Amanda
From Latin *amanda*, the female gerundive of *amare*, meaning 'lovable'. It was probably a 17th-century coinage, by the playwright Colley Cibber. Diminutives: Manda, Mandi, Mandie, Mandy.

Amaryllis
Latin, borne by several fair country girls in the works of Ovid and Virgil, among others, and in later pastoral works, such as Milton's *Lycidas*. Its use as the name of a genus of plants is modern.

Amber
From Old French *ambre*, ultimately derived from Arabic *anbar*, and denoting a semi-precious, translucent, orange-yellow resinous substance used for centuries to make jewellery and ornaments. One of several jewel names that became fashionable in the late 19th century, it was further boosted by the publication of the American writer Kathleen Winsor's novel *Forever Amber* (1944).

Ambrin
From Arabic, meaning 'ambergris', a sweetly smelling resinous substance produced by sperm whales.

Amelia
The strongest element is Old German, from *amal*, 'labour', influenced by the Latin name Aemelia, the source of Emily. However, Emily is used as a diminutive for Amelia. Diminutives: Emily, Millie, Milly. Variation: Amalia. See also: Emmeline.

Amice, Amicia
Exact origin uncertain; either French influenced by Latin (French form of the Latin name Amica), or Latin influenced by French (Latin form of the French name Aimée).

Amina
Arabic, meaning 'peaceful' or 'secure'; Amina bint-Wahab was the mother of the Prophet Muhammad. Variation: Ameena.

Aminta
A 17th-century British literary coining, probably from the Greek masculine name Amyntas, meaning 'protector'. It was used by several Restoration writers and dramatists. Diminutives: Minta, Minty. Variation: Araminta.

Amy
Anglicised form of Aimée. St Amata of Bologna was a 13th-century saint. This form was popularised by characters in Louisa M Alcott's *Little Women* (1868) and Sir Walter Scott's *Kenilworth*. Variations: Aimée, Ami, Amice, Amicia.

Anabel
Variation of Annabel.

Anaïs
French, from Greek, meaning 'fruitful'.

Anastasia
From Greek *anastasis*, 'rising up' or 'resurrection'. Borne by a Roman saint and matron said to have been beheaded with St Basilissa for having buried the bodies of St Peter and St Paul. The name is also popular in Eastern Europe, in honour of a 4th-century Dalmatian martyr. It was given to a daughter of the murdered Tzar Nicholas II of Russia; she probably died with the rest of her family in 1917, but in 1920 a woman claiming to be her came to public attention. The name is consequently often assumed to be Russian.

Andrea
(*an-dre-a*, *an-drey-a*) Feminine form of Andreas and Andrew, probably dating from the 17th century.

Angel
From the Latin form of Greek *angelos*, 'messenger'. Initially a boy's name, it is now more commonly given to girls.

Angela
Feminine form of Angel, itself no longer considered a boy's name. Diminutive: Angie. Variations: Angelina, Angeline.

Angelica
Latin, from *angelicus*, 'angelic'. Borne by the heroine of Matteo Boiardo's *Orlando Innamorato* (1487). Orlando's love for the beautiful but fickle Angelica drove him mad. It is also the name of a plant whose stalks are candied and used for decorating cakes. Diminutive: Angie.

Angelina, Angeline
Variations of Angela. Angelina is of Italian origin; Angeline of French origin. Diminutive: Angie.

Angelique
Variation of Angelica.

Angharad
(*ank-har-ad*) Welsh, meaning 'beloved'.

It is the name of a major figure in the collection of Welsh folk tales, the *Mabinogian*.

Angie
Diminutive of Angela, Angelica, Angelina or Angeline.

Anis
Early variation of Agnes. See also: Annes, Annice, Annis, Inez.

Anita
Spanish diminutive of Ann, used in its own right throughout the English-speaking world.

Ann
Variation of Anne.

Anna
Latin form of Anne, influenced by the Greek name Hannah. In classical legend Anna was sister to Dido, Queen of Carthage. In the New Testament it is the name of an elderly prophetess who, like Simeon, saw the infant Jesus when his parents took him to the temple (Luke 2:36-38).

Annabel, Annabelle
Variations of Amabel (not, as is sometimes assumed, derived from Ann- and the Latin adjective *bella*, 'beautiful'). Annabel Drummond, mother of King James I of Scotland, ensured the name's enduring popularity there. Annabelle is a 20th-century spelling.

Annabella
Latin form of Annabel, itself a variation of Amabel. Diminutive: Bella.

Annalise
Variation of Anneliese.

Anne
English form (also influenced by Latin and French) of the biblical name Hannah, from Greek *hanna*, meaning 'God has favoured me'. It was, according to the apocryphal Golden Legend, borne by the Virgin Mary's mother, known to the English-speaking world as St Anne. Ann(e) forms part of a myriad names throughout the world.

Anneka
Swedish form of Ann(e). Variation: Annika.

Anneliese
German, a compound of Anna and Liese (Elizabeth). Variation: Annalise.

Annes
Early variation of Agnes. See also: Anis, Annice, Annis and Inez.

Annette
Diminutive of Ann(e), widely used in its own right.

Annice
Early variation of Agnes. See also: Anis, Annes, Annis and Inez.

Annie
Diminutive of Ann(e), sometimes used as a name in its own right.

Annika
Swedish form of Ann(e). Variation: Anneka.

Annis
Early variation of Agnes. See also: Anis, Annes, Annice, Inez.

Annora
Variation of Honor.

Anona
Uncertain origin possibly from latin annona 'grain harvest' or a compound of Ann and Nona.

Anouk
French variation of Ann(e).

Anouska, Anoushka
Russian diminutives of Ann(e). Variation: Anouchka.

Anselma
Feminine form of Anselm.

Anthea
Greek, from antheios, meaning 'flowery'. In classical legend Anthea was an early name for Hera, Greek queen of the gods. The name underwent a brief revival in the 17th century, stimulated largely by pastoral poets. A further revival in the mid-20th century seems to have abated.

Antoinette
Feminine diminutive form of Antoine. Diminutives: Net, Nettie, Netty, Toinette, Toni.

Antonia, Antonina
Feminine form of Antony, itself adapted from Antonius, a Roman family name. Diminutives: Toni, Tony, Tonia, Tonya.

Anwen
Welsh, meaning 'very beautiful'.

Anya
Anglicised spelling of the Spanish form of Ann(e).

Aphra
Origin uncertain; either Hebrew *aphrah*, meaning 'dust', or a variation of Afra.

Aoife
(ee-fia) Irish and Scottish, probably from Irish Gaelic *aoibh*, meaning 'beauty'. It is borne by several figures of Irish legend. It can be anglicised as Eva or Eve.

Apollonia
Latin form (meaning 'of Apollo'), of the Greek name Apollonios. A 3rd-century martyr who, among many tortures, had her teeth knocked out, she is held as the patron saint of toothache.

Apple
Name given to Gwyneth Paltrow and Chris Martin's daughter.

April
Fourth month of the year, probably influenced by the French equivalent, Avril, or a contraction of the Old English name Averil. See also: June, May.

Arabella
Probably a variation of Annabel. Popular in Scotland since the 14th century and in England since the 18th century, it is rare outside Britain now.

Araminta
Probably an elaboration of Aminta.

Aranrhod
(*ar-an-throd*) Welsh, from archaic elements meaning 'large' and 'wheel'. In the collection of Welsh folk tales, the Mabinogian, Aranrhod is the mother of Dylan. It is now influenced by Arianrhod, a variation consisting of modern Welsh elements *arian*, 'silver', and *rhod*, 'wheel'. Variation: Arianrhod.

Areta, Aretha
Greek, meaning 'virtue'. The name is also related to Arethusa, a classical nymph who fled the attentions of a river

god by leaving Greece for Sicily, where she disguised herself as a freshwater spring that can still be seen today.

Ariadne
Greek, meaning 'most holy'. Borne in classical legend by the daughter of King Minos of Crete who gave Theseus a ball of wool so that he could find his way out of the Labyrinth after killing the Minotaur. She later went with him to Naxos, where he deserted her. She was found there by Dionysus, who married her. It was also the name of a 2nd-century Christian martyr.

Ariane
French form of Ariadne.

Arianna
Italian form of Ariadne.

Arianrhod
(*a-ree-an-throd*) Modern variation of Aranrhod, influenced by modern Welsh elements *arian*, 'silver' and *rhod*, 'wheel'.

Arianwen
(*a-ree-an-win*) Welsh, from *arian*, 'silver', and *gwen*, 'white, holy, fair, blessed'. Borne in the 5th century by a daughter of Brychan, a Welsh chieftain.

Ariel
See: Boys.

Arlene
Modern coinage, possibly from Charlene. It is mainly popular in the US and Australia.

Arlette
French, origin obscure; possibly from Charlotte, or another feminine form of Charles. Borne by William the Conqueror's mother, mistress of Duke Robert of Normandy, but rare in Britain until the 20th century.

Artemis
Greek counterpart of Diana, Roman goddess of the moon and hunting.

Ashley
Adopted surname, from *aesc*, 'ash', and *leah*, 'wood, clearing'. Initially used as a boy's name, it is now a popular girl's name in the English-speaking world, particularly in the US. Variations: Ashlea, Ashleigh, Ashlee, Ashlie, Ashly.

Ashling
Anglicised form of Aisling.

Asia
Modern, either after the continent, or as a diminutive of girls' names ending in -asia, such as Anastasia. See also: Africa.

Asma
Arabic, meaning 'most prestigious'. Borne by a woman who helped Muhammad and her father, caliph Abu-Bakr, escape from Mecca when their lives were threatened in 622.

Aspasia
From Greek meaning 'welcome'.

Astra
From Latin astralis 'of the stars'.

Astrid
Scandinavian, from Old Norse elements *ass*, 'god', and *frior*, 'beautiful'.

Atalanta
From Greek *atalantos*, meaning 'equal in weight'. Borne in Greek mythology by a fast-running woman who refused to marry unless the suitor first beat her in a

running race. Milanion (also known as Hippomenes) distracted her by dropping three golden apples, a gift of Venus, along the way. Atalanta stopped to pick them up and lost the race.

Athena
(*a-thee-nah*) Variation of Athene.

Athene
(*a-thee-nee*) Greek, from *a*, 'not', and possibly *thnetos*, 'mortal', meaning 'immortal', or *tithene*, 'nurse', meaning 'born without a nurse'. Supposedly born, fully armed, from the head of Zeus, Athene was considered in classical mythology to be goddess of the arts, war and wisdom, and patron of the city of Athens. Variations: Athena, Athina.

Athina
(*a-thee-nah*) Modern Greek variation of Athena.

Aubrey
Old French; form of the German name Alberic, itself from *alb*, 'elf', and *ric*, 'power'. Although originally a boy's name, in the US it is now more commonly used for girls.

Audrey
Old English, from *æthel*, 'noble', and *pryð*, 'strength'. It derives from the colloquial pronunciation of the name of St Etheldreda, 7th-century abbess of Ely. The word tawdry was first used to describe the tinny and worthless goods sold at St Audrey's annual fair, and this association contributed to the name's going out of fashion until the early 20th century. Variation: Audra (particularly in the US).

Augusta
Latin, the feminine form of Augustus. Originally given to female members of the Imperial families of Rome, it was popularised in Britain by the mother of George III and remained in regular use until the late 19th century.

Augustina
Latin, the feminine form of Augustine.

Aurea
From Latin aureus 'golden'. Possibly a variant of Aurora.

Aurelia
Latin, the feminine adaptation of Aurelius, a Roman family name derived from *aurum*, 'gold'. Variations: Auriel, Oriel.

Auriel
Variation of Aurelia.

Aurora
Latin, from *aurora*, meaning 'dawn'. Aurora was the Roman goddess of sunrise. See also: Dawn, Roxane.

Ava
(*ay-va, ar-va*) Origin uncertain, but probably a medieval Germanic diminutive for names beginning Av-. In the form Avia it was borne by 9th-century Frankish saint of royal birth. The name re-emerged in the 20th century, most notably with the American actress Ava Gardner (1922-90), possibly as a variation of Eva.

Aveline
Latinate form of the Norman French name Eveline. See also: Eileen, Eveline, Evelyn.

Averil
From the Old English name Everild, from *eofor*, 'boar', and *hild*, 'battle'. Borne by an obscure 7th-century

Yorkshire saint. It was common in the 17th century.

Avice
Variation of Avis.

Avis
Origin uncertain, although it has come (probably erroneously) to be associated with Latin *avis*, 'bird'. It was probably a Norman introduction to Britain. Variation: Avice.

Avril
From French *avril*, 'April', adopted in line with the fashion for month names. It may also be a contraction of Averil.

Ayesha
Form of Aisha used by H Rider Haggard in his novel *She* (1887), in which he gave the meaning as 'she who must be obeyed'.

Azalea
From Greek *azaleos*, 'dry', and referring to a species of flower that flourishes in dry soil. A late 20th-century coinage, and one of the more recent of the names derived from flowers.

Azania
Modern coinage; originally biblical (from Hebrew, meaning 'heard by God'), but adopted by African nationalists to refer to South Africa during the years of oppression.

Azaria
Hebrew, meaning 'helped by God'. A biblical name; borne by several (male) figures, including a king of Judah. A Puritan adoption, it is now used for girls.

B

Bab, Babs
Diminutives of Barbara.

Babette
French-influenced diminutive of Elizabeth.

Barbara
From Greek *barbaros*, 'strange' or 'foreign', originally an onomatopoeic word describing the babbling sound of an unintelligible foreign tongue. St Barbara was, it is said, a virgin martyr, handed over to the governor of Nicomedia by her father, a heathen. Her father was about to cut off her head when he was struck by lightning. She is hence invoked against lightning and is also considered the patron saint of architects and engineers, firework makers and gunpowder, arsenals and artillery. Her actual existence is in fact disputed. Diminutives: Bab, Babs, Barbie, Baubie, Bobby. Variation: Barbra (modern spelling).

Barbie
Diminutive of Barbara.

Bathsheba
Hebrew, meaning 'daughter of satiety' or 'voluptuous'. A biblical name; borne by the wife of Uriah the Hittite, who was spied bathing by King David. David arranged for Uriah to be killed in battle and married Bathsheba (2 Samuel 11). She became the mother of Solomon. A Puritan adoption, the name was used by Thomas Hardy for the heroine of his novel *Far From The Madding Crowd* (1874). Diminutive: Sheba.

Baubie
Scottish diminutive of Barbara.

Bea, Beattie, Beatty, Bee
Diminutives of Beatrice or Beatrix.

Beata
Latin, the feminine form of *beatus*, 'happy'. St Beata was martyred in France, and the name is mainly popular in continental Europe. It is also used as a pet name for Beatrice.

Beatrice
Variation and most common form of Beatrix. Beatrice, Dante's spirit-guide through Paradise in the *Divine Comedy* (c. 1309-20), was based on Beatrice Portinari, a young girl with whom Dante fell in love when she was only a child. She died in 1290, aged only 23. The name was used by Shakespeare in *Much Ado About Nothing* (1598). Variation: Beatrix. Diminutives: Bea, Beattie, Beatty, Bee, Tris, Trissie.

Beatrix
Latin, meaning 'bringer of joy'. It is mentioned in the Domesday Book. Diminutives: Bea, Beattie, Beatty, Bee, Trix, Trixie.

Becca, Beck, Becky
Diminutives of Rebecca.

Bedelia
Variation of Bridget. Diminutive: Delia.

Belinda
From the Old German name Betlindis, from *lindi*, meaning 'snake'. Diminutives: Bel, Bell, Belle, Linda, Lindy.

Bell, Belle
Diminutives of Annabel, Arabella, Belinda, Isabella or Sibella.

Bella
Diminutive of names incorporating the element -bella, such as Arabella, associated with the feminine form of the Italian adjective *bella*, 'beautiful'.

Benedicta
Feminine form of Benedict.

Benita
Spanish feminine form of Benedict.

Berenice
Interpreted as from the Greek name Pherenike, meaning 'bringer of victory', but actually Egyptian in origin. Borne by the wife of King Ptolemy III of Egypt (246-221 BC). A legend tells how Berenice vowed to cut off her hair if her husband was victorious over Asia. Her hair was therefore hung in the temple, but disappeared overnight. It is said that it was blown to heaven, where it formed a group of seven stars called Coma Berenices, near the tail of Leo. Diminutives: Bunnie, Bunny.

Bernadette
French feminine form of Bernard. It was popularised by the young St Bernadette of Lourdes (1844-79) after whose visions of the Virgin Mary a sacred shrine was erected. Diminutives: Bernie, Berny.

Bernadina, Bernadine
Feminine forms of Bernard.

Bernice
Contracted form of Berenice and the most common form of the name in the English-speaking world. A biblical name; borne by the sister of King Agrippa II (Acts 25, 26). A Puritan adoption.

Bernie, Berny
Diminutives of Bernadette or Bernice.

Berta, Bertha
From Old German *berht*, 'bright'. Borne

by the mother of Charlemagne and introduced by the Normans to Britain.

Beryl
From Old French *beril*, ultimately derived from Greek *berullos*, and denoting a precious pale green stone with light blue, yellow and white lights. One of several stone names that became fashionable in the late 19th century, it is rarely chosen in modern times.

Bess, Bessie, Bessy
Diminutives of Elizabeth dating from the 16th century.

Bet
Diminutive of Elizabeth.

Beta
Variant of Elizabeth.

Beth
Diminutive of Elizabeth, dating from the 19th century. It was popularised by Louisa M Alcott in *Little Women* (1868).

Bethan
Origin uncertain; possibly an elaboration of Beth, or a variation of Bethany.

Bethany
Anglicisation of the Hebrew beth te'ena, possibly meaning 'house of figs'. A biblical name, of a village near Jerusalem. It is a 20th-century adoption. Diminutive: Beth. Variation: Bethan.

Bethia
From Hebrew meaning 'daughter of God'.

Betsy
Diminutive of Elizabeth.

Bette
French diminutive of Elizabeth, popularised by actress Bette Davis (1908-89).

Bettina
Diminutive of Elizabeth, of Italian and Spanish origin. Borne as a nickname by the German writer Elisabeth von Arnim (1785-1859), wife of the poet Ludwig Achim von Arnim and author of, among other works, *Letters to a Child* (1835).

Bettrys
Welsh form of Beatrix.

Betty
Diminutive of Elizabeth, hugely popular throughout the English-speaking world in the 1920s.

Betty Kitten
Daughter to Jane Goldman and Jonathan Ross.

Beulah
Hebrew, meaning 'married'. Biblical name for the land of Israel (Isaiah 62).

Beverley, Beverly
Adopted surname and place name, from Old English *beofor*, 'beaver', and *leac*, 'stream'. First used as a masculine name in the 19th century, it gradually came to be used as a feminine name in the USA. It is now widespread as a girl's name throughout the English-speaking world.

Bianca
Feminine form of the Italian adjective *bianco*, 'white'. The name was used by Shakespeare for the gentle sister of Katharina, 'the shrew' in *The Taming of the Shrew* (1593), and for an impudent Cypriot courtesan in *Othello* (1604). See also: Blanche, Candida.

Biba
The name of a very fashionable clothes

shop that opened on London's Kings Road in the 1960s, this is occasionally used as a girl's name.

Biddy
Diminutive of Bridget.

Billie
Diminutive of William or Wilhelmina, sometimes used in its own right for girls, especially in the US.

Birdie
From pet name for 'bird' in occasional use as a first name.

Birgit, Birgitta
Swedish, possibly a variation of Bridget. The feast day of a Swedish St Birgitta (1304-73) falls on the same day as St Bridget. Diminutives: Birgit, Brita, Britt. Variation: Brigitta.

Blanche
Feminine form of the French adjective *blanc*, 'white'. It was brought to Britain in the 14th century and borne by Blanche of Lancaster, wife of John of Gaunt. See also Bianca, Candida.

Blodwedd
Welsh, meaning 'flower form'. Borne in Welsh legend by the wife whom Llew Llaw Gyffes made for himself, out of flowers.

Blodwen
Welsh, from *blodyn*, 'flower', and *gwen*, 'white, fair, holy, blessed'.

Blodyn
Welsh, meaning 'flower'.

Blossom
From Old English *blostm*, 'blossom'. It is a direct adoption from the English vocabulary, referring to the mass of flowers on a fruit tree. It was one of the less popular of the flower names adopted in the late 19th century.

Blythe
Adopted surname, from 'blithe'.

Bobbie, Bobby
Diminutives of Roberta or Barbara.

Bonita
Spanish, feminine form of the Spanish adjective *bonito*, 'pretty'. It is a modern coinage not used in Spain. Diminutives: Bonnie, Bonny.

Bonnie
Scottish dialect word meaning 'beautiful, healthy', from Latin *bonus*, 'good'. It is found mainly in the US, after Margaret Mitchell gave it to Scarlett O'Hara's daughter in *Gone With The Wind* (1936). It is also used as a diminutive of Bonita. Variation: Bonny.

Brandy
Modern American coinage after the spirit, influenced by the popular male name Brandon.

Branwen
Welsh, from *bran*, 'raven', and *gwen*, 'fair'. Borne in Welsh legend by the heroine of one of the tales of the *Mabinogian*, the daughter of Llyr and wife of Matholwch, king of Ireland.

Brenda
Origin uncertain, but it probably derives from Old Norse *brand*, meaning 'sword', or 'torch'. It is sometimes considered, and used, as a feminine form of Brendan, although the names are not, in fact, related.

Brianna
Irish/Gaelic 'strong'.

Briar
From Old English *brær*. A direct adoption from the English vocabulary, referring to a thorny bush of wild roses; one of the more recent names taken from flowers, appearing in the early 20th century.

Bride, Bridie
Variations of Bridget, particularly popular in Scotland and Ireland.

Bridget, Brigit
From the Irish name Brighid (*breed*), meaning 'high one', or 'strength'. The name of the Celtic goddess of poetry, St Brigid of Kildare (c. 450-525), an Irish abbess who founded a religious community for women and who is considered the second patron saint of Ireland, after St Patrick. She composed a series of meditations on the Passion, each beginning 'O Jesu', called the Fifteen Os of St Bridget. Her feast day is 1st February. Variations: Bedelia, Bride, Brigette, Brigid, Brigitta. Diminutives: Biddy, Bridie.

Brigid
Variation of Bridget incorporating the hard 'g' introduced by the Swedish form of the name, Birgitta.

Brigitta
Latinate form of Bridget.

Brigitte
French form of Bridget.

Briony, Bryony
Greek, meaning 'luxurious growth', used for a type of hedgerow plant with berries. It was adopted with the late 19th-century fashion for plant and flower names.

Brita, Britt
Diminutives of Birgitta.

Brittany
English name for Bretagne, an area of north-west France. First used in the 1960s, by the 1980s it was one of the most popular names for a girl in the US.

Britannia
From Britannia, the Latin name for Britain. It has been in occasional use as first name since the 18th century.

Bronwen, Bronwyn
Welsh, meaning 'white breast'. Long popular in Wales, the name has been widely used outside Wales since the mid-20th century. Diminutive: Bron.

Brooke
Adopted surname, meaning 'brook'. Popular in the US as a girl's name since the mid-1900s, and used as a boy's name the US and Britain for much longer.

Brunetta
Feminine form of Bruno.

Brunhild
From Old German *brun*, 'armour' and *hild* 'battle': in the medieval Teutonic epic poem *Nibelungenlied*, upon which Richard Wagner based his operatic *Ring* cycle (1876), Brunhild was the daughter of the king of Islant, beloved by Gunther. Famed for her superhuman strength, she vowed to marry the man who could make his way through the flames encircling her castle. Siegfried helped Gunther to win her by achieving the feat disguised as Gunther, for which she never forgave him. When she realised the trick that had been played on her, she had Siegfried killed then killed herself.

Bunty
Ancient English dialect word for a baby lamb, adopted as a pet name.

C

Cade
Pure and fair. Can also be a boy's name taking the meaning 'handsome'

Caítlin
Irish Gaelic form of Catherine. The traditional pronunciation *kat-leen* is slowly being eclipsed by the more modern *kayt-lin* as the name spreads to non-Irish communities.

Caítrin
(*kat-reen*) Irish Gaelic form of Catherine.

Cameron
Adopted Scottish surname, from Gaelic *cam srón*, 'crooked nose'. It is particularly popular in the US, Canada and Australia, and is also used for boys.

Camilla
Feminine form of the Roman family name Camillus, possibly meaning 'child acolyte'. In Roman mythology it was borne by a Volscian warrior queen who fought with Turnus against Aeneas. Virgil claimed in the *Aeneid* that she was such a fast runner that she could run over a field of corn without bending a single blade, and over the sea without getting her feet wet. Diminutives: Millie, Milly. Variation: Camille.

Camille
French form of Camilla or Camillus. It was used by Alexandre Dumas for the heroine of *La Dame aux Camélias* (1848). It is also given as a boy's name in France.

Candace, Candice
Hereditary title of the queens of Moroe, in Upper Nubia, Ethiopia, one of whom is mentioned in the Bible (Acts 8). Its origin is unknown but it spread to the English-speaking world in the 17th century. Diminutive: Candy.

Candida
Feminine form of the Latin adjective *candidus*, 'white'. Borne by several early saints, including a Neapolitan woman cured by St Paul. Diminutive: Candy. See also: Bianca, Blanche.

Candy
Diminutive of Candace or Candida, sometimes used in its own right.

Cara
Feminine form of Italian *caro*, 'dear', or from Irish Gaelic *cara*, 'friend'. It was a mid-20th century coinage. Variations: Carina, Carita, Kara, Karina.

Carey
Adopted surname and place name in Devon and Somerset. It was adopted as a girl's name in the later 20th century, possibly under the influence of Carrie. It is also used for boys.

Carina
Diminutive feminine form deriving from Italian *caro*, 'dear'. Variations: Carita, Karina.

Carla
Feminine form of Carl and ultimately Charles. It has been popular since the 1950s. Diminutive: Carly.

Carleen, Carlene
Modern feminine forms of Carl, probably coined under the influence of Darlene, Jolene etc.

Carlotta
Italian form of Charlotte, and ultimately a feminine form of Charles. Diminutive: Carly.

Carly
Diminutive of Carla, Carlotta or Caroline, and ultimately a feminine form of Carl and Charles.

Carmel
Hebrew, meaning 'garden'. Mount Carmel, near Haifa in Israel, was where Elijah summoned Israel to choose between God and Baal (I Kings 18). It was also traditionally the site of a church visited by the Virgin Mary with her child. In the 12th century the Carmelite order of mendicant monks was founded at Carmel, and an order of nuns was created in 1452. Variations: Carmela, Carmelita, Carmen.

Carmela, Carmelita
Variations of Carmel, of Italian origin.

Carmen
Variation of Carmel, of Spanish origin, probably associated with Latin *carmen*, 'song', or 'charm'. It was used by Prosper Mérimée for a short story (1847), upon which Bizet's opera *Carmen* (1875) was based. Carmen, a beautiful but fickle gypsy girl, is assigned to the custody of Don José after her arrest for fighting. He falls in love with her and allows her to escape. She attends a bullfight with the glamourous bullfighter Escamillo. José seeks her and asks her to come and live with him, but she refuses and he stabs her to death, at the very moment of Escamillo's triumph in the ring.

Carol
Feminine form of Charles, via the original Latin name Carolus. Initially most common as a boy's name, it is now generally used for girls, probably influenced by Caroline. It is occasionally used for Christmas babies, although there is no etymological connection with Christmas songs. Variations: Carola, Carole, Caryl.

Carola
Feminine form of Charles, via the original Latin name Carolus, occurring from the 17th century onwards.

Carole
French form of Carol.

Carolina
Latinate form of Caroline. Its adoption was possibly influenced by North and South Carolina in the US, named after the British king Charles I. Diminutive: Lina.

Caroline
Feminine form of Charles, via the Italian diminutive feminine form of the original Latin name Carolus. It was introduced to Britain by Caroline of Ansbach, German-born wife of the British king George II. Diminutives: Carly, Caro, Carrie, Caz. Variations: Carolina, Carolyn.

Carolyn
Variation of Caroline, from the early 20th century.

Carrie
Diminutive of Caroline, dating from the late 19th century.

Caryl
Variation of Carol or Carys. It is also used for boys.

Carys
Welsh, from *car*, 'love', plus the Welsh feminine ending -ys, as in Nerys. Variations: Caryl, Cerys, Cheryl.

Casey
Originally a boy's name (See Boys: Casey), it is now increasingly given to girls. It is occasionally used as a diminutive of Katherine. Variation: Cassie.

Cassandra
Greek, origin unknown, but possibly a feminine variation of Alexander. In Greek mythology it was borne by a Trojan princess, daughter of King Priam, who was endowed with the gift of prophecy. She refused Apollo's advances, which so enraged him that he arranged for her never to be believed. She appears in Shakespeare's *Troilus and Cressida* (1602). Diminutives: Cas, Cassie, Sandra.

Cassie
Diminutive of Cassandra, sometimes used in its own right.

Cath, Cathie, Cathy
Diminutives of Catherine.

Catherine
Greek, from Aikaterina, of uncertain origin. The Latin form, Katherine, is associated with Greek *katheros*, 'pure' or 'clear', now the name's accepted meaning. Borne by several early saints, including St Catherine of Alexandria, a 4th-century virgin martyr of noble birth who was condemned to die on a spiked wheel. The wheel miraculously broke, whereupon she was beheaded instead. She is the patron saint of wheelwrights and is usually depicted carrying a wheel, from which we derive the concept of a Catherine wheel. Her cult had spread to Britain by the 12th century. St Catherine of Siena (1347-80), who was instrumental in bringing about the return of the pope to Rome from Avignon, is considered the patron saint of Italy. Catherine is one of the most perennially popular names throughout the English-speaking world. Diminutives: Casey, Cate, Cath, Cathie, Cathy, Kate, Kath, Kathie, Kathy, Katie, Katy, Kay, Kit, Kitty, all also used in their own right. Variations: Caitlín, Cathleen, Cathryn, Catrin, Catriona, Karen, Katharine, Katherine, Kathleen, Kathryn.

Cathleen
Variation of Catherine, influenced by the Irish Gaelic name Caitlín. Variation: Kathleen.

Catrin
Welsh form of Catherine.

Catriona
(*cat-ree-ona*) Anglicisation of Caitríona or Caitríona, respectively Scottish Gaelic and Irish variations of Catherine. It was used by Robert Louis Stevenson for his novel *Catriona* (1893). Variation: Katrina.

Cecile
French feminine form of Cecil.

Cecilia
Latinate feminine form of Cecil. Borne in the 2nd century by a blind Roman martyr and saint, who is said to have invented the organ. She is regarded as patron saint of music and musicians. Her feast day is 22nd November. Diminutives: Cis, Ciss, Cissie, Cissy, Sissie, Sissy. Variations: Cecilie, Cecily, Cicely.

Cecilie
French feminine form of Cecil, and variation of Cecilia or Cecily.

Cecily, Cicely
Medieval anglicised forms of Cecilia.

Ceinwen
From Welsh meaning 'beautiful gems'.

Celeste
French, from Latin *caelestis*, 'heavenly', the source of several names popular among early Christians. It is used for both boys and girls in France but outside France is generally given only to girls.

Celestina, Celestine
Variations, originally diminutives, of Celeste. Celestine was borne by five popes, although the name is now used exclusively for girls.

Celia
Feminine form of the Roman family name Caelius, itself possibly derived from Latin *caelum*, 'heaven'. It was used by Shakespeare in *As You Like It* (1599). It is often considered a diminutive of Cecilia, although it is actually unrelated. Variations: Caelia, Sheila, Shelagh.

Celina
Variation of Selena.

Celine
From a French name, Céline, itself derived from Latin *caelum*, 'sky'. It is especially popular in Canada. Variations: Celine, Selena, Selina.

Ceridwen
Welsh, from *cerdd*, 'poetry', and *gwen*, 'fair, white, holy, blessed'. Borne by the Welsh goddess of poetic inspiration, the mother of Taliesin, who according to Welsh legend prepared the cauldron of knowledge.

Cerys
Variation of Carys.

Chandra
Indian, from Sanskrit, meaning 'moon'. The moon is generally considered a male deity, but the name is also used for girls.

Chandrakanta
Feminine form of the masculine Hindu name Chandrakant, from Sanskrit, literally meaning 'beloved by the moon' and referring to a semi-precious moonstone that features in Hindu texts. Borne in Hindu legend by the wife of the moon.

Chanel
Adopted French surname, from Old French, meaning 'wine amphora'. Its adoption as a first name is purely an association with Gabrielle 'Coco' Chanel (1883-1971), founder of the French fashion house that bears her name. It has been used as a first name, particularly in the US, since the mid-20th century. Variations: Chanelle, Shanel, Shanell, Shanelle.

Chantal
Adopted French surname and place name, after Chantal in Saône-et-Loire. It was first adopted at the beginning of the 20th century, probably in honour of St Jeanne-Françoise Frémiot (1572-1641), wife of the Baron de Chantal, who founded a holy order of nuns, the Visitandines. Variations: Chantel, Chantelle, Shantelle.

Charis
From Greek *charis*, 'grace'. Although grace is an important Christian concept, it was not adopted as a name until the 17th century, possibly influenced by an apparent (but erroneous) association with Charity.

Charity
From Old French *charité*, 'Christian

love', from Latin *caritas*. It is held to be the greatest of the three Christian virtues (1 Corinthians 13). It was a Puritan adoption, along with several of the abstract nouns denoting admirable personal qualities. Diminutives: Charrie, Chattie, Chatty, Cherry. See also: Faith, Hope.

Charlene
Feminine form of Charles. It is a modern coinage, popular in Australia and the US. Variations: Sharleen, Sharlene.

Charlie
Diminutive of Charlotte.

Charlotte
French feminine diminutive of Charles, used in Britain since the 17th century. It was popularised by Charlotte Sophia (1744-1818), wife of the British king George III, and is one of the most enduringly popular of girls' names. Diminutives: Charley, Charlie, Chattie, Chatty, Lottie, Lotty, Totty.

Charmaine
A 20th-century invention of uncertain origin, but possibly derived from Carminea, the feminine form of the Roman clan name Carmineus; or from charm, plus the feminine suffix -aine, as in Lorraine. Variation: Sharmaine.

Charmian
From Greek *kharma*, 'delight' or 'joy'. It was used by William Shakespeare for Cleopatra's attendant in *Antony and Cleopatra* (1606). Variation: Charmianne.

Chastity
From Latin *castus*, 'pure'.

Chastity Sun
Sonny Bono and Cher's daughter.

Chattie, Chatty
Diminutives of Charity or Charlotte.

Chelsea
Modern coinage, ostensibly derived from an area of south-west London that was particularly fashionable in the Swinging Sixties. Borne by the daughter of the US President Bill Clinton, who is said to have been named after the song Chelsea Morning, by the American singer-songwriter Joni Mitchell.

Cherie
From French *chérie*, 'darling'. Variations: Cher, Chère, Cherry, Sherri, Sherry.

Cherry
Originally a diminutive of Charity, it later became associated with the fruit, and later still began to be used as a variation of Cherie. Variation: Cheryl.

Cheryl
An early 20th-century coinage, possibly a variation of Cherry or Carys, influenced by Beryl. Variation: Sheryl.

Chesna
From Slavic meaning 'peaceful'

Chiara
(*kee-ar-a*) Italian form of Clara and Clare, and the form by which the several Italian saints known outside Italy as Clara or Clare would have been known. Most popular of these is St Clare of Assissi (c. 1193-1253), founder of the order of nuns known as the Poor Clares. This form is increasingly used in its own right throughout the English-speaking world.

Chiquita
From Spanish meaning 'little one'.

Chlöe

(*klow-ee*) From Greek, probably derived from *khloros*, 'green', and meaning 'green shoot'. Associated with Demeter, Greek goddess of agriculture and fertility, it was borne in Longus's Greek pastoral romance, *Daphnis and Chloe*, by a shepherdess loved by Daphnis, from which the name later developed into a generic term in literature for a rustic maiden. Alexander Pope used the name in his *Moral Essays* (1731-5). Chloe is also a biblical name, mentioned briefly in the New Testament (1 Corinthians 1:11). The name became popular in the 17th century, both with the Puritans and with those of a literary bent, and has remained in use ever since.

Chloris

From Greek *khloros*, 'green' or 'greenish'. Borne in Greek legend by a minor goddess of vegetation and fertility. The name appeared in the works of the Roman lyric poet Horace (65-8 BC).

Chris, Chrissie, Chrissy

Diminutives of Christabel, Christiana, Christina or Christine.

Christa

Latinate diminutive of Christabel, Christine or Christina. Probably a German diminutive originally, it is now well used in its own right in the English-speaking world.

Christabel

A 19th-century coinage combining the first element of Christine, plus -bel, from Latin *bella*, 'beautiful'. It was probably first used by Samuel Taylor Coleridge in his poem *Christabel* (1816). Diminutives: Bel, Chris, Christa, Christie, Christy.

Christiana

Medieval Latinate form of Christian. Used by John Bunyan for the wife of Christian in Part II of *The Pilgrim's Progress* (1684), who followed her husband from the City of Destruction, with their children. Diminutives: Chris, Christie, Christy.

Christie, Christy

Diminutive of all names beginning Christ-, such as Christabel, Christine, etc.

Christina

Feminine form derived from the Latin name Christianus, meaning 'follower of Christ'. Diminutives: Chris, Chrissie, Chrissy, Tina. Variations: Christine, Kristina, Kristine.

Christine

French form of Christina that spread to Britain in the late 19th century. Diminutives: Chris, Chrissie, Chrissy. Variations: Christeen, Christene, Christina, Kirsten, Kristen, Kristin, Kristina.

Chryseis

From Latin for 'golden daughter'.

Ciara

(*kee-ar-a*) Modern Irish feminine form of Ciaran.

Cicely

Common medieval English form of Cecily. Diminutives: Cis, Ciss, Cissie, Cissy, Sissie, Sissy. Variations: Cecilia, Cecily, Sisley.

Cilla

Diminutive of Priscilla.

Cindy

Diminutive of Lucinda, often used in its own right. Variation: Sindy.

Cis, Ciss, Cissie, Cissy,
Diminutives of Cecilia or Cicely, sometimes used in their own right.

Claire
Originally introduced to Britain as a French form of Clara by Norman invaders, it was revived in the 19th century as the French form of Clare. Variations: Clair, Clayre.

Clara
(*klair-a*, *klar-a*) Feminine form of the Latin adjective *clarus*, 'bright' or 'famous'. It has been largely replaced by Claire and Clare, and the increasingly popular Chiara. Variations: Clair, Claire, Clare, Claribel, Clarice, Clarinda, Clayre.

Clare
Common medieval English form of Clara. Variations: Clair, Claire, Clayre.

Claribel
Variation of Clara formed by the addition of -bel, from Latin *bella*, 'beautiful'. Edmund Spenser used the name for the bride of Phaon in *The Faerie Queene* (1590-6). Mrs Charlotte Alington-Barnard (1830-69), a popular ballad writer of her day, took the name as a pseudonym.

Clarice
Variation of Clara, of Italian and Spanish origin. Variation: Clarissa.

Clarinda
Variation of Clara formed by adding the feminine element -inda. First used by Edmund Spenser in *The Faerie Queene* (1590-6).

Clarissa
Latinate form of Clarice. It was used by Samuel Richardson for the heroine of his novel *Clarissa* (1748).

Clarrie
Diminutive of any feminine name beginning Clar-, such as Clarinda or Clarissa.

Claudette
French feminine and diminutive form of Claud.

Claudia
Feminine form derived from the Roman family name Claudius, itself derived from *claudus*, 'lame'. A biblical name; it is mentioned by St Paul (2 Timothy 4). Especially popular in Italy, it has been in use in the English-speaking world since the 16th century.

Claudine
French feminine and diminutive form of Claud.

Clemence, Clemency
From Latin *clemens*, meaning 'merciful, mild'. The name emerged in France and Britain in the Middle Ages, was popular with the Puritans but is uncommon in modern times.

Clementina, Clementine
Feminine forms of Clement, of German origin. Clementine is formed by the addition of the French feminine diminutive suffix -ine. Clementina is the Latinate form. Diminutives: Clem, Clemmie.

Cleo
Diminutive of Cleopatra, often used in its own right.

Cleopatra
From Greek *kleos*, 'glory', and *pater*, 'father', meaning 'born of a famous father'. Borne by several queens and princesses of the ruling Ptolemy family of Egypt, the most famous of which ruled Egypt (69-30 BC) as the sister and wife of

her brother, Ptolemy Dionysius. She became the lover of both Julius Caesar, by whom she had a son, and Mark Antony. When Mark Antony was defeated by Octavian, Cleopatra committed suicide by placing a poisonous asp at her breast. It is in occasional use as a first name.

Clíodhna
Original Irish Gaelic form of Cliona.

Cliona
Anglicised form of the Irish name Clíodhna, of uncertain origin. Borne in Irish legend by a beautiful fairy woman, one of three daughters of the poet Libra.

Clodagh
Modern adoption, from a river in County Tipperary, Ireland. It was probably first used by the Marquis of Waterford for his daughter.

Clotilda, Clotilde
Old German, from *hloda*, 'loud', and *hildi*, 'battle'. Borne by a 6th-century French saint.

Coco
Chosen by Courtney Cox and David Arquette for their daughter.

Cody
Adopted Irish surname, of uncertain origin. Probably first given in honour of the Wild West hero William Frederick Cody (1847-1917), otherwise known as Buffalo Bill, it has become common for both boys and girls in the US and Australia.

Colette
Diminutive of Nicolette, itself a French diminutive of Nicholas, used in its own right. Borne by a 15th-century French nun and saint, the name was popularised by the French writer Colette, whose full name was Sidonie Gabrielle Colette (1873-1954).

Colleen
Irish vernacular word, meaning girl. The name is not found in Ireland, but is popular in Australia.

Columbina, Columbine
Italian feminine diminutive forms of the Latin first name Columba, meaning 'dove'. Columbina is an Italian pet name for a lady-love. Columbine was the name borne, in the 15th-century Italian tradition of *commedia dell'arte*, by the daughter of Pantaloon, loved by Harlequin. Like Harlequin she was supposed to be invisible to mortal eyes. The character was subsequently adopted by the English pantomime tradition. However, modern usage is more likely to be part of the late 19th-century fashion for flower names, in this case after a hedgerow rambler.

Concetta
Italian form of a Latin name, Concepta, from *concepta*, 'conceived', a reference to the Immaculate Conception.

Conchita
Spanish form of Concetta.

Connie
Diminutive of Constance.

Constance
From Latin *constantia*, 'constancy'. It was a Norman introduction to Britain. Diminutive: Connie.

Constantia
Latin form of Constance. Diminutive: Connie.

Cora
Possibly from Greek *kore*, 'girl'. It was

invented by the American novelist James Fenimore Cooper for the heroine of *Last of the Mohicans* (1826). Variation: Coralie.

Coral
From Old French *corail*, ultimately from the Greek *korallion*, and denoting a hard calcareous substance secreted by some marine polyps, regarded as semi-precious and used for centuries to make jewellery. One of several jewel names that became fashionable in the late 19th century, it is unusual in modern times.

Coralie
Probably an elaboration of Cora, influenced by names such as Rosalie.

Cordelia
Origin uncertain, possibly from Latin *cor*, 'heart'. It was used by Shakespeare for the youngest daughter of King Lear. Diminutive: Delia.

Corinna, Corinne
From the Greek *kore*, 'maiden'. Corinna was an alternative name for Persephone, and the name of a 5th-century Greek poetess. It was used by the Roman poet Ovid in his love poetry, and later revived by 17th-century British poets. Corinne is the French form.

Cornelia
Feminine form of Cornelius, borne in the 2nd century BC by the devoted mother of the revolutionary reformers Tiberius, Gaius and Sempronia Gracchus. On their father's death in 154 BC she refused to marry again but dedicated herself to the upbringing of her children. According to legend, when asked to display her jewellery, Cornelia produced her sons, saying: 'These are the only jewels of which I can boast.'

Cosima
Feminine form of Cosmo.

Courtney
Adopted aristocratic surname, originally from a French place name, Courtenay. It is sometimes erroneously thought to derive from French *court nez*, 'short nose'. The name is very popular in the US.

Cressida
Greek, of complex origin. Borne in Greek mythology by a Trojan princess, daughter of Calchas and fickle mistress of Troilus. The name Briseis occurs for a captive Greek girl in the *Iliad* (8th century BC), then Benoît de Sainte-Maure, a 12th-century poet, adapted the name as Briseaida in his *Roman de Troie* (c. 1160). Boccaccio altered the name to Criseida, basing this on the name of another Greek captive girl, Chryseis, the daughter of Chryses. Chaucer retold the story in *Troilus and Criseyde*, from which Shakespeare derived the material for *Troilus and Cressida* (1601). Despite its negative associations the name has enjoyed a steady, quiet popularity.

Crystal
From Old French *cristal*, ultimately derived from Greek *krustallos*, meaning 'ice', and denoting a form of semi-precious clear quartz. One of several stone and mineral names that became fashionable in the late 19th century, it was probably influenced by Christel, a German form of Christine. A currency as a Scottish diminutive form of Christopher is now obsolete. Variation: Krystle.

Cynthia
From the Greek name Kynthia, meaning 'of Cynthos', a mountain on the island of Delos. It was an additional name for the Greek goddess Artemis, said to have been

born on Delos, and as such the name is also associated with the moon. Cynthia was one of many names applied to Elizabeth I by contemporary poets, and became popular in Britain during the 17th-century classical revival.

Cyrena
Classical Greek from Cyrene a water nymph who was the beloved of Apollo.

Cyrille
French form of Cyril.

Cytheria
From the Greek island Cythera which is associated with the goddess Aphrodite.

D

Daffodil
Altered form of the Greek *asphodelos*, 'asphodel', denoting a type of narcissus with yellow flowers indigenous to Western Europe. It was one of the less successful of the flower names adopted in the late 19th century. Diminutive: Dilly.

Dagmar
Scandinavian, from Old German *dag*, 'day', and *meri*, 'famous'. Borne by a Czech princess who became Queen of Denmark (d 1212), the name spread to Britain from Denmark in the 20th century.

Daisy
From Old English, meaning 'day's eye', a reference to the fact that the flower of the same name opens during the day. Daisy was first used as a diminutive of the French name Marguerite, which was adopted in the early 19th century to refer to a cultivated variety of daisy. It was further popularised by the late 19th-century fashion for flower names. Henry James used the name for the heroine of his novel *Daisy Miller* (1878), and it remains consistently popular. See also: Marguerite.

Daisy Boo
Julia and Jamie Oliver.

Dakota
Native American suggesting friendship.

Dale
Adopted surname, meaning 'valley', first used in the early 20th century. It is also used for boys.

Damaris
Greek, possibly from *damalis*, 'calf'. It was the Greek name of an Athenian woman converted by St Paul (Acts 17), and was adopted by the Puritans.

Dana
(*dah-na*, *day-na*) Celtic goddess of fertility. It is also used as a Scandinavian feminine form of Daniel.

Danaí
Borne in Greek legend by the daughter of Acrisius, king of Argos. Acrisius was told by the oracle that he would die by the hand of his daughter's son, so he locked her away in a tower so that she might never marry or have children. However, Zeus turned himself into a shower of gold and Danaí let him in, as a result of which Perseus was born. Mother and son were then set adrift, but rescued by Zeus. King Polydectes took them in but, being interested only in Danaí, he sent Perseus away on an apparently impossible mission to find the head of Medusa, which turned to stone all who looked on it. But he succeeded and returned, turning Polydectes to stone. He later accidentally killed his grandfather, Acrisius, with a discus, in fulfilment of the oracle. The name is

used occasionally in the English-speaking world.

Dandelion
Keith Richard's daughter.

Danica
Norse for the morning star.

Daniela, Daniella, Danielle
Feminine forms of Daniel. Danielle, the French form, has been in use in the English-speaking world since the mid-20th century. Daniella is the Latinate form. Diminutive: Dani.

Danita
Feminine form of Daniel.

Daphne
Greek, meaning 'laurel'. In Greek mythology borne by the daughter of the river god Peneus in Thessaly. Having vowed to die a virgin, Daphne fled the advances of Apollo. The gods took pity on her and turned her into a laurel tree. Apollo declared that henceforth he would wear laurel rather than oak, and exorted others to do the same. The name was very popular in the early 20th century.

Dara
From Hebrew meaning charity, compassion and wisdom.

Darcey, Darcy
Adopted Norman baronial surname (D'Arcy), introduced to Britain by the Normans. It is also used for boys.

Daria
Feminine form of Darius from Greek associated with Queen or wealthy woman.

Darlene
Modern coinage from the US, probably a modification of 'darling'.

Darrell
Adopted surname, from a French place name, Airelle, in the northern French region of Calvados. Originally a boy's name, its occasional use for girls may be due to Enid Blyton's use of the name (her married surname) for the central character of her *Malory Towers* series of children's books. Variations: Darell, Darrel, Darryl, Daryl.

Dassah
Diminutive of Hadassah.

Davida
Scottish feminine form of David, dating from the 17th century. Diminutive: Vida.

Davina, Davinia
Scottish feminine forms of David, dating from the 17th century. Diminutives: Vina, Vinia.

Dawn
Direct vocabulary adoption, dating from the mid-20th century. See also: Aurora.

Deane
Variation of Diane.

Deanna
Variation of Diana, popularised by the 1930s Canadian actress Deanna Durbin, who formed the name from her own given name, Edna.

Deb, Debbie, Debby, Debs
Diminutives of Deborah, sometimes used in their own right.

Deborah
Hebrew, meaning 'bee'. A biblical name;

borne by two figures of the Old Testament. One is the nurse of Rebekah (Genesis 35), the other a prophetess and judge who led the Israelites against the Sisera and the Canaanites (Judges 4). It was a Puritan adoption. Diminutives: Deb, Debbie, Debby, Debs. Variation. Debra.

Debra
Modern respelling of Deborah.

Decima
Feminine form of Decimus, in the past traditionally given to a tenth child, if a daughter, a rare occurrence today.

Dee
Diminutive of any name beginning with 'D'. It is also used in its own right.

Deirdre
Irish name of uncertain origin, probably meaning 'raging' or 'sorrowful'. In Celtic legend Deirdre was the daughter of the storyteller to Conchobhar, king of Ulster. At her birth it was prophesied that she would bring ruin to Ireland. Conchobhar wanted to marry her, and when she fell in love with Naoise, one of the sons of Usnech, he had him treacherously killed. Deirdre then killed herself. The legend was treated by the Irish poet W B Yeats in his 1907 poem *Deirdre*, and by the Irish playwright J M Synge in his play *Deirdre of the Sorrows* (1910).

Delia
From Greek *delos*, meaning 'visible' or 'clear'. The name derives from Delos, the smallest of the Greek islands of the Cyclades, where legend has it that Artemis and Apollo were born. It was used by several pastoral poets of the 17th century. It is also used as a diminutive of names ending in -delia, such as Cordelia.

Delilah
Hebrew, possibly meaning 'amorous'. A biblical name; borne in the Old Testament by the mistress of Samson, who betrayed him by cutting off his hair, source of his strength, as he slept (Judges 16). It was a Puritan adoption, rather surprisingly.

Della
Diminutive of Adela, often used in its own right since the late 19th century.

Delora
Latin 'from the seashore'.

Delphine
French, from the Latin name Delphina, meaning 'woman of Delphi', the site in Greece of Apollo's oracle, itself from Greek *delphis*, 'dolphin'. A later association, ultimately from the same source, is with the flower, delphinium.

Delwen, Delwyn
Welsh, from *del*, 'neat', and *wyn*, 'white, fair, blessed, holy'.

Delyth
From Welsh meaning neat and pretty

Demelza
Adopted Cornish place name, meaning 'hill fort of Maeldaf'. It was made famous by Winston Graham in his series of *Poldark* novels, adapted for television in the 1970s.

Dena
North American Indian meaning 'a valley'.

Denise
(*den-ees*, *den-eez*) French feminine form of Denis, first used in Britain in the 12th century.

Dervla
From the Irish Gaelic name Deirbhile, from *der*, 'daughter', and *file*, 'poet'. It is also associated with Dearbhail, meaning 'daughter of Fal', which is anglicised as Derval. It is undergoing a revival in Ireland.

Deryn
Welsh, probably from *aderyn*, 'bird'.

Desdemona
Latinate form of Greek *dysdaimon*, 'ill-starred, miserable'. It was used by Shakespeare for the wronged wife of *Othello* (1604), a Venetian noblewoman who marries Othello against her father's wishes. The wicked Iago constructs a scenario in which she appears to be unfaithful, for which Othello kills her. It is in occasional use in the English-speaking world.

Desiree
From *desirée*, 'desired', French form of the Latinate name Desideria.

Devon
Adopted surname and English county name, widely used in the US for boys and girls, where pronunciation tends to stress the second syllable. Variation: Devonne.

Di
Diminutive of Diana or Diane.

Diamond
From the name of the precious stone.

Diana
Roman goddess of fertility, hunting and the moon (counterpart of the greek godess Artemis), whose name was probably derived from Latin *divinus*, 'divine'. In use since the 16th century, the name has not experienced the revival that might have been expected after the death of the widely admired Diana, Princess of Wales, although there has been a noticeable increase in the use of the names William and Harry for boys. Variations: Deanna, Diane, Dyan.

Diane
French form of Diana dating from the Renaissance. Variation: Dyan.

Dilys
Welsh, meaning 'genuine'. A mid-19th century coinage.

Dinah
Hebrew, from *din*, 'judgement'. A biblical name; borne by a daughter of Jacob and Leah. A Puritan adoption, it has been very popular in the US.

Dione, Dionne
From Greek *dios*, 'divine'. Borne in Greek mythology by the daughter of Oceanus and Tethys, and mother of Jupiter and Venus. The name is also used for Venus herself. It is also regarded by some as a feminine form of Dion, a variation (originally a diminutive) of Denis. Variations: Deon, Deonne.

Dionysia
Feminine form of Dionysius, source of Denis and hence Denise. The name has another meaning: Dionysus (NB a different spelling) was the god of wine, the Greek equivalent of Bacchus, hence Dionysia is the vocabulary equivalent of Bacchanalia, the extreme sensual rites held in honour of the gods of wine.

Dodie
Diminutive of Dorothy.

Doll, Dolly
Diminutives of Dorothy, dating from the

16th century, and sometimes used in their own right.

Dolores
Spanish, from *Maria de los Dolores*, 'Maria of the Sorrows' (from Spanish *dolor*, 'sorrow'), a reference to the Virgin Mary. Diminutives: Lola, Lolita.

Domenica, Dominica
Feminine forms of Dominic.

Dominique
French form of Dominic, popular throughout the English-speaking world since the 1950s.

Donalda
Feminine form of Donald.

Donna
From Italian *donna*, 'woman'. It was an American coinage of the 1920s. See also: Madonna.

Dora
Diminutive of Dorothea, Dorothy, Pandora, Theodora, etc, used in its own right since the 19th century. Variations: Doreen, Dorette, Dorinda, Dorita.

Dorcas
Greek, meaning 'gazelle'. A biblical name; Dorcas (also called Tabitha) was raised from the dead by St Peter (Acts 9:36-41). A Puritan adoption, it is particularly popular in the US.

Doreen
Origin disputed; either from the Irish name Doirean, possibly meaning 'sullen', or an elaboration of Dora, itself a diminutive of Dorothy.

Dorette
Variation of Dora.

Doria
Feminine form of Dorian.

Dorice
Variation of Doris.

Dorinda
Invented by George Farquhar for his 1707 play *The Beaux Stratagem*, probably influenced by names such as Belinda and Clarinda. Variations: Dora, Dorothy.

Doris
Place name of an area of Ancient Greece, and also, in Greek mythology, the name of the mother of the fifty sea nymphs called the Nereids (all of whom are named by Edmund Spenser in *The Faerie Queene* IV xi: 48-51). It is also seen as a variation of Dora and Dorothy. Particularly popular in the 19th century, it is rare today. Variations: Dorice, Dorita.

Dorita
Variation of Dora or Doris.

Dorothea
Greek, from *theos*, 'god', and *doron*, 'gift'. St Dorothea was a virgin martyr, killed under Diocletian in c. 300. Her feast day is 6th February. She is generally depicted carrying roses and fruit, a reference to the story that, as she was walking to her execution, the judge's secretary laughingly asked her to send him back roses and fruit from Paradise. No sooner had she died than an angel presented the man with a basket of fruit and roses, saying: 'From Dorothea, in Paradise', whereupon he was immediately converted. The name spread to Britain in the 15th century and underwent a 19th-century revival after the publication of George Eliot's 1872 novel *Middlemarch*, whose heroine is Dorothea. Diminutives: Dora, Thea. Variations: Dorothy, Theodora.

Dorothy
Variation of Dorothea most popular in the English-speaking world. A 16th-century adoption, and hugely popular in the early 20th century. Diminutives: Dodie, Doll, Dolly, Dora, Dot, Dottie. Variations: Doreen, Dorinda.

Dorrie
Diminutive of any name beginning Dor-.

Dot, Dottie
Diminutives of Dorothy.

Dowsabel
Anglicisation of Dulcibella, from Latin *dulcis*, 'sweet', and *bella*, 'beautiful'. In 16th-century poetry it became a common name for a sweetheart, especially a simple rustic girl.

Dreda
Diminutive of Eldreda or Etheldreda.

Drew
Diminutive of Andrew but occasionally used for girls, especially in the US.

Drusilla
Feminine diminutive of the Roman family name Drusus, possibly meaning 'firm'. Borne in the 1st century BC by Emperor Caligula's sister and mistress. A biblical name; borne by a convert of St Paul (Acts 24), and later adopted by the Puritans.

Dulce
Diminutive of Dulcie.

Dulcie
From Latin *dulcis*, 'sweet'. A late 19th-century coinage, it was possibly a diminutive of an earlier name Dulcibella. (See also: Dowsabel).

Durga
Indian, from Sanskrit, meaning 'inaccessible'. An epithet of the wife of Shiva, Hindu goddess of death and destruction, it is a reference to her talent for prolonged meditation. When disturbed she presents a terrifying and angry form.

Dusty
Apparently a diminutive of Dustin originally, it is now used as a first name for both girls and boys. It was popularised in the 1960s by the singer Dusty Springfield.

Dymphna, Dympna
Latinate anglicised form of the Irish name Damhnait, of uncertain origin but possibly meaning 'suitable' or 'little deer'. St Dymphna, a medieval Flemish saint, is regarded as patron saint of the insane. She is said to have been the daughter of an Irish chieftain with incestuous intentions, from which she fled to Gheel in Belgium. Her father eventually tracked her down and killed her.

E

Eartha
From Old English *eorthe*, 'earth'.

Ebony
After the type of dense black wood. The name has been used in Afro-American communities since the 1970s.

Eda
Variation of Ada.

Eden
Hebrew, meaning 'place of delight'. A biblical name; scene of the blameless

existence of Adam and Eve before the Fall, traditionally supposed to be in Mesopotamia. A Puritan adoption, it is also used for boys.

Edie
Diminutive of Edith.

Edina
Either a contracted form of Edwina, or possibly a variation of Aithne, the feminine form of Aidan. Diminutive: Ena.

Edith
From the Old English name Easgyth, from *ead*, 'rich', and *gyth*, 'war'. Borne by a 10th-century nun, illegitimate daughter of King Edgar. It was one of few early Anglo-Saxon names to survive the Norman Conquest. Diminutives: Eda, Edie.

Edna
Origin disputed; the name appears in the Apocrypha's Book of Tobit, borne by the stepmother of Tobias, and may be derived from Hebrew, meaning 'pleasure' or possibly 'rejuvenation'. Its modern use may be more as a contracted form of Edwina.

Edwina
Feminine form of Edwin. Variation: Edna.

Effie
Diminutive of Euphemia, also used in its own right.

Eileen
Anglicised form of the Irish name Eibhlin, derived originally from the Norman French name Aveline. Variations: Aileen, Eveleen, Eveline, Evelyn. Diminutive: Eily.

Eilwen
Old Welsh, from *eil*, 'brow', and *gwen*, 'fair, blessed, holy, white'.

Eily
Diminutive of Eileen.

Eira, Eirwen
Modern Welsh, from *eira*, 'snow', Eirwen also including the common Welsh element *gwen*, 'fair, blessed, holy, white'.

Eithne, Ethna, Ethne
(*ee-na*, *et-na*, *en-ya*) Irish Gaelic, origin disputed; either a direct adoption of *eithne*, meaning 'kernel', or diminutives derived from Aodh, Celtic god of fire, hence meaning 'little fire'. The name is borne by many figures in Irish legend. Variations: Aine, Aithne, Ena, Ethnea.

Elain
Welsh meaning 'fawn' or 'young hind'.

Elaine
Old French form of Helen, long used in its own right. In Arthurian legend it was borne by the Lily Maid of Astolat, beautiful mother of Lancelot's son, Sir Galahad. Her unrequited love for Sir Lancelot was 'that love which was her doom' (Tennyson, *Lancelot and Elaine*, 1870). The name underwent a popular revival in the late 19th century, along with many other pre-Conquest names.

Eldreda
Feminine form of Eldred. Diminutive: Dreda.

Eleanor, Elinor
Old French form of Helen, brought to Britain in the 12th century by Eleanor of Aquitaine, wife of Henry II and reinforced by Edward I's wife, Eleanor of Castile (1246-90). Elinor is a 17th-centu-

ry respelling, used by Jane Austen in her 1811 novel *Sense and Sensibility*. Diminutives: Ellie, Nell, Nellie, Nelly. Variations: Eleanora, Lenore, Leonora.

Eleanora
Variation of Eleanor. Diminutives: Ellen, Nora, Norah.

Elena
Variation of Helen dating from the 12th century, now considered an Italian or Spanish form of Helen.

Eleonora
Variation of Leonora.

Elfreda, Elfrida
From the Old English name Aelfthryth, from *aelf*, 'elf', and *thryth*, 'strength', borne by the mother of Ethelred the Unready. It was revived in the 19th century. Diminutive: Freda. Variation: Alfreda.

Elisabeth
Variation of Elizabeth, used in the New Testament and in most European languages.

Elise
French diminutive of Elizabeth widely used in its own right since the late 19th century.

Elissa
In classical mythology an alternative name for Dido, queen of Carthage, but now considered a variation of Elizabeth.

Eliza
Diminutive of Elizabeth dating from the 18th century, and now widely used in its own right.

Elizabeth
From the Hebrew name Elisheba, meaning 'oath of God', borne in the Old Testament by the wife of Aaron. In the New Testament Greek form Elisabeth it was borne by the wife of Zacharias, mother of John the Baptist. The name has been hugely and enduringly popular throughout the English-speaking world since the 16th century. Diminutives: Bess, Bessie, Bessy, Beth, Bethan, Betsey, Betsy, Bette, Betty, Eliza, Libby, Lisbeth, Liz, Liza, Lizbeth, Lizzie, Lizzy, Tetty. Variations: Babette, Beta, Bettina, Elise, Elissa, Elsa, Elsie, Elspeth, Ilsa, Ilse, Isabel (in its various forms), Leisel, Leisl, Lisa, Lise, Lisette, Lysette.

Ella
From the Old German name Alia, meaning 'all'. A Norman introduction, it was revived in the 19th century and is currently undergoing a further revival. It is also sometimes used as a diminutive of names beginning El-, or ending -ella.

Ellen
Most common variation of Helen in the Middle Ages, now used in its own right. It is also used as a diminutive of Eleanor. Diminutives: Ellie, Nell, Nellie, Nelly.

Ellie
Diminutive of Eleanor or Ellen, also used in its own right.

Elma
Possibly a compound of Elizabeth and Mary or a diminutive of Thelma.

Eloisa
Latin and Italian forms of Eloise.

Eloise
Origin disputed; contenders are a form of the Old German name Helewise, and a modification of Aloysia, the Latinate form of Louise. Variations: Eloisa, Lois.

Elsa
Originally a German diminutive of Elisabeth, used in its own right. Variation: Ailsa.

Elsie
Originally a diminutive of Elspeth, the Scottish form of Elizabeth, now used in its own right.

Elspeth
Scottish form of Elizabeth. Diminutives: Elsie, Elspie.

Elspie
Diminutive of Elspeth.

Eluned, Elined, Eiluned
Old Welsh, derived from *eilun*, 'idol'. Variations: Lynette and related names.

Elvira
Spanish name of Germanic origin, albeit obscure. Popularised in the 18th century as the wife of Don Juan in Mozart's opera *Don Giovanni* (1789) and Lord Byron's epic poem, *Don Juan.*

Emanuela, Emmanuela
Feminine forms of Emanuel and Emmanuel respectively.

Emer, Emir
(*ee-mer*) Irish Gaelic, of uncertain meaning. Borne in Irish legend by the woman beloved of Cuchulainn.

Emerald
From Old French *esmeraude*, denoting a bright green precious stone. One of several stone names that became fashionable in the late 19th century, it is rarely found in modern times.

Emily
Feminine form of the Roman family name Aemilius. The 14th-century Italian writer Boccaccio popularised the form Emilia, and Chaucer used the name in the form Emelye in The Knight's Tale. It was very popular in the 18th century and in Victorian times, and has enjoyed a new vogue in the late 20th century. Diminutives: Millie, Milly.

Emina
Origin uncertain but meaning 'daughter of a noble house' or 'highly placed maiden'.

Emlyn
Welsh, originally a boy's name, but now commonly used for girls, as a derivative of Emmeline.

Emma
From Old German *ermin* or *irmin*, meaning 'universal'. Introduced to Britain in the 11th century by Emma of Normandy, wife of Ethelred the Unready and subsequently of King Canute, it experienced an 18th-century revival possibly spawned by Jane Austen's *Emma* (1815). Since the 1970s it has been one of the most favoured names for girls in Britain.

Emmeline
Old French form of the Old German name Ameline, from *amal*, 'work'. A Norman introduction to Britain, it is sometimes erroneously associated with Emily. See also: Amelia.

Ena
Origin uncertain, but probably as a diminutive of any number of names ending -ena or -ina, such as Philomena or Edina. Variation: Ina.

Enid
Welsh, from *enaid*, 'soul'. Borne in Arthurian legend by Enid the Fair, or Enid the Good, daughter of Yniol and wife of

Prince Geraint, a knight of the Round Table. The name underwent a revival following Tennyson's retelling of her story in 'Geraint and Enid', published in *Idylls of the King* (1870).

Eppie
Diminutive of Euphemia or Hephzibah.

Erica, Erika
Feminine form of Eric, sometimes associated with the species of plants called *erica*, which includes heather and rhododendrons and as such reflecting the late 19th-century fashion for plant names. Erika is the German spelling.

Erin
Ancient poetic name for Ireland, from the Irish Gaelic name Éirinn. It is now widely used, especially in the US, with no reference to Ireland.

Ermintrude
Old German, from *ermin*, 'universal', and -trude, the common suffix for German female names, derived from Old German *prup*, meaning 'strength'.

Ernestina, Ernestine
Feminine forms of Ernest.

Esmé, Esmée
Old French, from Latin *aestimatus*, 'esteemed'. Introduced to Scotland from France in the 16th century, it was originally given to both boys and girls but is now almost exclusively used for girls.

Esmeralda
Spanish vocabulary word for 'emerald'. The name was used by Victor Hugo for the heroine of *The Hunchback of Notre Dame* (1831).

Essylt
From Welsh meaning 'beautiful to behold'.

Estella, Estelle
Old French form of Latin *stella*, 'star'. It was used by Charles Dickens for the heroine of *Great Expectations* (1861). Estelle is the modern French form. See also: Stella.

Esther
Biblical; borne in the Old Testament by a Hebrew woman, adopted daughter of Mordecai, who became queen of Persia in the 5th century BC when she married Ahasuerus after he had rejected his disobedient wife, Vashti. The name's origin is disputed; her Hebrew name was Hadassah, 'myrtle', and Esther may be its Persian form, or it may be an independent Persian name, meaning 'star'. Her story is told in the Old Testament book that bears her name, and in the Apocrypha's Rest of Esther. Diminutives: Ettie, Etty. See also: Stella, Vanessa, Vashti.

Étain
Traditional Irish Gaelic name, borne in Irish legend by a fairy princess whose wooing by the mortal King Eochaidh was the subject of a popular opera, The Immortal Hour (1914).

Ethel
Old English, from *aethel*, 'noble'. Originally a diminutive of names beginning Ethel-, such as Etheldreda, it has long been used in its own right.

Etheldreda
Old English, from *æthel*, 'noble', and *pryð*, 'strength'. St Etheldreda, later known as St Audrey, founded an abbey at Ely in the 7th century. Diminutives: Dreda, Ethel. See also: Audrey.

Ethelinda
Old English from Aethelind. Athal 'noble' and lindi 'snake'.

Ethne
Variation of Eithne.

Etta
Either from the Old German element *eda*, meaning 'happy', or a diminutive of names ending in -etta, such as Henrietta.

Ettie, Etty
Diminutives of Esther or Henrietta.

Eudora
Greek, ostensibly from *eu*, 'good', and *doron*, 'gift', although it is probably a learned 19th-century coinage.

Eugenia
Feminine form of Eugene. St Eugenia was an early Roman martyr of whom little is known.

Eugénie
French form of Eugenia. Empress Eugénie (1826-1920), wife of Napoleon III, popularised the name throughout the English-speaking world.

Eulalia, Eulalie
From Greek *eulalos*, meaning 'sweetly speaking'. The name was borne by two 4th-century saints, Eulalia of Barcelona and Eulalia of Merida, both probably put to death by Diocletian. Eulalie is the French form.

Eunice
Greek, from *eu*, 'good', and *nike*, 'victory'. A biblical name; borne in the New Testament by the mother of Timothy (2 Timothy 1). Variation: Unis.

Euphemia
Greek, from *eu*, 'good', and *phenai*, 'to speak'. Borne by a 4th-century martyr, it was first used in Britain in the 12th century and became very popular in the 19th century, particularly in Scotland. Diminutives: Effie, Eppie, Phemie.

Eurwen
Welsh from gwyn 'fair' and aur 'gold' meaning 'beautiful golden girl'.

Eustacia
Feminine form of Eustace.

Eva
Latinate form of Eve. It was popularised by the heroine of Harriet Beecher Stowe's novel *Uncle Tom's Cabin* (1852), whose full name was Evangeline. Diminutives: Evie, Evita.

Evadne
Greek, of uncertain meaning beyond the common element *eu*, 'good'. Borne in Greek mythology by the wife of Capaneus, who loyally threw herself on his funeral pyre.

Evangelina
Latinate form of Evangeline.

Evangeline
Fanciful 19th-century coinage derived from Greek elements *eu*, 'good', and *angelma*, 'news'. Henry Longfellow may have coined the name for his 1847 poem *Evangeline*, or he may have modified an existing Italian name, Evangelista. Harriet Beecher Stowe used the name for the heroine of *Uncle Tom's Cabin* (1852).

Eve
Latin form of a Hebrew name derived from *hayya*, 'alive'. A biblical name; borne in the Old Testament by the first

woman on earth, 'the mother of all living'. Diminutives: Eveleen, Evie.

Eveleen
Irish variation of Eileen, Evelina or Evelyn, and also a diminutive of Eve.

Evelina, Eveline
Variations of Evelyn; Evelina is the Latinate form, Eveline the French. See also: Aveline.

Evelyn
Anglicised form of the Norman French feminine name Aveline. Adopted as a boy's name in the 17th century, it is now more commonly used for girls. Variations: Eileen, Eveleen, Evelina, Eveline.

Evie
Diminutive of Eva, Eve and any names beginning Ev-.

Evita
Diminutive of Eva.

Ezit
Variation of Isolde.

F

Fabia
Latin, feminine form of the Roman family name Fabius. It probably derives from *faba*, 'bean'. See also: Fabiana, Fabiola.

Fabiana
Latin, feminine form of the Roman family name Fabius. See also: Fabia, Fabiola.

Fabiola
Latin, feminine form of the Roman family name Fabius. St Fabiola, a 4th-century member of the Fabius family, opened a hostel for pilgrims to Rome. See also: Fabia, Fabiana.

Fae
Variation of Fay(e).

Faith
One of the three great Christian virtues (with hope and charity), and one of several abstract nouns denoting admirable personal qualities that became popular as names among the Puritans in the 17th century. See also: Charity, Hope.

Fallon
Adopted surname, itself an anglicised form of the Irish surname O Fallamhain, meaning 'leader'. It was popularised by a character in the American television series *Dynasty*, made in the 1980s.

Fanny
Diminutive of Frances.

Farah
Arabic, meaning 'joy' or 'cheerfulness'.

Farrah
A modern coinage, apparently by the parents of the American actress Farrah

Fawcett, who claim they were unaware of the existence of the Arabic name Farah.

Fatima
Arabic, meaning 'abstainer', and hence 'chaste'. An alternative meaning is 'weaner' or 'she who breastfeeds'. Borne by the Prophet Muhammad's favourite daughter, wife of Haidar, by whom she had two sons, Hasan and Husayn. The name is also borne in the ancient and widespread tale of Bluebeard by the last of his wives, the one who discovers the cupboard full of the bodies of his previous wives. He is about to cut her head off when her two brothers rush in and kill him.

Faustina
From Latin faustus 'fortunate'.

Fay, Faye
Origin uncertain; either a diminutive of Faith, or from the English folk word *fay*, 'fairy'.

Fedora, Feodora
Russian forms of Theodora, itself a feminine form of Theodore.

Felda
Teutonic 'from the field' or for one born at harvest time.

Felice, Felicia
Feminine forms of Felix. Popular in Britain from the Middle Ages until the 19th century, they are rarely found today.

Felicity
From Latin *felicitas*, meaning 'good fortune' or 'happiness'. It was one of several abstract nouns denoting admirable personal qualities that became popular with the Puritans in the 17th century.

Fenella
Anglicised Scottish form of the Irish Gaelic name Fionnuala. Variations: Finella, Finola.

Fenn
Adopted surname, originally given to boys, particularly in the US, but now used also for girls.

Fergie
Diminutive of Fergus and popularised by Sarah Ferguson, Duchess of York.

Fern
From Old English *fearn*, denoting a species of foliage plant. One of the more recent of the plant and flower names adopted, it is increasing in popularity.

Ffion
Welsh form of Fiona.

Fidelma
Latinate form of the traditional Irish Gaelic name Feidhelm, of uncertain origin. In Irish legend it was borne by a daughter of Conchobhar mac Nessa, a female warrior renowned for her beauty. It was also borne by the daughter of King Laoghaire and sister of St Eithne, also renowned for her beauty.

Fifi
French pet form of Josephine, but often used as a diminutive of Fiona.

Fifi Trixi Belle
Bob Geldof's daughter

Fina
Italian, of uncertain origin. Borne in the 13th century by a woman of San Gimignano, considered by some as the dullest of all saints. She was technically not a martyr because she did not die vio-

lently, but rather endured apparently endless physical disease until her death. Her feast day is 12th March.

Finella
Anglicised Scottish form of the Gaelic name Fionnuala. Variations: Fenella, Finola.

Finola
Irish- and Scottish-influenced anglicisation of Fionnuala. Variations: Fenella, Finella.

Fiona
Scottish, the Latin form of Gaelic *fionn*, 'white, fair'. Probably first used by James Macpherson (1736-96) in his Ossianic poems, it was later adopted by William Sharp (1855-1905) as a pseudonym. Diminutives: Fi, Fifi.

Fionnuala
(*fya-noo-la*) Irish Gaelic, from *fionn*, 'white, fair', and *guala*, 'shoulder'. Borne in Irish legend by the daughter of King Lir, who was transformed into a swan and condemned to wander over the lakes and rivers until Christianity came to Ireland.

Flavia
Latin, the feminine form of the Roman family name, Flavius, meaning 'yellow (haired)'. See also: Fulvia.

Fleur
Old French name, meaning 'flower'.

Flick
Byname from Felicity.

Flo
Diminutive of Flora or Florence.

Floella
Modern coinage, combining Flo and Ella. It is particularly popular among Afro-Caribbean families.

Flora
Latin, from *flos*, 'flower'. Borne by the Roman goddess of spring and flowers, whose festivals, the Floralia, were held 28 April to 3 May. Diminutives: Flo, Florrie.

Florence
Latin, medieval form of the Latin name Florentius, itself from *florens*, 'flourishing, blooming'. The popularity of the name in the 19th century was in tribute to Florence Nightingale (1820-1910), who was born in Florence. It has enjoyed a late 20th-century revival. Diminutives: Flo, Florrie, Floss, Flossie, Floy

Florinda
Variation of Flora.

Florrie
Scottish diminutive of Flora, or diminutive of Florence.

Floss, Flossie, Floy
Diminutives of Florence.

Flower
From the vocabulary word. See also: Fleur.

Fortune
Latin, from *fortuna*, 'good luck'. It was adopted in the 17th century by the Puritans.

Fran
Diminutive of Frances or Francesca.

Frances
Feminine form of Francis, itself an anglicised form of the Italian name Francisco,

meaning 'French'. Diminutives: Fanny, Fran, Francie, Frankie, Frannie.

Francesca
Italian feminine form of Francisco (Francis). Borne in the 13th century by Francesca da Rimini, the daughter of Guido da Polenta, Lord of Ravenna, who married Giovanni Malatesta, Lord of Rimini, although she loved his brother Paolo. When she and Paolo were discovered together they were put to death, c. 1289. The story has been repeatedly retold in literature; Dante told the story in his *Inferno* v, Leigh Hunt treated it in his poem *The Story of Rimini* (1816), and several tragic plays were written on the subject.

Francie
Diminutive of Frances.

Francine
Familiar form of Françoise, the French form of Frances.

Francisca
Spanish form of Frances.

Françoise
French form of Frances, meaning 'French'.

Frannie, Franny
Diminutives of Frances, Francesca or Francine.

Freda
Diminutive of several names deriving from the Old German element *frid*, 'peace', such as Winifred, but also used in its own right. Variation: Frieda.

Frederica, Fredrica
Latinate feminine form of Frederick, itself deriving from Old German *frid*, 'peace', and *ric*, 'ruler'. Variations: Frederika, Fredrika.

Freya
Old Norse, from *frouwa*, 'lady' or 'mistress'. In Scandinavian mythology Freya (or Freyja) is the goddess of love, marriage and the dead. She is the sister of Freyr, god of fruitfulness, crops, rain and sun, and the wife of Odin. The name is particularly popular in Scotland, especially in Orkney and Shetland, where Scandinavian connections remain strong.

Frieda
Diminutive of several names deriving from the Old German element *frid*, 'peace', such as Winifred, but also used in its own right. Variation: Freda.

Fronde
From Latin 'leaf of the fern'.

Fulvia
Latin, feminine form of the Roman family name Fulvius, meaning 'tawny (haired)'. See also: Flavia.

G

Gabby
Diminutive of Gabriela, Gabriella or Gabrielle. Variation: Gaby.

Gabriela, Gabriella, Gabrielle
Feminine forms of Gabriel. Gabriela is the Latinate form, Gabriella the Italian and Gabrielle the French.

Gaby
Diminutive of Gabriela, Gabriella or Gabrielle. Variation: Gabby.

Gae
Variation of Gay. Gay is now more or less obsolete (owing to association with the late 20th-century sense of 'homosexual'), but Gae survives. See also: Gay.

Gaenor
Variation of Gaynor.

Gaia
From Greek, *ge*, 'earth'. Borne in Greek mythology by the goddess of the earth, who gave birth to the sky, mountains and sea. The name has never been common, but is in occasional use today, particularly among those concerned with environmental issues.

Gail, Gale, Gayle
Diminutives of Abigail, which became popular in their own right in the US, and spread to Britain in the 1950s.

Gala
Diminutive of Galina.

Galina
From the Greek name Galen, meaning 'calm'.

Gauri
Indian, from Sanskrit, meaning 'white'. It was a byname of Shiva's previously dark-skinned wife, who acquired a fair complexion after meditating in the Himalayas.

Gay, Gaye
Old French, from *gai*, 'cheerful'. The name is now more or less obsolete, owing to association with the late 20th-century sense of 'homosexual'. See also: Gae.

Gayle
Diminutive of Abigail.

Gaynor
Medieval English form of Guinevere.

Gavrila
From Hebrew 'heroine'.

Gelasia
From Greek for 'laughing water' one like a fresh and rippling stream.

Gemma
Modern coinage, from the Old Italian word for 'jewel'. Borne by the Italian poet Dante's wife, and, more importantly, by Gemma Galgani (1878-1903), an Italian saint. Variation: Jemma.

Gene
Modern variation of Jean, also used for boys.

Genette
Variation of Jeanette.

Geneva
Recent coinage of uncertain origin, but either after the Swiss capital city, a variation of Jennifer or a variation of Geneviève.

Geneviève
French, of Celtic or Germanic origin, possibly from the Germanic name Genowefa, from *geno*, meaning 'race' or 'tribe', and *wefa*, 'woman' (source of the English word 'wife'). St Geneviève (c. 422-512), patron saint of Paris, is said to have defended Paris against Attila the Hun with prayer. Her church in Paris has since become the Panthéon. She is generally represented in art with the keys of Paris at her girdle, and her feast day is 3rd January.

Gentian
From violet or blue flower possibly named

after Gentius, king of Illyria who discovered the plant's medicinal properties.

Georgene
Variation of Georgine, influenced by the feminine ending -ene.

Georgette
French feminine form of George.

Georgia
Feminine form of George influenced by the name of the US state, itself named for George II of England.

Georgiana
Feminine form of George, particularly popular in the 18th and 19th centuries.

Georgie
Diminutive of Georgene, Georgette, Georgia, Georgiana, Georgina or Georgine.

Georgina
Feminine form of George, popular in Britain since the 18th century, though not elsewhere.

Georgine
French form of Georgina, now used in the English-speaking world in its own right.

Geraldine
Feminine form of Gerald, coined by the 16th-century Henry Howard, Earl of Surrey, in his poems to Lady Elizabeth Fitzgerald, 'the Fair Geraldine'. Diminutives: Geri, Gerry.

Gerda
Scandanavian, probably from Old Norse *garthr*, meaning 'enclosure' or 'guardian'. It was borne in Norse mythology by the giant daughter of the frost giant Gymir and wife of Freyr, god of peace. She was so beautiful that her naked arms illuminated the air and the sea. Its occasional use in the English-speaking world is due to its use by Hans Christian Andersen in his story *The Snow Queen*.

Geri
Modern variation of Gerry, popularised in the 1990s by Geri Halliwell, at one time a member of the Spice Girls.

Germaine
Feminine form of the French name Germain, meaning 'German'. Germaine Cousin (1579-1601) was a French saint. See also: Boys: Jermaine, Jerman.

Gerry
Diminutive of Geraldine. Variation: Geri.

Gert, Gertie
Diminutives of Gertrude.

Gertrude
Old German, from *ger*, 'spear' and -trude, the common suffix for German female names derived from Old German *prup*, meaning strength. It was introduced, probably from Northern Europe, in the late Middle Ages. St Gertrude of Nivelles (d 664), daughter of Pepin of Landen, was abbess of Nivelles and was said to know most of the Bible by heart. Her feast day is 17th March. Diminutives: Gert, Gertie, Trudie, Trudy.

Ghislain, Ghislaine
(*ghi-layne*, *gil-an*) French, apparently a byname from Giselle.

Gigi
Diminutive of Gilberte, a French feminine form of Gilbert. Colette's novel *Gigi* (1944) tells the story of a young Parisian girl instructed by her aunt in becoming a courtesan.

Gilberte
French feminine form of Gilbert.

Gilda
Uncertain origin popularised in the US film Gilda starring Rita Haywort

Gill
Diminutive of Gillian. It was so common in the Middle Ages as to be used as a general term for a girl. Variation: Jill. See also: Jack.

Gillaine
Modern coinage, an altered form of Gillian, probably influenced by Ghislaine.

Gillian
Feminine form of Julian, very popular in the Middle Ages. Variations: Gillean, Jillian. Diminutives: Gill, Gillie, Gilly.

Gillie, Gilly
Diminutives of Gillian.

Gina
Diminutive of girls' names ending -gina (usually Georgina), and also used in its own right.

Ginette
French variation of Geneviève, also used as a variation of Jeanette.

Ginger
Diminutive of Virginia. The Hollywood dancer Ginger Rogers was born Virginia McMath.

Ginnie, Ginny
Diminutives of Virginia.

Gisela
Old German, from *gisil*, 'pledge'.

Giselle
French variation of Gisela. It was popularised by Théophile Gautier's 1841 ballet of that name.

Gita
Indian name, from the Sanskrit word for 'song'.

Glad
Diminutive of Gladys.

Gladys
Welsh, from *gwledig*, 'ruler'. Contrary to some claims, there is no connection with Claudia. Diminutive: Glad.

Glenda
Modern coinage, from Welsh elements *glan*, 'clear, holy', and *da*, 'good'. It is distinct from the Scottish element *gleann*, 'valley'.

Glenn
Adopted surname, originally Scottish Gaelic, from *gleann*, 'valley'. It is most commonly given to boys (usually in the version Glen), but is sometimes given to girls in this form, as with the American film star Glenn Close.

Glenna
Feminine form of Glen(n).

Glenys
Modern coinage, from Welsh elements *glan*, 'clear, holy' and the feminine ending -ys, as in Gladys. It is distinct from the Scottish element *gleann*, 'valley', and from Welsh *glyn*, also meaning 'valley', the root of Glynis.

Glenys Pearl Y-Felin
Singer Cerys Matthews's daughter; *y-Felin* is Welsh for the mill near her family home in Trefin, Pembrokeshire.

Cerys Gloria
From Latin, meaning 'glory'. It was first used by George Bernard Shaw in his 1898 play *You Never Can Tell.*

Glory
Anglicised form of Gloria.

Glynis
From Welsh *glyn*, 'valley', and meaning 'little valley'.

Godwin
From Anglo Saxon 'gift of God'.

Goldie
Modern byname for one with blonde hair, popularised by the American actress Goldie Hawn.

Govindi
Feminine form of Govind.

Grace
From the abstract noun drawn from Latin gratia, meaning 'heavenly favour'. It was one of several abstract nouns denoting admirable personal qualities that became popular as names among the Puritans in the 16th century. Having fallen out of favour in the 18th century it was revived in the 19th, has been in regular use since then and has recently undergone a surge in popularity. In Ireland it is sometimes used as an anglicised form of Gráinne.

Gracie
Diminutive of Grace.

Gráinne
(*gron-ya*) Irish Gaelic, possibly from *grán*, 'grain', although the meaning 'love' has been suggested. In Irish legend Gráinne was the daughter of King Cormac, and beloved by Finn, although she eloped with his nephew Diarmait. It is sometimes anglicised as Grace.

Grania
(*gra-nia*) Latinate form of Gráinne. Variation: Granya.

Granya
Variation of Grania, probably influenced by the feminine ending -ya, as in Tonya.

Greer
Adopted Scottish surname, itself originally a contraction of Grigor. The film actress Greer Garson (b 1908) was given her mother's maiden name. Variation: Grier.

Greta
(*gree-ta*, *gret-ta*) German and Swedish diminutive of Margareta, the Latinate form of Margaret. It was popularised by the film actress Greta Garbo (1905-92).

Gretchen, Gretel
German diminutive forms of Margaret, used independently.

Grier
Variation of Greer.

Griselda
Probably from Old German *gris*, 'grey', and *hildi*, 'battle', albeit a meaning at odds with the name's medieval association with 'patient Griselda', the long-suffering wife of whom Boccaccio wrote in his *Decameron* (1353). Chaucer retold the story in his *Clerk's Tale* (c. 1387). Diminutives: Grizzie, Zelda. Variations: Grizel, Grizzel.

Grizel, Grizell
Scottish variation of Griselda.

Guda
From Anglo Saxon meaning 'the good one'.

Gudrun
Old Norse, from *gud*, 'god' or 'good', and *rune*, 'wisdom'. Borne by a heroine of German epic poetry and Norse mythological poetry. The 13th-century German epic poem *Gudrun* tells the story of the daughter of King Hettel, carried off by Hochmut of Normandy and eventually rescued by her brother. In England the name is probably best known from Gudrun Brangwen, one of the main characters in D H Lawrence's *Women in Love* (1920). Variation: Kudrun.

Guendolen
Variation of Gwendolen.

Guinevere
Old French form of the Welsh name Gwenhwyfar, from *gwen*, 'fair, blessed, holy, white', and *hwfar*, 'smooth, yielding'. Borne in Arthurian legend by Arthur's unfaithful wife, the paramour of Sir Lancelot du Lac. Variations: Gaenor, Gaynor, Genevra, Ginevra, Guenevere, Guinever, Jenifer, Jennifer.

Gussie, Gusta
Diminutives of Augusta.

Gwen
Welsh, from *gwen*, 'fair, blessed, holy, white'. Originally a diminutive of Gwendolen, it has been used in its own right since the 19th century. See also: Boys: Gwyn.

Gwenda
Modern coinage, from Welsh elements *gwen*, 'fair, blessed, holy, white', and *da*, 'good'.

Gwendolen
Welsh, from *gwen,* 'fair, blessed, holy, white', and *dolen*, 'circle'. In Welsh legend Gwendolen was the wife of the Welsh king Locrine, in Arthurian legend the wife of Merlin. It was widely used in England in the mid-19th century, and further boosted by Oscar Wilde's use of the name in his 1895 play, *The Importance of Being Earnest*. Diminutive: Gwen. Variations: Guendolen, Gwendolin, Gwendoline, Gwendolyn.

Gwendolin, Gwendoline
Variations of Gwendolen.

Gwenllian
Welsh, from *gwen*, 'fair, blessed, holy, white', and *lliant*, 'flaxen'.

Gwenyth
Variation of Gwyneth.

Gwyn
Diminutive of Gwyneth.

Gwyneth
Welsh, either an altered form of Gwynedd, the medieval name for an area of North Wales, now restored, or possibly meaning 'blessed' or 'happiness'. It has been popular from the late 19th century. Venetia is taken by some to be a much-altered variation. Diminutive: Gwyn.

H

Hadassah
Hebrew form of Esther, a Persian name. A biblical name; borne by Esther, after whom an Old Testament book is named. Diminutive: Dassah.

Hagar
Hebrew, meaning 'forsaken'. A biblical name; borne in the Old Testament by the Egyptian-born servant of Abraham's barren wife, Sarah, and mother of his first child, Ishmael (Genesis 16:22). When Sarah later bore Isaac, she feared that Ishmael might become a rival heir and so she had mother and son banished into the desert where God sustained them until Ishmael had grown up.

Haidee
Invented by Lord Byron for his epic poem *Don Juan* (1819-24), possibly derived from the Greek *aidoios*, 'modest', or from the Greek name Haidoo, meaning 'to caress'. It is now sometimes erroneously considered a variation of Heidi.

Hailey
Ironically, Hailey is today considered merely a variation of Hayley. However, the original surname from which the first name developed was most probably derived from the village of Hailey in Oxfordshire.

Hal
Diminutive of Harriet.

Hannah
Hebrew, from *hanna*, meaning 'God has favoured me'. A biblical name; borne by the mother of Samuel (I Samuel 1). It was adopted by the Puritans in the 17th century, and was one of the most popular girls' names in the 1980s and 1990s.

Harley
Old English 'from the long field'.

Harper
Adopted surname, originally an occupational name for someone who played the harp. It was made famous by the US writer Harper Lee, author of *To Kill a Mockingbird* (1960).

Harriet
Anglicised form of Henriette, the French form of Henrietta, which was introduced to Britain when Charles I married the French princess Henriette Marie in 1625. Diminutives: Hal, Hattie, Hatty, Hettie, Hetty.

Hattie, Hatty
Diminutives of Harriet or Henrietta.

Hayley
Adopted surname, from a place name derived from *heg*, 'hay', and *leah*, 'wood, clearing'. It was the name given by Mary Hayley Bell and John Mills to their daughter, Hayley Mills, born in 1946. Since then it has become one of the most popular girl's names in the English-speaking world. Variation: Hailey.

Hazel
From Old English *hæsel*, denoting a species of nut-bearing tree. It was a 19th-century introduction, and one of the more successful of the names coined at that time from plant names. Its enduring popularity is probably due to the fact that it can also refer to an eye colour.

Heather
From Old English *hadre*, denoting a species of moorland shrub with purple or white flowers. It is one of the more consistently popular of the flower names fashionable at the very end of the 19th century,

particularly in Scotland, where heather is abundant. See also: Erica.

Heavenly Hiraani Tigerlily
Bob Geldof's daughter.

Hebe
(*hee-bee*) Greek name, meaning 'youthful beauty'. In Greek mythology Hebe was a daughter of Zeus and Hera, goddess of youth and spring and cup-bearer to the gods. The name was adopted for a species of evergreen shrub indigenous to New Zealand in the 19th century and is occasionally found as a first name in the English-speaking world.

Hebsibah
Variation of Hephzibah.

Hedda
Diminutive of Hedwig. Used by Henrik Ibsen in his 1890 play, *Hedda Gabler*. Variations: Hedy,

Hedwig
German, from elements meaning 'refuge in war'. Diminutives: Hedda, Hedy. Variations: Hedewig, Hedwige.

Heidi
Swiss diminutive of Adelheid, itself the German form of Adelaide. It was popularised by Johanna Spyri, who gave the name to the orphaned heroine of her 1881 novel for children. See also: Adelaide.

Helen
Anglicised form of the Greek name Helene, itself possibly drawn from the Greek *helios*, 'sun', and meaning 'sunbeam'. In classical legend Helen was the daughter of Leda and Jupiter and the wife of Menelaus. She was abducted by Paris, an act that sparked the Trojan War. Diminutives: Ena, Hels, Lena, Nell, Nellie, Nelly. Variations: Eibhlin (Irish Gaelic, and the source of Aileen, Eileen and Evelyn), Elaine, Eleanor, Elena, Elidh (Scottish Gaelic), Ellen, Helena, Helène, Ilana or Ilona (Hungarian), Iliana (Romanian).

Helena
Latinate form of Helen. St Helena (c. 248-328) was the mother of Constantine the Great, a woman venerated for finding the True Cross at Jerusalem. She is usually depicted wearing royal robes and an imperial crown, sometimes carrying a cross and the three nails by which Christ was nailed to the cross. Her feast day is 18th August.

Helène
French form of Helen.

Helga
Old Norse, from *heilagr*, 'holy'. It became rare in Britain, but is being reintroduced via Germany and Scandinavia. See also: Olga.

Héloïse
Origin uncertain; either from the Old German name Helewise, or from the same source as Louise. The name was popularised by the true story of the French scholar Peter Abelard (1079-1142) and his seventeen-year-old lover, Héloíse, neice of Canon Fulbert of Notre Dame. They had a child and were secretly married, but were discovered by Fulbert, who had Abelard castrated. Abelard entered the monastery of Saint-Denis, while Héloíse became a nun. On her death in 1164 she was buried beside him at Paraclete, but both were moved to Père Lachaise cemetery in Paris in 1817.

Hen, Hennie, Henny
Diminutives of Henrietta or Henriette.

Henrietta, Henriette
Feminine forms of Henry. Henriette is the French form, introduced to Britain when Charles I married the French princess Henriette Marie in 1625. Henrietta is the Latinate form. Diminutives: Etta, Ettie, Etty, Hen, Hennie, Henny, Hettie, Hetty.

Hephzibah
Hebrew, meaning 'my delight is in her'. A biblical name; borne by the wife of Hezekiah, king of Judah, and used by Isaiah to refer to the state of Israel. Diminutives: Eppie, Heppie, Heppy, Hepsey, Hepsie, Hepsy. Variation: Hepsibah.

Hermia
Latinate feminine form of Hermes, the Greek messenger god. It was used by Shakespeare in *A Midsummer Night's Dream* (1595-6).

Hermione
Derived from Hermes, the Greek messenger god, and possibly meaning 'daughter of Hermes'. In classical mythology Hermione was the daughter of Helen and Menelaus, and the name was also used by Shakespeare in *A Winter's Tale* (1611).

Hero
Borne in Greek legend by a priestess of Venus beloved by Leander, who swam to her nightly across the Hellespont. One night Leander drowned and the desolate Hero drowned herself in the same sea. The name was used by Shakespeare in *Much Ado About Nothing* (1598).

Hester
Variation of Esther. Diminutives: Hettie, Hetty.

Hettie, Hetty
Diminutives of Harriet, Henrietta or Hester.

Hilary
Medieval form of the late Latin name Hilarius, from *hilaris*, 'cheerful'. Variations: Hilaire (French), Hillary (especially in the US). It is given to both boys and girls, although it is increasingly rare for boys.

Hilda
Old German, from *hildi*, 'battle'. A 7th-century saint, Hilda, founded an abbey at Whitby, in Yorkshire. Variation: Hylda.

Hildegard
From Old German derived from hildi 'battle' born in the 12th century by the German Abbess St Hildegard.

Hillary
Variation of Hilary, found particularly in the US.

Hina
From Hebrew 'female deer'.

Holly
From Old English *holen*, and denoting a species of evergreen plant with glossy, prickly leaves. It was one of the many flower and plant names that became popular at the very end of the 19th century, and it is often given to girls born at Christmastime. However, Holly Golightly, the fascinating heroine of Truman Capote's novella *Breakfast at Tiffany's* (1958), had a calling card that stated: 'Miss Holiday Golightly. Travelling'.

Honesty
Modern coinage, a direct adoption from the English vocabulary, ultimately from the Latin *honestas*. Its adoption was prob-

ably influenced in part by the flower of the same name.

Honor
Latin, meaning 'honour'. The elaborate form Honoria was in use in the 11th century. The diminutive was one of several abstract nouns denoting admirable personal qualities that became popular among Puritans in the 16th century, when it was used for both genders. Variations: Annora, Honora, Honoria, Nora, Norah.

Honora, Honoria
Variations of Honor.

Honey
Term of endearment sometimes used as a first name.

Hope
One of the three great Christian virtues (with faith and charity), and one of several abstract nouns denoting admirable personal qualities that became popular among Puritans in the 16th century. See also: Charity, Faith.

Horatia
Feminine form of Horatio, itself from the Roman clan name Horatius. It was given to the daughter of Horatio, Lord Nelson and Emma, Lady Hamilton. Diminutive: Horry.

Hortense
Popular French form of Hortensia.

Hortensia
Feminine form of the Latin clan name Hortensius, meaning 'gardener'.

Huldah
Hebrew, meaning 'weasel'. A biblical name; borne by a prophetess who predicted the fall of Jerusalem (2 Kings 22).

Hyacinth
From the Greek name Hyakinthos, the name of a dark lily. In Greek legend dark lilies grew where the blood of Hyacinthus spread after he was accidentally killed by Apollo. Originally a boy's name, it is now used for girls, probably influenced by the fashion for flower names in the late 19th century.

Hylda
Variation of Hilda.

Hypatia
Greek, from *hypatos*, 'highest'. Borne by a 5th-century Alexandrian woman philosopher who was killed by a Christian mob, and was subsequently the subject of Charles Kingsley's novel *Hypatia* (1853).

I

Ianthe
(*i-an-thee*) From Greek *ion*, 'violet', and *anthos*, 'flower', meaning 'violet flower'. Borne in Ovid's *Metamorphoses*, written in the 1st century, by a Cretan girl who married Iphis, a young girl who had been changed into a young man. Percy Bysshe Shelley used the name in his poem *Queen Mab* (1813). Lord Byron dedicated Canto I of his *Childe Harold's Pilgrimage* (1818) to 'Ianthe', by which he meant Lady Charlotte Harley, and also gave it to his eldest daughter (1813-76). See also: Iolanthe, Violet.

Ida
From Old German *id*, 'work'. A Norman introduction to Britain, it was used by Alfred, Lord Tennyson in his 1847 poem *The Princess*.

Idonia, Idonea
(*i-doan-ea*) Possibly from Old German *id*, 'work', or from Latin *idoneus*, 'suitable', or after the Norse goddess Iduna, guardian of the Apples of Youth.

Ilana, Ilona
Variations of Helen, of Hungarian origin.

Ilsa, Ilse
Diminutives of Elizabeth, of German origin.

Iman
Arabic, meaning 'faith' or 'belief'.

Imelda
Italian form of the German name Irmhild, from Old German *irmin* (or ermin), 'universal', and *hildi*, 'battle'.

Imogen
First used by Shakespeare in *Cymbeline* (1609). It was possibly a misreading of his source, Holinshed's *Chronicles*, which has Innogen, possibly from Latin *innocens*, 'innocent', or Gaelic *inghean*, 'girl'.

Ina
Diminutive of names ending in -ina, such as Christina or Georgina. Variation: Ena.

India
From the name of the country. It was used by Margaret Mitchell in *Gone With The Wind* (1936), and is a favourite in British families who have an association with India.

Inez
(*ee-nez*) Spanish variation of Agnes. Other variations: Anis, Annes, Annice, Annis.

Ingrid
Of Norse origin, from Ing, a Norse fertility god, and *frior*, 'fair'.

Innes
Adopted Scottish surname, or an anglicised form of Aonghas (Angus). It is also used for boys.

Iolanthe
(*eye-oh-lan-thee*) From Greek *ion*, 'violet', and *anthos*, 'flower', meaning 'violet flower'. It was popularised by Gilbert and Sullivan's opera of that name (1882) and, as in the cases of Ianthe and Iole, may have been chosen as a learned response to the 19th-century fashion for flower names. Variations: Ianthe, Yolande.

Iole
(*eye-oh-lee*) From Greek, 'violet'. In classical mythology Iole was beloved by Heracles. The name may have been chosen as a learned response to the 19th-century fashion for flower names.

Iona
Origin uncertain; either after the Scottish island, or from Greek *ion*, 'violet'.

Ione
From Greek *ion*, 'violet'. The name may have been chosed as a learned response to the 19th-century fashion for flower names.

Irene
(*eye-reen*, *eye-ree-nee*) From Greek *eirene*, 'peace'. Borne by a minor deity of Greek mythology, the goddess of peace and wealth, who is usually depicted as a young woman carrying Plutus, the god of riches, in her arms. Diminutives: Reenie, Rene, Renie.

Iris
From Greek *iris*, 'rainbow'. In Greek mythology Iris was goddess of the rainbow and messenger of the gods, particularly Juno. She used a rainbow as a bridge between the gods and mortal man. The name was revived during the late 19th-century fashion for flower names, the flower having been so named because there are as many different shades of the iris as there are colours of the spectrum.

Irma
From Old German *irmin*, 'universal'. It has been used in the English-speaking world since the early 19th century. See also: Emma.

Isa
Diminutive of Isabel.

Isabel, Isabelle
Variations of Elizabeth, of medieval Spanish origin, and brought to Britain from France in the form Isabella by the French-born wife of Edward II (1296-1358). Until the end of the 17th century Isabel and Isabelle were common in England, while Isobel took a hold in Scotland. The Latinate version, Isabella, was introduced in the 18th century. Variations: Ishbel, Isla. Diminutives: Bel, Bell, Bella, Belle, Ib, Ibbie, Ibby, Isa, Iz, Izzie, Izzy, Tibby.

Isabella
Latinate form of Isabelle, popular in Britain from the 18th century. See also: Isabel.

Isadora, Isidora
Feminine form of Isidore, itself the English form of Isidoros, meaning 'gift of Isis'. It was popularised by Isadora Duncan (1878-1927). Diminutives: Dora, Iz, Izzie, Izzy.

Iseult
French form of Isolde.

Isla
(*eye-la*) Modern coinage, after a Scottish river, or a modification of the Hebridean island, Islay.

Ismay
Name of uncertain origin. Variation of Esme.

Isobel
Scottish form of Isabel. See also: Isabel.

Isolde
Origin uncertain, possibly Welsh, meaning 'beautiful'. Borne in Arthurian legend by Ysolde the Fair, the daughter of the king of Ireland, betrothed to King Mark of Cornwall. As the result of a love potion she fell in love with Tristan, with tragic consequences. Their story was retold by Richard Wagner in his opera *Tristan und Isolde* (1865). Variations: Esyllt (Welsh), Ezit, Iseult, Isold, Isolt, Ysold, Ysolda, Ysolde, Yseult, Yseut.

Isra
Arabic name, meaning 'night journey', a reference to Muhammad's journey to Jerusalem during which he met Jesus and Moses.

Ita
From Gaelic 'desire for goodness and knowledge'.

Ivana, Ivanka
Modern coinages, probably feminine forms of Ivan.

Ivy
From Old English *ifig*, and denoting a species of evergreen creeper with dark green, shiny leaves, associated in

Christian symbolism with everlasting life. It was one of many names popularised during the late 19th-century fashion for flower names.

Iz, Izzie, Izzy
Diminutives of several names beginning Is-, such as Isabel or Isadora.

J

Jacinta, Jacinth, Jacynth
Spanish form of Hyacinth. Like Hyacinth it was originally used for both sexes, but today is almost exclusively given to girls.

Jackie, Jacky, Jacqui
Diminutives of Jacqueline, sometimes used in their own right.

Jaclyn
Variation of Jacqueline.

Jacoba, Jacobi, Jacobina
Feminine forms of Jacob.

Jacqueline, Jacquelyn
Feminine forms of Jacques, introduced to Britain in the 13th century. Diminutives: Jackie, Jacky, Jacqui.

Jacquetta
Feminine form of Jacques.

Jade
Name of a type of stone, derived from archaic Spanish *piedra de ijada*, meaning 'stone of the side', a reference to the supposed ability of the stone to cure renal colic. The stone's other name, nephrite, is from Greek *nephros*, 'kidney'. Unlike the majority of stone names, Jade was not adopted in the late 19th century, but in the 1950s, and has enjoyed a recent vogue.

Jaden
From Hebrew 'God has heard'.

Jael
Hebrew, meaning 'wild goat'. A biblical name; borne by a nomadic woman who offered Sisera shelter and then murdered him by plunging a tent peg through his temples (Judges 4:17-21). Rather surprisingly, it was a Puritan adoption.

Jamila
Feminine form of Jamil.

Jamesina
Feminine form of James.

Jamie
Diminutive of James, used in its own right as a girl's name.

Jan
Diminutive of Janet, or name beginning Jan-.

Jancis
A 20th-century coinage, a combination of Jan and Frances. It was probably first used by Mary Webb in her novel *Precious Bane* (1924).

Jane, Jayne
Feminine form of John, from the Old French name Jehane. It was popularised in Britain in the 16th century by Jane Seymour, third wife of Henry VIII (d 1537). Very popular from the mid-18th century, it was further boosted by publication of Charlotte Brontë's *Jane Eyre* (1847). It is now more common as a second given name or as the second element of a compound name, e.g. Sarah Jane.

Janet
Feminine form of John, originally a medieval diminutive of Jane, under the influence of Jeanette. It remained popular in Scotland then

experienced a general revival in the mid-20th century. Diminutives: Jan, Jennie, Jenny. Variations: Janetta, Janette.

Janetta
Latinate variation of Janet.

Janette
French form of Janet.

Janey, Janie
Diminutives of Jane.

Janice
Originally a diminutive of Jane, influenced by the -ice ending of girl's names such as Candice. It has been popular in its own right from the early 20th century. Variation: Janis.

Janine
Most common form of Jeannine.

Janis
Variation of Janice.

Jasmine
From Arabic *jasamine*, and denoting a species of ornamental flowering climbing shrub with yellow and white flowers. It was one of many names popularised during the late 19th-century fashion for flower names. Variations: Jessamine, Jessamy, Jessamyn, Yasmin.

Jaswinder
Sikh, derived from Sanskrit, meaning 'Indra of the thunderbolt'.

Jay
Diminutive of any name beginning with 'J', and also used in its own right.

Jayne
Variation of Jane.

Jaz Elle
Daughter of Andre Agassi and Steffi Graf.

Jean
Feminine form of John, from the Old French form, Jehane (See also: Jane). Largely confined to Scotland until the late 19th century, its popularity spread widely in the 1930s. Diminutives: Jeanette, Jeanie, Jeannette, Jeannie. Variation: Jeanne.

Jena
From Arabic 'small bird'.

Jeanette, Jeannette
Diminutives of Jean, originally French diminutives of Jeanne, now in regular use in their own right. Variations: Genette, Ginette.

Jeanie, Jeannie
Diminutives of Jean, sometimes used in their own right.

Jeanne
French feminine form of John, from the Old French name Jehane. Diminutives: Jeannette, Jeannine.

Jeannine
Diminutive of Jeanne. Variation: Janine.

Jemima
Hebrew, meaning 'dove'. A biblical name; borne in the Old Testament by one of Job's daughters. It was adopted by the Puritans. Diminutives: Jemma, Mima.

Jemma
Diminutive of Jemima, and variation of Gemma.

Jen
Diminutive of Jennifer, or any name beginning Jen-.

Jennifer
Variations of Guinevere, of Cornish origin. Not found outside Cornwall before the early 20th century, by 1950 it had spread throughout the English-speaking world. Diminutives: Jen, Jennie, Jenny. Variation: Jenifer.

Jenna, Jennai
Variations of Jenny.

Jennie, Jenny
Diminutives of Jane, Janet or Jennifer, and often used in their own right. Diminutive: Jen. Variations: Jenna, Jennai, Jinny.

Jess
Diminutive of Jessamine, Jessica, Jessie, or any name beginning Jess-.

Jessamine, Jessamy, Jessamyn
Variations of Jasmine. Diminutives: Jess, Jessie.

Jessica
Hebrew, meaning 'God beholds'. Probably a Shakespearean invention for the daughter of Shylock in *The Merchant of Venice* (1596), possibly derived from an obscure biblical name Iscah, or Jesca (Genesis 11:29). It has enjoyed a recent surge in popularity. Diminutives: Jess, Jessie.

Jessie
Scottish diminutive of Janet dating from the 18th century, sometimes used in its own right. It is also used as a a diminutive of Jessica. Diminutive: Jess.

Jewel
One of the less successful of the names associated with precious stones adopted in the late 19th century.

Jill, Jilly
Diminutives of Jillian, and modern variations of Gill and Gilly respectively.

Jillian
Modern variation of Gillian. Diminutives: Jill, Jilly.

Jinny
Variation of Jenny, or a diminutive of Virginia.

Jo
Diminutive of Joanna, Joanne, Josephine, or any name beginning Jo-.

Joakima
From Hebrew 'the lord's judge' also Joachima.

Joan
Feminine form of John, derived from the Latin name Johanna. It was given to the daughter of Henry II and Eleanor of Aquitaine in the 12th century, and was the name of the only female pope, supposedly of the 13th century, but whose existence is still in dispute. It had been largely replaced by Jane by the 17th century, which is why the French form of Joan of Arc, Jeanne, is also the commonly accepted French form of Jane. Joan was revived, however, in the early 20th century. Diminutives: Joanie, Joni. Variation: Siobhán.

Joanna
Feminine form of John, derived from the Latin name Johanna. A biblical name: borne in the New Testament by one of Jesus's followers, who brought news of

the Resurrection to the apostles (Luke 8 and 24). A Puritan adoption, it was revived in the 18th century and has been particularly popular in the late 20th century. Diminutive: Jo, Joey.

Joanne
From the Old French name Johanne, itself derived from the Latin name Johanna. Adopted first in French-speaking communities in the US, it became immensely popular in Britain and elsewhere from the 1950s. Diminutives: Jo, Joey.

Jobina
Feminine form of 'Job' from Hebrew 'the afflicted'.

Jocasta
Greek, meaning 'shining moon'. In Greek mythology it was borne by the wife of King Laius of Thebes, who became the mother of Oedipus. Despite all attempts to avert the fulfilment of a prophecy that Oedipus would kill his father and marry his mother, she did indeed eventually - and unknowingly - become the wife of her son. When the truth was discovered she hung herself.

Jocelin, Joceline, Jocelyn
From the Old French name Joscelin, derived from an Old German masculine name, meaning 'of the tribe of Goths'. First introduced to Britain by the Norman invaders, it was not used for girls until the early 20th century, when it was probably influenced by the popularity of the feminine name, Joyce. Diminutives: Joss, Jossy.

Jodie, Jodi, Jody
Diminutive of Judith, used in its own right in the US, Canada and Australia since the 1950s.

Joella, Joelle, Joely
Feminine forms of Joel. Diminutives: Jo, Joey.

Johanna
Original Latinate and feminine form derived from Johannes (John).

Jolene, Joleen
Mid-20th century invention, derived from Jo-, plus the feminine element -lene.

Jonquil
From Spanish *junquillo*, itself derived from Latin *juncus*, meaning 'rush', and denoting a type of narcissus with rushy leaves. One of the more recent and less common of the flower names taken as first names, it was popular in the 1940s and 1950s.

Jordan
From the name of the river in the Middle East where Christ was baptised by John the Baptist. The Hebrew name, Hayarden, means 'to flow down'. It is also used for boys.

Josa
Diminutive of Josephine, also used in its own right.

Josepha
Feminine form of Joseph.

Josephine
Feminine form of Joseph, originally a French diminutive of Josepha. It was popularised throughout Europe by Empress Joséphine (1763-1814), wife of Napoleon Bonaparte. Diminutives: Fifi, Jo, Joey, Josa, Josette, Josie, Josy, Posie, Posy. Variations: Josefina, Josefine, Josephina.

Josette
French diminutive of Josephine, dating from the 19th century.

Josie
Diminutive of Josephine.

Joss
Diminutive of Jocelyn.

Jovita
Feminine form of Jove from Latin 'joyful one'.

Joy
Direct adoption from the English vocabulary. Popular with the Puritans, it was revived in the 19th century.

Joyce
Originally a Norman French masculine name, it was borne by a St Joisse, (Jodocus in Latin), a 7th-century Breton saint. Used for both sexes for a while, it then fell out of favour as a girl's name until a late 19th-century revival.

Juanita
Feminine version of Juan, the Spanish form of John.

Jude
Diminutive of Judith.

Judith
Hebrew, meaning 'Jewess'. A biblical name; borne in the Old Testament by a wife of Esau, and by the central figure of the Apocrypha's Book of Judith. Always popular with Jews, it has been used by non-Jewish families, particularly during the 18th century and mid-20th century. Diminutives: Jodi, Jodie, Jody, Judi, Judy.

Judy
Diminutive of Judith, sometimes used in its own right. Variation: Judi.

Jules
Diminutive of any girl's name beginning Jul-, such as Julia or Julie.

Julia
Feminine form of the Roman family name Julius, Italian in origin. It was used by Shakespeare in *The Two Gentlemen of Verona* (1594), was very popular in Britain in the 18th century, and has undergone a late 20th-century revival. Diminutive: Jules. Variations: Julie, Juliet, Julietta.

Juliana
Feminine form of Julian dating from the Middle Ages. St Julian, a 14th-century woman anchorite of Norwich, was also known as Juliana. It has been largely replaced by Gillian.

Julianne
Mid-20th century coinage, a combination of Julie and Anne.

Julie
French form of Julia. First used in Britain in the early 20th century it became one of the most popular girl's names of the 1970s. Diminutive: Jules.

Julienne
French feminine form of Julian.

Juliet
Variation of Julia, an anglicised form of Giulietta, the Italian diminutive. It was most famously used by Shakespeare in *Romeo and Juliet* (1595).

Juliette
French form of Juliet.

Julietta
Variation, originally a diminutive, of Julia. It was the name of a 3rd-century Christian martyr, killed at Tarsus with her son.

June
Sixth month of the year, probably named from the Latin Iunius, or the family name Junius, from *juvenis*, 'young'. Some associate it with Juno. It was the most successful of the names derived from months adopted in the early 20th century. See also: April, May.

Juno
Variation of Una, influenced by the name of the Roman goddess Juno, wife and sister of Jupiter and the queen of heaven. She is identified with the Greek goddess Hera, patron of marriage and women.

Justina
Feminine form of Justin, borne by two early Christian martyrs.

Justine
Feminine form of Justin, originally a French form of the Latinate Justina. It was popularised by the English novelist Lawrence Durrell in *Justine* (1957), the first novel of his Alexandria Quartet.

K

Kali
Indian name, from Sanskrit *kala*, meaning 'black'. It was the cult name of Durga, the Hindu goddess of death and destruction, and wife of Shiva. Her representation is fearful: black and smeared in blood, with red eyes, four arms, matted hair, fangs and a protruding, bleeding tongue. She wears a necklace of skulls.

Kamala
Feminine form of the Sanskrit name, Kamal, meaning 'pink', associated with the lotus flower. In classical Hindu texts Kamala is a byname of the goddess Lakshmi. It is also borne by the wife of Shiva.

Kamin
Iranian, meaning 'my soul'.

Kara
Variation of Cara.

Karel
Variation of Carol

Karen
Variation of Katherine, originally a Danish diminutive. It was taken to the US from Denmark by early 20th-century immigrants and became one of the most popular girls' names in Britain in the 1970s. Variations: Karena, Karin.

Karin
(*car-in*) Swedish variation of Karen.

Karina
Variation of Carina.

Kate
Diminutive of Katherine and many related names, and also used in its own right.

Kath, Kathie, Kathy
Diminutives of Katherine and many related names. Variations: Cath, Cathy.

Katherine, Katharine
Latin form of Catherine. Katherine is the English spelling, Katharine the Scottish. Variations: Caítlin, Caítrin, Catherine, Cathleen, Catriona, Karen, Kathleen, Kathryn. Diminutives: Casey, Cath, Cathie, Cathy, Kate, Kath, Kathie, Kathy, Katie, Katrina, Katrine, Katy, Kay, Kit, Kitty, all also used in their own right.

Kathleen
Variation of Catherine, influenced by the Irish Gaelic name Caítlin. Variation: Cathleen.

Kathryn
Variation of Katherine.

Katie, Katy
Diminutives of Katherine, also used in their own right and highly popular in the late 20th century.

Katrina
Variation of Catriona or Catrina.

Katrine
French form of Katherine.

Katya
Russian form of Katherine.

Kay, Kaye
Diminutives of Katherine or Kathleen, also used in their own right.

Kayla
Variation of Kay 'great rejoicing'.

Kelda
Uncertain but possibly from Scandinavian word for 'spring' or 'fountain'.

Kellie, Kelly
Adopted Irish surname, possibly meaning 'warlike'. A recent adoption, it has been hugely popular in the English-speaking world in the 1980s and 1990s. Variations: Kayleigh, Keleigh, Keeley, Kelley, Kylie.

Kelsey
Adopted surname, from the Old English masculine name Ceolsige, from *ceol*, 'ship', and *sige*, 'victory'. It is used for boys and, more commonly, for girls, probably influenced by the girl's name, Elsie.

Kendra
Probably derivation of Ken and Sandra.

Keturah
From Hebrew meaning 'fragrance'.

Keren
Diminutive of Kerenhappuch.

Kerenhappuch
From Hebrew, meaning 'container of kohl'. A biblical name; borne in the Old Testament by one of Job's daughters.

Kerenza
Cornish, meaning 'love' or 'affection'.

Kerry
Name of an Irish county, from Irish Gaelic, meaning 'descendents of Ciar'. First used by Irish immigrants to Australia for their sons, it has more recently been used for girls throughout the English-speaking world. Variations: Keri, Kerri, Kerrie.

Ketan, Ketana
Indian name, meaning 'home'.

Kezia, Keziah
From the Hebrew word for a cassia tree.

A biblical name; borne in the Old Testament by one of Job's daughters. Diminutives: Kez, Kissy.

Khadija
Ancient Arabic name, originally a byname meaning 'premature child'. Khadiya bint-Khuwaylid was the first wife of the Prophet Muhammed and mother of all his children. Variations: Khadeeja, Khadeejah, Khadiga, Khadijah.

Kiara, Kiera
Modern coinage, possibly derived from Kieran. Variation: Kiera.

Kimberley
Given initially to boys (See Boys: Kimberley), but then increasingly to girls. It is one of the most popular girl's names in the US today, with any number of fanciful spellings, such as Kimberlie, Kimberlee or Kimberleigh.

Kirby
Taken as a first name from a place name but originally from Old Norse meaning 'church farm'

Kirsten
Scandinavian form of Christine.

Kirstie, Kirsty
Scottish diminutives of Christina or Christine.

Kitty
Diminutive of Katherine and related names.

Kristen, Kristin
Variations of Christine.

Kristina, Kristine
Scandinavian form of Christina or Christine.

Kylie
Of modern Australian origin, probably coined as a feminine form of Kyle, influenced by the popular girl's name Kelly. It sprang to sudden prominence and popularity in the English-speaking world in the 1980s, as the name of an actress in the Australian soap opera *Neighbours*, and appears to be fading in popularity almost as fast.

L

Laetitia
(*le-tish-a*) From Latin *laetitia*, 'joy'. Diminutives: Lettie, Letty, Tisha. Variations: Laeticia, Leticia, Letitia, Lettice.

Laila, Lailah
(*lay-la*) Variations of Leila.

Lakeisha
Modern coinage, probably an elaborated form of Keisha, itself an elaborated form of Aisha. Particularly popular in the Afro-American communities, it reflects the fashion for the prefix La- that appears to have begun in the 1970s. See also: Latasha, Latisha, LaToya.

Lakshmi
Indian name from Sanskrit, meaning 'lucky sign' or 'lucky mark', as in a birthmark, and indicating prosperity. Borne by the goddess of beauty, good fortune and wealth, wife of Vishnu and mother of Kama.

Lalage
(*lal-a-dgee, lal-a-ghee*) Greek, from *lalagein*, 'chatter'. It was given by the Roman lyric poet Horace (65-8 BC), to the object of his affections. Diminutives: Lallie, Lally.

Lana
Modern coinage, probably by the American film actress Lana Turner (b 1920). It is also possibly a diminutive of Alana, or an anagram of Alan.

Lani
(*lah-nee*) Polynesian, meaning 'sky, heaven'. It is common in Hawaii, and popular in the US generally.

Lanna
(*lan-na*) Diminutive of Alanna.

Laoise
(*lee-sha*) Irish Gaelic, of uncertain origin.

Lara
Diminutive of the Russian name Larissa. It was popularised by Boris Pasternak's 1957 novel *Dr Zhivago* and, more particularly, the 1965 film of the book.

Laraine
Modern coinage, either a variation of Lorraine, or from French *la reine*, 'the queen'. Variation: Larraine. See also: Lauraine.

Larch
From the name of the tree. Most tree names were late 19th-century introductions, but this is much more recent, and mainly confined to the US.

Larissa
Russian, of uncertain origin, although possibly after an ancient town, now dis appeared. It was borne by a Greek martyr of the Eastern Church.

Lark
From the name of the bird. It was introduced in the mid-20th century, and is mainly confined to the US.

Larraine
Variation of Laraine and Lorraine. See also: Lauraine.

Latasha
Recent coinage, a blending of Latisha and Natasha and reflecting the fashion for the feminine prefix La- that began in the 1970s in Afro-American communities. It is mainly popular among those communities in the US.

Latisha
Recent coinage, a respelling of Laetitia reflecting the fashion for the feminine prefix La- that began in the 1970s in Afro-American communities.

LaToya
Modern coinage, apparently by the mother of pop singer LaToya Jackson (sister of Michael Jackson), reflecting the fashion for the feminine prefix La- that began in the 1970s in Afro-American communities.

Laura
Latin, the feminine form of *laurus*, 'laurel', symbol of victory. It was the name of the ethereal object of the love poetry of Petrarch (1304-74), whom he first espied in the church of St Clare, Avignon in April 1327. A 19th-century import to Britain from Italy, it is now one of the most popualr names for a girl. Variations: Lauraine, Lauren, Lauretta, Laurette, Laurinda, Loren, Loreto, Loretta, Lorinda, Lorrina.

Lauraine
Variation of Lorraine, influenced by Laura. See also: Larraine

Laurel
From the name of the tree. It was a late 19th-century introduction, probably influenced by Laura.

Laurelle
Elaboration of Laurel.

Lauren
Variation of Laura, popularised by the American actress Lauren Bacall (b 1924). Variation: Loren.

Laurencia, Laurentia
Feminine forms of Laurence.

Lauretta
Medieval Italian diminutive of Laura. Variation: Loretta.

Laurette
French variation or diminutive of Laura.

Laurey, Laurie
Diminutives of Laura or Laurel.

Laurina
Variation or diminutive of Laura or Laurel. Variation: Lorina.

Laurinda
Variation of Laura.

Lavena
Medieval variation of Lavinia.

Lavender
From Middle English *lavendre*, and denoting a small flowering shrub with pungent flowers indigenous to the Mediterranean. It was one of several flower names that became popular at the very end of the 19th century.

Laverne
Origin uncertain, possibly after La Verne, California. It has been popular amongst Afro-Americans, with several other names beginning La-, possibly reflecting a French influence.

Lavina
Medieval variation of Lavinia.

Lavinia
Borne in classical mythology by the daughter of Latinus, king of the Latini. She became the wife of Aeneas and the ancestress of Romulus and Remus. The name became common in the English-speaking world after the Renaissance, and very popular during the 18th century.

Layla
Arabic, meaning 'wine' or 'intoxication'. It was borne by the woman beloved of the Arabic poet Qays ibn-al-Mulawwah (d 688). It also has a currency as a variation of Leila.

Lea
Pronounced *le-ah* or *lay-ah*, this is a variation of Leah and Lia, or a diminutive of Azalea; pronounced *lee*, it is a variation of Lee or Leigh.

Leaf
From the part of a plant. It was one of the names from nature adopted in the hippy 1960s. It may also be influenced by Leif, a Scandinavian boy's name meaning 'heir'.

Leaf Joaquin
Daughter of Arlyn and John Phoenix.

Leah
Hebrew, probably meaning 'cow'. A biblical name; borne by the elder sister of Rachel. Jacob wanted to marry Rachel but was tricked into marrying Leah first (Genesis 29). Variations: Lea, Lia.

Leanna, Leanne
Either a recent coinage blending Lee and Anna or Anne, or a variation of Liane.

Leanora
Variation of Eleanora, the Italian form of Eleanor.

Leda
Borne in Greek mythology by the wife of Tyndarus, king of Sparta, who was ravished by Jupiter in the shape of a swan. She gave birth to two eggs, which hatched into the heavenly twins Castor and Pollux, and Helen of Troy and Clytemnestra. Some accounts have Helen and Clytemnestra as the daughters of Tyndarus.

Lee
Adopted surname; from Old English *leah*, 'meadow' or 'wood'. Its popularity as a first name originated in the US, in honour of the Confederate general Robert E Lee (1807-70), but it spread worldwide in the later 20th century in various forms, for both boys and girls.

Leesa
Variation of Lisa, influenced by Lee.

Leigh
Variation, more fanciful, of Lea or Lee.

Leila
Persian, meaning 'night'. It was popularised by Lord Byron in his poem *The Giaour* (1813). Variations: Laila, Lailah, Layla, Lila, Lilah.

Lela
Either a variation of Leila, or a variation of Lelia.

Lelia
Latin, from the Roman family name Laelius. It was popularised by George Sand's novel *Lélia* (1833).

Lena
(*lay-na*, *lee-na*) Byname from female names ending in -lena, such as Helena, and a name in its own right.

Lenora
Contracted form of Leonora, the Italian form of Eleanor.

Lenore
German variation of Eleanor.

Leona, Leone, Leonie
Feminine forms of Leon. Variations: Liona.

Leonora
Variation of Eleanora, the Italian form of Eleanor. It was borne by the heroine of Beethoven's opera *Fidelio* (1814). Diminutives: Leo, Nora, Norah.

Leontia
Feminine forms of Leon. Variation: Leontine.

Leontine
Feminine forms of Leon. Variation: Leontia.

Lesley
Variation of Leslie, a Scottish surname derived from a place called Lesslyn in Aberdeenshire. Probably first used by Robert Burns in his poem *Bonnie Lesley*, this form is generally accepted as the feminine.

Leta
From Latin letus 'glad'.

Leticia, Letitia
Variation of Laetitia. Diminutives: Lettie, Letty, Ticia.

Lettice
Medieval anglicised form of Laetitia. It was popular in Britain until the early 20th

century, but is now rare. Diminutives: Lettie, Letty.

Lettie, Letty
Diminutives of Lettice.

Lex, Lexie, Lexy
Diminutives of Alexa, Alexandra, Alexandria, Alexandrina, Alexia or Alexis.

Leya
From Spanish ley 'upholder of principles'.

Lia
Variation of Lea or Leah.

Lian, Liane, Lianne
Origin uncertain. Possibilities include: forms of Eliane (a French name derived from the Latin name Aeliana), variations of Leanne, or diminutives of names ending in -liana, such as Juliana.

Liana
Diminutive of names ending -liana, such as Juliana.

Libby
Diminutive of Elizabeth, sometimes used in its own right.

Liddy
Diminutive of Lydia.

Liesel, Liesl
German diminutives of Elizabeth, sometimes used in their own right.

Lil
Diminutive of Lilian, Lillian, Lillie or Lily.

Lila, Lilah
Variations of Leila.

Lilac
Ultimately from the Persian *lilak*, from nil, 'blue', and the diminutive *ak*, and denoting a small tree of the olive family with fragrant blue or white flowers. It was one of the less common of the flower names that became popular at the very end of the 19th century.

Lili
German diminutive of Elizabeth, often used in its own right – brought to attention outside Germany by the popularity of the Second World War song, *Lili Marlene*, composed in 1938. See also: Lilian, Lily.

Lilian, Lillian
Latin, from *lilium*, 'lily'; or an expanded form of Lili as a diminutive of Elizabeth. Diminutive: Lily. Variations: Lilias, Lillias, Lillie, Lilly, Lily.

Lilias, Lillias
Scottish Gaelic forms of Lilian or Lillian.

Lilith
In Jewish folklore Lilith is the 'ugly demon', and in the Bible the name means 'night monster' (Isaiah 34:14). In medieval Jewish mythology Lilith is Adam's first wife, who refused to obey him and was transformed into a demon as punishment. That it became a popular name is probably an erroneous association with Lily. It was adopted as a mascot by some sections of the women's movement.

Lilla, Lillah
Variations of Lily, or diminutives of Elizabeth.

Lillie
Variation of Lily, and the spelling generally used by Lillie Langtry, born Emily Charlotte Langtry (1852-1929), society

beauty, actress and intimate of the Prince of Wales, later Edward VII. She was also known as the 'Jersey Lily'.

Lily
From Greek *leirion*, and denoting a species of tall, slender plants with trumpet-shaped flowers, the Christian symbol of purity. It has been one of the most perennially popular of the flower names that became popular at the very end of the 19th century. Variations: Lillie, Lilly.

Lina
(*ly-na, lee-na*) Diminutive of several names ending -lina, including Carolina or Selina.

Linda
A 19th-century coinage, of uncertain origin. Suggestions include: a byname from Belinda, or from any girl's name including the element -lind (e.g. Rosalind); or from Spanish *linda*, 'pretty'. Diminutives: Lindie, Lindy. Variation: Lynda.

Lindie, Lindy
Diminutives of Linda.

Lindsay
Adopted Scottish surname, probably meaning 'Lincoln's marsh'. First taken to Scotland from Lindsey, Lincolnshire, by Sir Walter de Lindesay, it is used as a boy's name in Scotland. Variations: Lindsey, Linsay, Linsey, Lynsey.

Linette
Variation of Lynette.

Linnet
Variation of Lynette, influenced by the songbird.

Liona
Modified form of Leona, influenced by Fiona.

Liorah
From Hebrew 'I have light'.

Lis
Variation of Liz.

Lisa
Variation of Liza, influenced by Liese (German) and Lise (French), and hugely popular in the second half of 20th century.

Lisbet
Pet name for Elizabeth.

Lise
Diminutive of Elizabeth.

Lisette
French diminutive of Lise, itself a diminutive of Elisabeth.

Lisha
Modern coinage, influenced by names with the phonetic ending -isha, such as Laetitia.

Lissa
Diminutive of Alisa, Alissa or Melissa.

Little Pixie
Bob Geldof's daughter. (He also has a daughter called Peaches Honeyblossom).

Liv, Livy
Diminutives of Olivia or Livia.

Livia
Now considered a diminutives of Olivia, it actually has independent roots as a feminine form of the Roman clan name Livius.

Liz
Most common diminutive of Elizabeth.

Liza
Either (*ly-za*) a diminutive of Eliza; or (*lee-za*), a variation of Lisa.

Lizanne
Compound of Liz and Anne.

Lizzie, Lizzy
Diminutives of Elizabeth.

Lois
Origin unknown. A biblical name; borne in the New Testament by the grandmother of Timothy.

Lola
Spanish diminutive of Dolores.

Lolicia
Recent coinage; an elaboration of Lola influenced by other girl's names ending in -icia, such as Patricia. It is mainly popular in Afro-American communities in the US.

Lolita
Spanish diminutive of Lola (itself a diminutive of Dolores). It was common in the US (owing to the country's Hispanic population) until Vladimir Nabokov's 1955 novel *Lolita*, after which the name became associated with underage promiscuity.

Lolly
Diminutive of Laura.

Lora
German form of Laura.

Lorelei
From Lurlei, meaning 'fairy cliff'. The name of a steep rock on the right bank of the River Rhine, south of Koblenz. Some 130m high, it has a remarkable echo and is thc traditional haunt of a siren with long blonde hair, called Lorelei, whose song is said to lure boatmen to their deaths. It is in occasional use as a first name.

Loren
Variation of Lauren.

Loreto
Italian town to which, according to medieval legend, the holy house of the Virgin Mary was miraculously transported from Recanati in 1295 (having been earlier transported from Nazareth to Dalmatia in 1291, and to Recanati in 1294). The house can still be seen. The name is in occasional use in Roman Catholic families.

Loretta
Variation of Lauretta, informed by Loreto.

Lori
Either a pet form of Lorraine, or a variation of Laurey or Laurie.

Lorinda
Modern coinage; an elaboration of Lora using the feminine suffix -inda (as in Belinda).

Lorna
Invented by R D Blackmore for his 1869 novel *Lorna Doone*, probably derived from Lorne, an area of Argyll, Scotland.

Lorraine
Adopted French surname derived from Alsace-Lorraine, a district of north-eastern France, itself derived from the Old German place name Lotharingia, meaning 'Lothar's place'. The name was first used in Scotland, for reasons unclear, but is now widespread throughout the English-speaking world. It is, however, not used in France. Variations: Laraine,

Larraine, Lauraine.

Lorri
Variation of Laurey, Laurie or Lori.

Lottie, Lotty
Pet forms of Charlotte.

Lou
Diminutive of Louise.

Louanne
Modern coinage, a blending of Louise and Anne. See also: Luella.

Louella
Modern coinage, a blending of Louise and Ella. See also: Luanne.

Louisa
Latinate feminine form of Louis. It replaced Louise as the most popular form of the name in the late 17th century, but in the 1990s Louise has regained ascendancy. Diminutives: Lou, Louie, Lulu.

Louise
French feminine form of Louis. It was only adopted in Britain in the 17th century, despite its long popularity in France before then. Diminutives: Lou, Louie, Lulu.

Lourdes
A town in southern France, site of a shrine established after a young peasant girl, Bernadette Soubirous, had eighteen visions of the Virgin Mary in 1858. It became, and is still, a popular pilgrimage destination. The name is largely restricted to daughters of Roman Catholic families, but it has come to recent prominence as the name given to Madonna's daughter.

Loveday
Loveday was a medieval tradition, whereby neighbours who had quarrelled met to discuss their grievances. Common in the Middle Ages for both boys and girls, it is now usually (albeit rarely) given to girls. It is chiefly confined to Cornwall.

Lucasta
Invented by the poet Richard Lovelace (1618-58) in poems addressed to Lucy Sacheverell, supposedly derived from *lux casta*, 'chaste light'.

Lucia
Feminine form of the Latin name Lucius, itself probably from *lux*, 'light'. St Lucy was a Sicilian martyr revered in the Middle Ages. Variations: Lucilla, Lucinda, Lucy.

Luciana
Feminine form of Lucien. Also Lucienne

Lucie
Old French form of the Italian name Lucia.

Lucilla, Lucille
Variations of Lucia. Lucilla is a Latin byname from Lucia, borne by several minor saints. Lucille is the French form, particularly popular in the US.

Lucina
Roman goddess of childbirth.

Lucinda
A form of Lucia, expanded with the feminine suffix -inda. It first occurred in Cervantes's *Don Quixote* (1605), becoming popular in the late 18th century. Diminutives: Luce, Luci.

Lucretia
Feminine form of the Roman family name Lucretius. In Roman legend

Lucretia, the beautiful wife of a nobleman, was raped by Tarquin, ruler of Rome, after which she committed suicide. As a result the Tarquin family was expelled from Rome and the Roman republic declared. Shakespeare treated the story in *The Rape of Lucrece* (1594). Variation: Lucrezia.

Lucy
Anglicised form of the Old French name Lucie, itself derived from the Italian name Lucia, derived from *lux*, 'light'. It has been consistently one of the most popular names for girls in Britian over several centuries, and remains so. Diminutives: Loose, Luce. Variation: Luci.

Ludmila, Ludmilla
Slavonic, from *lud*, 'people', and *mil*, 'grace'. St Ludmila (d 921) was grandmother of St Wenceslas. Ludmilla is the anglicised spelling.

Luella
Variation of Louella.

Luisa, Luise
Variations of Louise. Luisa is the Spanish form, Luise the German form.

Lulu
Byname of Luisa and Luise, the Spanish and German forms of Louise. It is now used as a diminutive of all related names (such as Louisa or Louise) and as a name in its own right.

Lydia
Greek, meaning 'woman of Lydia', a town in Asia Minor. A biblical name; borne by a woman who was converted by St Paul (Acts 16:14).

Lyn, Lynn, Lynne
Origin uncertain; either from the French feminine element -line (as in Adeline), or an altered form of Linda.

Lynda
Variation of Linda.

Lyndsey
Variation of Lindsay.

Lynette, Lynnette
Adapted from the medieval French form of Eluned. The modern form first appeared in *Idylls of the King*, by Alfred, Lord Tennyson (1859-85). Variations: Linnet, Linnette. See also: Eluned.

Lynsey
Variation of Lindsay.

Lyra
Modern coinage, from Latin *lyra*, 'lyre'. It was possibly influenced by names such as Myra.

Lys
Variation of Liz.

Lysandra
From Greek lysander 'liberator of men'.

Lysette
Variation of Lisette.

Lyssa
Diminutive of Alyssa.

M

Mab
Diminutive of Mabel or Mable. It is also the name of Queen Mab, in folklore the midwife of the fairies whose job is to deliver mankind of their dreams. (In this instance queen derives from Old English *cwen*, meaning 'woman'.)

Mabel, Mable
Originally diminutives of Amabel, established in their own right since the Middle Ages. Variations: Mabella, Mabelle

Mabella, Mabelle
Variations of Mabel, influenced by French *ma belle*, 'my lovely'. Mabella is the Latinate form, Mabelle the French. Variations: Maybella, Maybelle.

Mackenzie
Adopted Scottish surname, from Gaelic Mac Coinnich, meaning 'son of Coinneach'. Originally a boys' name, its use for girls is largely confined to the US.

Maddie, Maddy
Diminutives of Madelaine, Madeleine or Madeline.

Madelaine, Madeleine, Madeline
Medieval French forms of Magdalene.

Madge
Diminutive of Margaret, which came to be used as an alternative name for a barn owl or a magpie.

Madison
Old English 'son of Maud'. Also after US president James Madison the name was popular for boys from the 1800s and for girls from 1966.

Madonna
Italian, meaning 'my lady', used in reference to the Virgin Mary. It is popular in the US among families of Italian descent, and has in recent years been particularly associated with the phenomenally successful singer.

Mae
Variation of May.

Maev, Maeve
From the Irish Gaelic name Meadhbh, meaning 'she who intoxicates'. Borne in Irish legend by an early queen of Connaught, wife of Ailill and mother of Findabair. Variation: Meave.

Magda
German diminutive of Magdalen(e).

Magdalen, Magdalene
Hebrew; meaning 'woman of Magdala', a village by the Sea of Galilee. A biblical name; borne by St Mary Magdalene, reformed prostitute and follower of Jesus. An early variation, Maudlin, is now no longer used as a first name, although it survives in the pronunciation of Magdalen College, Oxford and Magdalene College, Cambridge.

Maggie
Diminutive of Margaret.

Magnolia
Derived from Pierre Magnol (1638-1715), the botanist who first identified this species of Asian and North American tree with large flowers. It was one of the many flower names that became popular at the end of the 19th century, particularly in the US.

Mahalia, Mehalia
Hebrew; from *mahala*, 'tenderness'. Variations: Mahala, Mahalah, Mehala.

Mai
Variation of May.

Maia, Maya
Variations of Mary. The former may be influenced by Maia, in Roman mythology the eldest and most beautiful of the Pleiades and mother, by Jupiter, of Mercury. In Buddhist philosophy Maya gave birth to Buddha in the shape of a little white elephant.

Maidie
Old English, of uncertain origin, but either a nickname meaning 'little maid', or a Scottish diminutive of Margaret or Mary.

Mair
Welsh form of Mary.

Máire
Irish Gaelic form of Mary, with the same pronunciation. Variations: Maura, Moira, Moyra.

Mairead, Máiréad
(*my-raid*, *ma-raid*) Respectively, Scottish and Irish Gaelic forms of Margaret. Pronunciation varies from place to place.

Máirin
(*my-rin*) Diminutive of Máire, and also a variation of Maureen.

Maisie
Diminutive of Margaret, Marjorie or Mary. Variation: Mysie.

Mallory
Adopted surname, originally from French, meaning 'ill-starred'. It is a recent adoption, having been brought to the attention of American television watchers as the name of a character in the soap opera *Family Ties* in the 1990s.

Malvina
Used (and probably invented) by James Macpherson (1736-96), some of whose writings purported to be 'translations' of an ancient Gaelic bard, Ossian. Variations: Malvena, Melvina.

Mamie, Mame
Diminutives of Mary. Used as names in their own right, particularly in the US.

Mandi, Mandy
Diminutives of Amanda.

Manon
French diminutive of Marie.

Manuela
Feminine form of Manuel.

Mara, Marah
Hebrew, meaning 'bitter'. A biblical name; adopted by Naomi after the death of her husband and sons (Ruth 1:20).

Marcella, Marcelle
Feminine form of a Roman family name Marcellus. Marcelle is the French form.

Marci, Marcie
Diminutives of Marcia.

Marcia
Feminine form of the Roman family name Marcius. Diminutives: Marcie, Marcy. Variation: Marsha.

Marea
Variation of Maria.

Mared
Welsh form of Margaret.

Maree
Variation of Marie.

Maretta
Scottish, anglicised form of Mairead, the Scottish Gaelic form of Margaret.

Margaret
From the Latin name Margarita, itself derived from Greek *margaron*, 'pearl'. St Margaret of Antioch, a 3rd-century virgin martyr, fought the devil in the shape of a dragon. The archetype of feminine meekness, she is known as St Marina to the Greeks and her feast day is 20th July. St Margaret of Scotland (c. 1045-93), daughter of Edmund Ironside of England and the wife of Malcolm III, was noted for her piety. Her feast day is 16th November. The name has been perennially popular since the Middle Ages. Margaret was also a country name for a magpie or a barn owl. Variations: Margery, Marguerite, Marjorie. Diminutives: Daisy, Madge, Maggie, Marge, Margie, Margy, Marji, Marjie, May, Meg, Meggie, Peg, Peggy.

Margarita
Spanish form of Margaret, used throughout the English-speaking world in its own right.

Margery, Marjery
Variations of Marjorie.

Margherita
Italian form of Margaret.

Margie
Diminutive of Margaret.

Margot
French diminutive of Marguerite, used in its own right. Variation: Margaux.

Marguerite
French variation of Margaret. The name was adopted in the early 19th century to refer to a variety of cultivated daisy. Marguerite derives from Old French, meaning 'pearl', and it was intended to reflect the pearly whiteness of the flower. Marguerite d'Angoulême (1492-1549), wife of Henri, king of Navarre, is known to history as Marguerite des Marguerites, 'pearl of pearls', or Queen Margot. Diminutive: Margot. See also: Daisy.

Mari
Welsh form of Mary.

Maria
Latinate form of Mary. Variations: Marea, Marya.

Mariah
Elaborated form of Maria.

Mariamne
Hebrew form of Miriam. Variations: Mariam, Miriam.

Marian, Marianne, Marion
Marian and Marion, originally French diminutives of Marie, have been used in their own right since the Middle Ages. Marianne, an elaborated form of Marian dating from the 18th century, gave rise to Mary Anne, probably the first double name. Marianne is also used as a name for the French Republic, and a slang term for the guillotine. Variations: Mariana, Mariann, Marianna, Maryann, Maryanne.

Marie
French form of the Latin name Maria used throughout the English-speaking world in its own right. Diminutive: Manon.

Mariel, Mariella
Variations of Mary, originally German diminutives.

Marietta, Mariette
Elaborated diminutive forms of Mary, of Italian origin. Mariette is the French form.

Marigold
Derived from Mary (a reference to the Virgin Mary), plus 'gold', and denoting a species of garden plant with orange daisy-like flowers. It was one of the more popular of the flower names adopted at the end of the 19th century.

Marilyn
Variation of Mary, originally a diminutive influenced by the feminine suffix -lyn. It was widely popularised by the American actress Marilyn Monroe (1926-62).

Marina
Origin uncertain, possibly from Latin *marinus*, 'of the sea', or derived from a Latin family name related to Marius. It was borne by a 14th-century martyr of the Greek church.

Marisa, Marissa
Diminutives of Mary, of Continental European origin.

Marjorie, Marjory
Variations of Margaret, from a diminutive of the French form, Marguerite. Variation: Margery. Variations: Margery, Marjery.

Marlene
Contraction of Mary Magdalene, of German origin. It was introduced to the English language by the German song *Lili Marlene* (*mar-layn*), popular during the Second World War, and further popularised by German-born actress Marlene (*mar-lay-na*) Dietrich (1901-92). The pronunciation *mar-leen* is a later development.

Marnie
Probably a diminutive of Marna, a Scandinavian form of Marina.

Marsha
Variation of Marcia.

Marta
Variation of Martha, originally German in origin.

Martha
Aramaic, meaning 'lady'. A biblical name; borne in the New Testament by the sister of Lazarus and Mary of Bethany, who was busy with serving her guests while Mary listened to Christ (Luke 10:38) and is therefore associated with housework. She is depicted with keys at her girdle and a ladle in her hand, and sometimes with a bound dragon. Her feast day is 29th July. The name was popularised in the US in the 18th century by the wife of President George Washington. Variation: Marta.

Martina, Martine
Feminine forms of Martin. Martina is the Latinate form, Martine the French. It was borne by two saints, whose feast days are celebrated on the 1st January and 30th January.

Mary
Medieval anglicisation of the French name Marie, itself from the Latin name Maria, ultimately a form of the biblical name Miriam, probably of Hebrew origin, or possibly Egyptian. It is traditionally taken to mean 'star (or dew) of the sea' (a translation of Stella Maris, a title given to the Virgin Mary), although some cite connections with 'rebellious' or 'bitter'. Borne in the Bible by the mother of Christ, by Mary Magdalene and by Mary of Bethany, sister of Martha and Lazarus.

Mary Magdalene, a reformed prostitute, is the patron saint of penitents. Her feast day is 22nd July. Mary remains one of the most enduringly popular of all girl's names. Diminutives: Maidie, Maisie, Mamie, May, Mimi, Minnie, Moll, Molly, Poll, Polly.

Marya
Variation of Maria.

Matilda, Mathilda
From Old German *mahti*, 'strength', and *hildi*, 'battle'. It was introduced to Britain by Queen Matilda, wife of William the Conqueror. Diminutives: Mattie, Matty, Tilda, Tilly.

Mattie, Matty
Diminutives of Matilda.

Maud, Maude
Medieval French variations of Matilda. A Norman introduction, Maud was obsolete by the 15th century but revived after Alfred, Lord Tennyson used it in his poem *Maud* (1855).

Maura
English phonetic spelling of Máire, the Irish Gaelic form of Mary. Variations: Moira, Moyra.

Maureen
English phonetic spelling of Máirin, diminutive of Máire, the Irish Gaelic form of Mary.

Mavis
Alternative name for a songthrush, derived from Old French. It was adopted in the 1890s in line with the fashion for names associated with birds, being first used by Marie Corelli in her novel *The Sorrows of Satan* (1895).

May
Diminutive of Mary and, more recently, one of the names of months adopted in the early 20th century. In this case it derives from the Latin Maius, probably from Maia, goddess of growth and increase. See also: April, June.

Maya
Variation of Maia.

Maybelle, Maybelline
Altered and elaborated forms of Mabel, influenced by two other names, May and Belle. Variations: Mabella, Mabelle.

Maxine
Feminine form of Max.

Meave
Variation of Maeve.

Meg, Meggie
Diminutives of Margaret.

Megan
Welsh diminutive of Meg. Variations: Meghan, Meaghan (especially in the US, Canada and Australia, as if it were of Irish origin).

Mehetabel, Mehitabel
Hebrew, meaning 'God makes happy', or 'God benefits'. A biblical name; borne by a figure mentioned briefly in a geneaology in the Old Testament (Genesis 36:39). It is probably now more often associated with the name of the cat befriended by Archy the cockroach in Don Marquis's collection of poems, *Archy and Mehitabel* (1927).

Mel
Diminutive of Melanie, Melinda, Melissa or Melody.

Melanie
French, derived from the Latin name Melania, from Greek *melas*, 'dark'. It was borne by two early Roman saints and introduced to Britain in the 17th century. Diminutives: Mel, Melly. Variations: Melany, Meloney, Melony.

Melba
Derived from the Australian place name Melbourne. Used as a surname by Australian opera singer Dame Nellie Melba.

Melinda
Modern coinage, a combination of Mel and Linda, influenced by Melissa and its association with honey and honey bees.

Melissa
From Greek *melissa*, 'bee'. Borne in Greek mythology by a Cretan princess who introduced mankind to honey and helped nurse the infant Zeus. In Ariosto's narrative poem *Orlando Furioso* (1532) the name is borne by a good witch who releases Rogero from the power of the bad witch Alcina. Rarely used in the English-speaking world until the 18th century, it has since been in regular use and underwent a popular revival in the latter half of the 20th century.

Melody
Direct adoption from the English vocabulary, denoting a musical tune.

Melvina
Variation of Malvina or feminine form of Melvin.

Mena
Diminutive of Philomena or of Wilhelmina.

Mercedes
Spanish, from Maria de las Mercedes, a Spanish title for the Virgin Mary, originally derived from Spanish *merced*, 'mercy'. Diminutives: Mercy, Sadie.

Mercia
Latinate elaboration of Mercy, coincident in form with the name of the Anglo-Saxon kingdom of Mercia, stretching south of the Humber, north of the Thames and incorporating East Anglia. Mercia arose under Penda (c. 577-655) and came to dominate England during the 8th century under Offa. The name derives from Old English *mearc*, 'border, march', a reference to the Marches, or frontier against the Britons (the Welsh).

Mercy
Direct adoption from the English vocabulary. It was one of the admirable abstract character qualities adopted as names by Puritans in the 17th century. It is also used as a diminutive of Mercedes.

Meredith
Adopted Welsh surname, from Maredudd, probably meaning 'great lord'. It is also used for boys; use as a girl's name is a 20th-century innovation. Diminutive: Merry.

Meriel
Variation of Muriel.

Merle
Either a contracted form of Meriel, or from Old French *merle*, 'blackbird', adopted in line with the fashion for bird names. It is also used for boys in the US. See also: Merlin

Merlin
Originally an anglicisation of the Old Welsh name Myrddin, meaning 'sea fort'.

It was borne most famously in Arthurian legend by the magician Merlin Ambrosius. However, its modern use for girls is probably more an association with the bird, a species of small falcon, in line with the trend for taking bird names. See also: Merle, Robin.

Meryl
Modern coinage, possibly a variation of Muriel influenced by comparable names, such as Beryl or Cheryl.

Meta
Variant or diminutive of Margaret.

Mhairi
Scottish Gaelic form of Mary.

Mia
Either a Scandinavian diminutive of Maria, or the Italian and Spanish word for 'my'.

Michaela
(*mi-kay-la*, *mi-kiy-la*) Feminine form of Michael, in regular use since the mid 20th century.

Michelle
Feminine form of the French name Michel, itself a variation of Michael. The name was popularised by a Beatles song and became a favourite for girls in the 1970s in Britain. Diminutives: Chelle, Mich, Michy, Shell, Shelley, Shelly.

Mignon
From French *mignon*, 'sweet', 'dainty', 'darling'. Borne by the heroine of Goethe's novel *Wilhelm Meisters Lehrjahre* (*William Meister's Apprenticeship*, 1795), on which the French composer Ambroise Thomas based his opera *Mignon* (1866). It is occasionally found in English-speaking countries.

Mildred
Old English, from *mild*, 'gentle', and *pryð*, 'strength'. It was borne by a 7th-century English abbess and saint. Diminutives: Millie, Milly.

Millicent
Norman French, from Old German *amal*, 'labour', and *swinth*, 'strength'. It was a Norman introduction.

Millie, Milly
Diminutives of Camilla, Mildred or Millicent.

Mimi
Diminutive of Mary.

Mina
Diminutive of Philomena or Wilhelmina.

Minerva
Roman goddess of wisdom, arts and crafts and war.

Minna
Diminutive of Wilhelmina, of Scottish origin.

Minnie
Diminutive of Mary or Wilhelmina.

Minta, Minty
Diminutives of Araminta.

Mira
Variation of Myra.

Mirabel, Mirabella, Mirabelle
From Latin *mirabilis*, 'wonderful'. It was popular in medieval Britain, when it was also regularly used for boys. It is rare in modern times.

Miranda
From Latin *mirari*, 'to admire', meaning

'admirable'. It was used by Shakespeare for the heroine of *The Tempest* (1612), the innocent daughter of Prospero who falls in love with Ferdinand.

Miriam
Old-fashioned form of Mary, of uncertain origin, possibly Egyptian. A biblical name; borne by the sister of Moses and Aaron. It was adopted by the Puritans. Variations: Mariam, Mariamne.

Mitzi
Variant of Maria, originally a German diminutive of the name.

Modesty
From the English word modesty. Associated with the comic strip heroine Modesty Blaise.

Mohana
Feminine form of the Indian name Mohan, from Sanskrit, meaning 'attractive' or 'enchanting'.

Moira
English phonetic spelling of Máire, the Irish Gaelic form of Mary. Variations: Maura, Moyra.

Moll, Molly
Diminutives of Mary.

Mona
Anglicised form of the Irish Gaelic name Muadhnait, meaning 'noble'. Its adoption was possibly influenced by its use as the Latin name for both the Isle of Man and Anglesey. It is sometimes used as a diminutive of Monica.

Monica
Origin uncertain; contenders are Greek *monos*, 'alone', or Latin *monere*, 'to advise'. It was the name of the powerful mother of St Augustine. Variations: Monika (Scandinavian), Monique (French).

Monique
French form of Monica.

Morag
Anglicised form of the Scottish Gaelic name Mórag, from *mór*, 'large'.

Morgan
Common Welsh name surname and boy's name, derived from Morcant, an old Welsh name itself derived from elements meaning 'sea' and 'bright'. It was borne in Arthurian legend by Arthur's wicked half-sister, Morgan Le Fay.

Morna
From Gaelic *muirne*, 'beloved' or 'gentle'. Variation: Myrna.

Morven
Scottish, derived from an area of north-western Scotland. The name could come from the Gaelic *mór bheinn*, meaning 'big peak', or from *a' Mhorbhairne*, meaning 'a large gap'. James Macpherson used the name for Fingal's kingdom in his Ossianic poems.

Morwenna
Welsh, probably from *morwyn*, 'maiden'. It was the name of a 5th-century Cornish saint.

Moyra
English phonetic spelling of Máire, the Irish Gaelic form of Mary. Variations: Maura, Moira.

Muriel
Anglicised form of the Celtic name Muireall, from *muir*, 'sea', and *eall*, 'bright'. A Norman introduction, it

underwent a revival in the 19th century. Variations: Meriel, Merrill, Meryl.

Myfanwy
(*mi-van-wee*) Welsh, meaning 'my precious one'.

Myra
Invented by the English poet Fulke Greville (1554-1628). Its origin is uncertain; it is possibly an anagram of Mary, or perhaps from Latin *mirari*, 'to admire', root of Miranda.

Myrna
Irish Gaelic; from *muirne*, 'beloved'. Variations: Merna, Morna.

Myrtle
From Latin *myrtillius*, and denoting a species of evergreen shrub indigenous to southern Europe, with white sweet-scented flowers, source of the precious substance myrrh. It was one of the flower names that became popular at the end of the 19th century. A classical legend seeks to explain the many tiny holes in the leaf of myrtle: Phaedra, the wife of Theseus but the lover of Hippolytus, is said to have passed one period of her beloved's absence by sitting in a myrtle tree, piercing the leaves with a hairpin.

N

Nadia
Anglicisation of Nadya, diminutive of the Russian name Nadezhada, meaning 'hope'. The name has enjoyed a sustained popularity throughout the English-speaking world in the 20th century, and even the full form has been used.

Nadine
French diminutive of Nadia. In common with many names of Russian origin, it was first used in Europe around 1909, when Diaghilev's Ballets Russes was established in Paris.

Naida
From Latin Naiada 'water nymph'.

Nairne
From Gaelic meaning 'from the river'.

Nan
Originally a nursery form of Anne, now more generally seen as a diminutive of Nancy.

Nancy
Probably originally a diminutive of Constance, but it became to be regarded as a diminutive of Anne in the 18th century, since when it has been used in its own right. It was particularly popular in the US from the 1920s to the 1960s. Diminutives: Nan, Nance. Variations: Nanci, Nancie.

Nanette
Elaborated form of Nan, with the feminine diminutive suffix -ette.

Naomh
(*neev*) Irish Gaelic, meaning 'holy' or 'saintly'. Despite the similarity, it is not to be confused with Niamh.

Naomi
Hebrew, meaning 'pleasant'. A biblical name; borne in the Old Testament by the mother-in-law to whom Ruth was devoted. A Puritan adoption, it has long been a favourite Jewish name but it began to be used in non-Jewish families around the 1960s and its popularity has continued to grow.

Natalia, Natalya
Russian, from Latin *natale domini*, 'birthday of the Lord', and used particularly for children born near Christmas. St Natalia, wife of St Adrian, was an inhabitant of Nicomedia who is said to have given succour to the martyrs who suffered there under Diocletian c. 303. She was not herself martyred, but is nevertheless regarded as a Christian saint. Diminutives: Talia, Talya, Tally.

Natalie
French form of Natalya, dating from around 1909, when Diaghilev's Ballet Russes was established in Paris. Although, like Natalya, it is associated with Latin *natale domini*, 'birthday of the Lord', and used for children born near Christmas, it is more common for there to be no such connection. Variation: Nathalie.

Natasha
Russian, originally a diminutive of Natalya, now far more widely used in its own right. It was used by Leo Tolstoy for the heroine of his epic novel *War and Peace* (1865-9) Diminutives: Tash, Tasha. Variations: Nastassja, Natasja, Natacha.

Nell
Medieval diminutive of Eleanor, Ellen or Helen. Nell Gwyn (1650-87), popular mistress of the British king Charles II, was christened Eleanor. Diminutives: Nellie, Nelly.

Nell Marmalade
Name given to Helen Baxendale and David Eliot's daughter.

Nerissa
Probably from Greek *nereis*, 'sea sprite'. It was used by Shakespeare for Portia's maid in *The Merchant of Venice* (1596).

Nerys
Welsh, a recent coinage, probably from *ner*, 'lord', plus the feminine suffix -ys, thus meaning 'lady'.

Nessa
Scottish Gaelic, a diminutive of Agnes. It was borne in Scottish legend by the mother of Conchobhar.

Nesta
Welsh, the Latinate form of Nest, itself a Welsh diminutive of Agnes. Borne in the 12th century by the grandmother of the Welsh chronicler, Gerald the Welshman.

Netta
Latinate form of Nettie.

Nettie
Diminutive of all girls' names ending -net, particularly Janet, or -ette, such as Annette.

Neva
Uncertain origin but probably from Spanish nevar 'to snow'.

Neve
English phonetic form of Niamh.

Ngaio
(*nye-oh*) New Zealand, from a Maori word simultaneously meaning 'clever' and 'tribe'.

Niamh
(*neev, nee-uv*) Irish Gaelic, meaning 'brightness', or possibly 'fairy'. Borne in Irish mythology by the lover of Oisín, son of Finn mac Cumhaill (Finn McCool), who carried him off to the land of eternal youth. See also: Boys: Ossian.

Nicky
Diminutive of Nicola. Variations: Nicki, Nickie, Niki, Nikki.

Nico
Modern diminutive of Nicola.

Nicola
Latinate and Italian feminine form of Nicholas. Diminutives: Nic, Nik, Nicki, Nickie, Nicky, Niki, Nikki. Variations: Nichola, Nikola.

Nicole
French feminine form of Nicholas.

Nicolette
French diminutive form of Nicole, used in its own right. Diminutive: Colette, and all those for Nicola.

Nigella
Latinate feminine form of Nigel, probably influenced by *nigella*, the horticultural genus of the flower love-in-a-mist.

Nikita
Russian masculine name, from the Greek name Aniketos, 'unconquered'. Borne by an early pope, it is now regarded as a girl's name in the English-speaking world, an elaboration of Nik- with the feminine diminutive suffix -ita.

Nina
Russian, originally a diminutive of girls' names ending-nina, it is now widely used in its own right throughout the English-speaking world. Diminutive: Ninka.

Ninette
French diminutive of Nina dating from around 1909, when Diaghilev's Ballets Russes was established in Paris. It was adopted by the dancer, choreographer and founder of Britain's Royal Ballet, Ninette de Valois (born Edris Stannus in 1908).

Noelle
Feminine form of Noel, itself derived from Old French *noel*, 'Christmas'.

Nola
Diminutive of Fionnuala, and hence a variation of Nuala. It is also regarded as a feminine form of Nolan.

Nolene
Modern coinage, probably from Noel plus the feminine suffix -ene. It is mainly popular in the US and South Africa.

Nona
Feminine form of Latin *nonus*, 'ninth'. In the days of big families the name was sometimes used for the ninth child or ninth daughter.

Nonie
Diminutive of Ione, Nona or Nora.

Nóra
Irish Gaelic form of Nora, introduced to Ireland after the Norman Conquest.

Nora, Norah
Diminutives of Leonora, Honora and other names incorporating the element. Diminutive: Nonie. See also: Honor.

Noreen
Anglicisation of Nóirín, Irish Gaelic diminutive of Nóra.

Norma
Origin uncertain; possibly derived from Latin *norma*, 'standard' or 'rule', although it is now regarded as a feminine form of Norman.

Nova
Latin novus 'new'. May have been influenced by the use of the term nova to describe a type of star.

Nuala
(*noo-la*) Irish, originally a diminutive of Fionnuala but now used in its own right.

Nyree
English phonetic spelling of the Maori name Ngaire.

O

Octavia
Feminine form of Octavius, from Latin *octavus*, 'eighth'. In the days of large families it was sometimes given to the eighth child or eighth daughter.

Odessa
From Greek meaning 'long journey'.

Odette
Feminine diminutive form of the Old French masculine name Oda, from Old German *od*, 'prosperity', 'heritage' or 'riches'. Odette and Odile are the names of the White Swan and Black Swan in the Tchaikovsky ballet *Swan Lake*. Variation: Ottilie.

Odile
Feminine diminutive form of the Old German masculine name Odila, from Old German *od*, 'prosperity', 'heritage' or 'riches'. St Odilia, an 8th century Alsatian abbess, is patron saint of Alsace. Odette and Odile are the names of the White Swan and Black Swan in the Tchaikovsky ballet *Swan Lake*. Variations: Otilia, Otilie, Ottilie, Ottoline.

Ofra
Variation of Ophrah.

Olethea
From Latin meaning 'truth'. Also Alethea, Oleta.

Olga
Russian, from Old Norse *heilagr*, 'holy'. It was introduced by Scandinavian explorers who founded Russia in the 9th century. The conversion of St Olga, regent of Kiev (d 969), was an important step in the introduction of Christianity to Russia. See also: Helga.

Olive
From Latin *oliva*, 'olive'. The olive tree, long a symbol of peace, was sacred to the goddess Athene in Ancient Greece, and a crown of olive leaves was the highest prize in the Olympic Games. It was one of the earliest and most successful of the plant and flower names adopted during the late 19th century, but it has not shared in the revival experienced by other such names.

Olivia
Origin uncertain, but probably the Latinate feminine form of Oliver, influenced by Latin *oliva*, 'olive'. St Oliva was venerated from early times in Italy as patron saint of olive trees. An early liter-

ary use in Britain was by Shakespeare in *Twelfth Night* (1599). It became very popular in Britain in the late 1990s.

Olwen
Welsh, from *ol*, 'footprint', and *gwen*, 'white, holy, fair, blessed'. Borne in Welsh legend by a giant's daughter in whose footsteps trails of white clover grew.

Olympia
Modern adoption, with learned intentions, of the ancient name of a valley in Elis, Peloponnesus, site of the early Olympic Games.

Onawa
American Indian meaning 'wide awake maiden'.

Oona, Oonagh
Irish and Scottish, anglicised forms of the Irish Gaelic name Úna. Variation: Una.

Opal
Type of semi-precious stone, from Greek *opallios*, itself probably derived from Sanskrit *upala*, 'gem'. Opals have long been associated with bad luck, which may be why it was one of the less common of the names adopted in the late 19th century in line with the then fashion for names associated with gemstones.

Ophelia
Feminine form of Greek *ophelos*, 'help'. It was used by Shakespeare for Hamlet's ill-fated lover in *Hamlet* (1601).

Ophrah
Hebrew, meaning 'gazelle'. A biblical name; borne by several male figures, although it now tends to be used for girls. Variation: Oprah.

Orea
From Greek 'of the mountains'.

Oriana
From Latin *oriri*, 'to rise', and sometimes interpreted as 'sunrise' or 'dawn'. The name first appeared in a 14th-century romance, *Amadis de Gaul*, borne by the beloved of the eponymous hero. Popular in 16th-century literature as a poetic name for Queen Elizabeth, it is only rarely used as a name in modern times.

Oriel
From Old German *aus*, 'fire', and *hildi*, 'battle'. It was a Norman introduction to Britain.

Orla
Irish Gaelic, meaning 'princess'.

Otilie, Ottilie
Variations of Otilia, itself a variation of the Old German masculine name Odila, from Old German *od*, 'prosperity', 'heritage' or 'riches'. Diminutive: Ottoline.

Ottoline
French diminutive of Ottolie. This form was popularised by the literary hostess Lady Ottoline Morrell (1873-1938).

Owena
From Welsh 'well born'.

P

Paddy
Diminutive of Patricia.

Paige
Adopted surname, originally an occupational name for an attendant. It has

become popular in the US in the latter half of the 20th century, and is spreading.

Paloma
Spanish, meaning 'dove'.

Pam
Diminutive of Pamela.

Pamela
Invented by the poet Sir Philip Sidney (1554-86), and taken by Samuel Richardson for his 1740 novel *Pamela*. Variation: Pamella.

Pamelia
Variation of Pamela.

Pamella
Modern variation of Pamela.

Pandora
Greek, meaning 'all-giving', from *pan*, 'all' and *doron*, 'gift'. In classical mythology the beautiful but foolish Pandora was created by the Greek god of fire to avenge the theft of fire by Prometheus. She was given a box but was forbidden to open it; she could not resist, however, and on opening it she released from the box all the ills of the world, hope following them last of all.

Pansy
A flower name, itself derived from French *pensée*, 'thought'. One of several flower names that became popular at the end of the 19th century, it has fallen out of favour in modern times, owing to a later 20th-century association with a homosexual man.

Parthenia
From Greek parthenos 'virgin'.

Pascale
Feminine form of the French name Pascal, meaning 'pertaining to Easter'.

Pat, Patti, Pattie, Patty
Diminutives of Patricia.

Patience
One of several abstract nouns denoting admirable personal qualities that became popular among Puritans in the 16th century.
Patrice
French form of Patricia.

Patricia
Latin, the feminine form derived from *patricius*, 'nobleman'. Diminutives: Pat, Patsy, Pattie, Patty, Tricia, Trish.

Patsy
Diminutive of Patricia.

Paula
Feminine form of Paul. A 4th-century St Paula founded a number of convents in and around Bethlehem.

Paulette
French diminutive form of Paula.

Paulina
Latinate diminutive form of Paula.

Pauline, Pauleen
French form of Paulina.

Peace
Adopted from the English word peace.

Pearl
Semi-precious gemstone produced by oysters and one of several names derived from gemstones that became popular in the late 19th century. However, a much longer history is as a byname for

Margaret, which derives from the Greek for pearl. Peninnah is a traditional Jewish name also meaning 'pearl'. See also: Margaret.

Peg
Pet form of Margaret and a variation of Meg. The mutation from 'M' to 'P' is not fully understood. Diminutive: Peggy.

Penelope
From Greek, but of uncertain origin, possibly from *pene*, 'bobbin', or from *penelops*, 'duck'. In Greek mythology Penelope was the wife of Odysseus, who passed his ten-year absence in spinning, loyally refusing all suitors. She was the mother of Telemachus, and the model of all domestic virtues. Diminutives: Pen, Penny.

Peninnah
Hebrew, meaning 'coral' or 'pearl' in modern Hebrew.

Penny
Diminutive of Penelope.

Pepita
Feminine form of Joseph, from the Spanish diminutive form, Pepito.

Perdita
From Latin *perditus*, 'lost'. It was first used by Shakespeare in *The Winter's Tale* (1610) for the daughter of Leontes and Hermione, abandoned on the orders of her jealous father. Brought up by a shepherd, she meets and falls in love with Prince Florizel of Bohemia. The match is forbidden and they flee to Sicily, where the full story is revealed, Perdita is reunited with her parents and she and Florizel marry.

Perpetua
From Latin perpetuus 'perpetual'. Also from St Perpetua who was martyred in the 3rd century.

Persephone
Greek goddess associated with spring. The name is also associated with Corinna.

Persis
From Greek, meaning 'Persian woman'. A biblical name; borne by a woman mentioned in the New Testament by St Paul in his letter to the Romans (Romans 16:12).

Pet
Diminutive of Petula, Petra or Petronella and also used as a general term of endearment, especially in northern England.

Peta
Modern feminine form of Peter.

Petal
Vocabulary word for a part of a flower. It is also used as a general term of endearment.

Petra
Feminine form of Peter, derived from Greek *petra*, 'rock'.

Petronella, Petronilla
Feminine form of the Roman family name Petronius. A 1st-century St Petronilla was thought by some to be the daughter of St Peter.

Petrova
Russian feminine form of Peter.

Petula
Origin unknown, possibly from the Latin *petulare*, 'to ask, to seek'.

Phil, Phillie, Philly
Dinimutives of Philippa, Phillida, Philomena, Phyllis and related names.

Philippa
Feminine form of Philip. Diminutives: Phil, Phillie, Philly, Pip, Pippa, Pippi, Pippy.

Phillida
Variation of Phyllis. Variation: Phyllida.

Philomena
From Greek, meaning 'beloved', and borne by two early Roman saints. Diminutives: Mena, Mina, Phil, Phillie, Philly.

Phoebe
From Greek *phoibos*, 'bright', meaning 'shining one'. In classical legend it was one of the titles given to Artemis, Greek goddess of the moon and sister of Apollo. It was also borne by a female Titan, the daughter of Uranus and Gaia. Variation: Phebe.

Phyllida
Variation of Phyllis. Variation: Phillida.

Phyllis
From Greek, meaning 'leafy'. In Greek legend Phyllis was changed on her death into an almond tree, which put out leaves only on the return of her lover. Diminutives: Phil, Phillie, Philly.

Pia
Feminine form of the Latin adjective *pius*, 'pious'.

Pilar
Spanish, from Nuestra Señora del Pilar, 'Our Lady of the Pillar', a reference to a legendary appearance of the Virgin Mary standing on a pillar at Saragossa. It is in occasional use in the English-speaking world.

Pippa
Pet name for Philippa.

Poll, Polly
From Molly and Moll, themselves pet names for Mary. They have long been used in their own right, although it is uncertain when or why the 'M' transmuted to 'P'. It was given by John Gay to the heroine of his *Beggar's Opera* (1728).

Pollyanna
Invented by E H Porter for the insistently cheerful and optimistic heroine of her eponymous book for children (1913). The name has come to describe an unduly – some might say maddeningly – optimistic person.

Poppy
From Old English *popig*, ultimately from Latin *papaver*, and denoting the species of flower with papery leaves, usually scarlet. One of several flower names that became popular at the end of the 19th century, it remains in regular use today.

Poppy Honey
Julia and Jamie Oliver's daughter.

Portia
Feminine form of the Roman family name Porcius. It was borne by the wife of Marcus Brutus, co-conspirator against of Julius Caesar, and was used by Shakespeare for the heiress and heroine of *The Merchant of Venice* (1596).

Posy
Pet form of Josephine. It is also used in its own right in the vocabulary sense of a bunch of flowers, itself originally derived from a contracted form of poesy, indicating a collection of verses. This connection probably arose from the custom of sending flowers and verses together. The

name was adopted in keeping with the 19th-century fashion for flower names, and is still current today.

Primrose
From Latin *prima rosa*, 'first rose', and denoting an early-flowering variety of the primula. Its pale yellow flowers can be seen on banks and in woodlands in the early spring. One of several flower names that became popular at the end of the 19th century, it remains in occasional use today.

Priscilla
Feminine diminutive of the Roman family name Priscus, from priscus, 'ancient'. A biblical name; St Paul stayed with Priscilla in Corinth (Acts 18: 2). It was adopted by the Puritans. Diminutives: Cilla, Pris.

Pris, Prissy
Diminutives of Priscilla.

Pru, Prue
Diminutives of Prudence or Prunella.

Prudence
From the Roman family name Prudentius, from prudens, 'provident'. It was one of the admirable abstract personal qualities adopted as names by Puritans in the 17th century.

Puma
Erykah Badu's daughter.

Prunella
From Latin, meaning 'little plum'. It emerged with the 19th-century fashion for names derived from plants.

Psyche
From Greek 'of the soul' or possibly 'of the mind'.

Q

Queenie
From Old English *cwen*, 'woman'. It is a pet form of Queen that was used by contemporaries to refer to Queen Victoria and was popular as a given name and nickname for girls during her lifetime. See also: Regina.

Querida
From Spanish 'beloved one'. Also Cherida.

Quincey, Quincy
Adopted surname, originally a baronial name from Cuinchy in northern France. Its use in the US is after a prominent New England family after which Quincy, Massachusetts is named. It tends to be more commonly used for boys.

R

Rachel
Hebrew, meaning 'ewe'. A biblical name; borne in the Old Testament by the wife of Jacob. Initially barren, she eventually became the mother of Joseph and Benjamin, after whose birth she died (Genesis 29-35). Since the 1970s it has been one of the most popular girls' names in Britain. Diminutives: Rach, Rae. Variations: Rachael (spelling influenced by Michael), Rachelle, Racquel, Racquelle, Raquel, Raquelle.

Rachelle
Modern elaboration of Rachel.

Radha
Indian, from Sanskrit, meaning 'success'. It was the name of a cowherd who became the favourite consort of Krishna.

Rae
Diminutive of Rachel, sometimes used in its own right.

Rafaela, Raffaela, Raphaela
Feminine forms of Raphael.

Rainbow Joan of Arc
Called 'Rain' as diminutive. Name for Arlyn and John Phoenix's daughter (they also have a daughter called Summer Joy).

Raine
Modern coinage, possibly a respelling of French *reine*, 'queen'. See also: Regina.

Ramona
Feminine form of Ramon, the Spanish form of Raymond.

Raquel
Spanish form of Rachel.

Rebecca
Latin form of the Hebrew name Rebekah, and the most favoured form in the English-speaking world. The name was popularised in this form in the mid-20th century, probably in response to Daphne du Maurier's novel, *Rebecca* (1938), made into a film by Alfred Hitchcock in 1940. It became one of the most popular girls' names in the English-speaking world in the 1990s. Diminutives: Becca, Becky.

Rebekah
Hebrew, of uncertain origin. A biblical name; born in the Old Testament by the wife of Isaac and mother of twin sons, Jacob and Esau (Genesis 24-28). The name was adopted by the Puritans and was very popular in the 17th century. Diminutives: Bec, Becca, Becky. Variation: Rebecca.

Reenie
Variation of Renée.

Regan
Origin uncertain. It was used by Shakespeare for one of the king's three daughters in *King Lear* (1605).

Regina
(*rej-een-a*, *rej-eye-na*) From Latin *regina*, 'queen'. It was popular in Victorian Britain. Diminutive: Gina. See also: Queenie.

Renata
From Latin *renatus*, 'reborn'. It was a Puritan adoption. See also: Renée.

Rene, Renie
Diminutives of Irene.

Renée
French, from Latin *renatus*, 'reborn'. See also: Renata.

Rhea
Origin uncertain. Borne in Greek legend by the daughter of Zeus and Gaia and, by her brother, Kronos the Titan, mother of Zeus, Hades, Poseidon, Hera, Hestia and Demeter. Identified with Cybele, she is also known as Agdistis. Variation: Ria.

Rhiannon
Welsh, probably meaning 'goddess' or 'great queen'. The name was borne by a figure in the *Mabinogian*, the collection of Welsh legends.

Rhoda
From Greek *rhodon*, 'rose', or possibly meaning 'woman of Rhodes'. A biblical

name, it is briefly mentioned in Acts 12:13 as the name of a girl who opened a door to Peter.

Rhona
Origin uncertain, but most probably after the Scottish island of Rona, the 'h' added in line with the spelling of Rhoda. Other contenders are as a feminine form of Ronald, or as a contracted form of Rowena. It was first used in Scotland in the late 19th century. Variation: Rona.

Rhonwen
Welsh, generally interpreted as meaning 'slender as a lance'. Variation: Rowena.

Ria
Variation of Rhea, or a diminutive of any girl's name ending -ria, such as Maria.

Rica, Rika
Diminutives of any girl's name ending -rica, such as Erica or Frederica.

Ricarda
Feminine form of Richard.

Richenda
Feminine form of Richard.

Ricki, Rikki
Diminutives of Erica or Richenda.

Rilla
Origin unknown but possibly Teutonic meaning 'stream' or 'brook'.

Rina
Diminutive of any girl's name incorporating the element -rina, such as Katrina or Marina. Variation: Rena.

Rita
Originally a diminutive of Margarita, the Spanish form of Margaret, but long used in its own right. St Rita (1380-1457) is regarded as patron saint of unhappy marriages and desperate cases.

Riva
From French 'riverbank'

Roberta
Feminine form of Robert. Diminutives: Bobbie, Bobby.

Robin
A 20th-century adoption of a well-established boy's name for girls, in line with the fashion for bird names. Variations: Robina, Robyn, Robynne. See also: Merlin.

Rochelle
Origin uncertain, but possibly a variation of Rachel, or derived from the French port, La Rochelle. It is mainly popular in the US.

Róisín
(*roe-sheen, rosh-een*) Irish Gaelic, meaning 'little rose'. It is anglicised as Rosheen, and sometimes Rosaleen.

Roma
Probably a direct adoption of the Italian name for Rome, adopted in the late 1800s.

Romaine
French, originally meaning 'woman of Rome'.

Romey, Romy
Diminutives of Rosemary.

Romily, Romilly
Adopted English surname, in occasional use as a given name. The British painter Augustus John (1878-1961) gave the name to one of his daughters.

Ros
Diminutive of Rosalind, Rosamund, or any name beginning Ros-.

Rosa
Latinate form of Rose.

Rosaleen
Variation of Rosalind, sometimes used as an anglicisation of Róisín.

Rosalia
Latinate form of Rosalie.

Rosalie
French name derived from Latin *rosa*. St Rosalie was a 12th-century virgin martyr of Palermo, Sicily.

Rosalind
Norman French form of the Old German name Rosalindis, probably derived from *hros*, 'horse', and *lindi*, 'snake'. A later, medieval, association with 'rose' and the Spanish *linda*, 'pretty', persists today. It was used by Shakespeare for one of the heroines of *As You Like It* (1599). Diminutives: Ros, Roz. Variations: Rosaleen, Rosaline, Rosalyn.

Rosaline
(*roz-a-lin*, *roz-a-line*) Variation of Rosalind.

Rosalyn
(*rose-a-lyn*) Variation of Rosalind.

Rosamond
Variation of Rosamund dating from the Middle Ages. 'Fair Rosamond' was a 12th century beauty from Woodstock in Oxfordshire who became Henry II's mistress and was probably murdered by his wife, Eleanor of Aquitaine.

Rosamund
Norman French, from Old German *hros*, 'horse', and *munda*, 'protection'. A later, medieval, association with the Latin *rosa mundi*, 'rose of the world', an epithet given to the Virgin Mary, persists. Diminutives: Ros, Rosa, Roz. Variations: Rosamond, Rosamonde, Rosamunde.

Rosanna
An 18th-century coinage combining Rose and Anna.

Rosanne
A mid-19th-century coinage combining Rose and Anne. Variations: Roseanne, Rozanne.

Rose
Ostensibly from Latin *rosa*, but more probably from Old German *hros*, 'horse' (see also: Rosamund). The name denotes a shrub of the genus *rosa*, generally with thorny stems and bright, fragrant flowers. It has been in regular use since the Middle Ages and was boosted by the 19th-century fashion for flower names. It remains very popular in modern times, particularly in its diminutive form. Diminutive: Rosie.

Rosemary
From the name of the herb, derived from Latin and meaning 'dew of the sea'. As Venus, the goddess of love, was born from the foam of the sea, rosemary is said to have amatory qualities. In her madness, Ophelia says in *Hamlet*: 'There's rosemary, that's for remembrance.' This is confirmed by the herbalist Culpeper, who wrote that rosemary 'quickens a weak memory, and the senses'. It was adopted as a name in the 19th century. Diminutives: Romey, Romy.

Rosetta
Variation of Rose, originally an Italian diminutive dating from the 18th century.

Rosheen
Anglicisation of the Irish Gaelic name Roísín.

Rosie
Diminutive of all names containing the element 'Rose'.

Rosina
Variation of Rose, originally a Spanish diminutive.

Rowan
Long used as a boy's name, when used for girls Rowan derives from the rowan, or mountain ash, a striking tree with red berries that was revered by Druids and was formerly known as witchen, because it was thought to protect against witches.

Rowena
Either the Latinate form of a Saxon name, derived from Old German *hrod*, 'fame, and *wynn*, 'joy', or a variation of the Welsh name Rhonwen.

Roxane, Roxanne
Most likely Persian in origin, meaning 'dawn'. Borne by the Persian wife of Alexander the Great. Diminutive: Roxy. See also: Aurora.

Roxy
Diminutive of Roxana or any of its variants

Roz
Variation of Ros.

Rozanne
Variation of Rosanne or Roseanne.

Rubina
Variant of Ruby.

Ruby
From Latin *rubus*, 'red'. The name of a precious red stone considered by the Ancients to be an antidote to poison and a protection from plague, it was popularised in the late 19th century in line with the fashion for stone names, and remained common until the 1950s. It has recently undergone a small revival.

Ruth
Hebrew, meaning 'friend'. A biblical name; borne in the Old Testament by the loyal wife of Boaz and daughter-in-law of Naomi. Her story is related in the Old Testament book of the name. It was popular with Puritans. Diminutives: Ruthi, Ruthie.

S

Sabina
Feminine form of the Latin name Sabinus, derived from the Sabine tribe living near Rome whose women were abducted by Roman soldiers. It was also borne by three early Christian saints.

Sabrina
Roman name for the River Severn. According to Geoffrey of Monmouth in his *Historia Regum Britanniae* (c. 1136), it was borne by the illegitimate daughter of King Locrine of Wales, drowned in the Severn by her father's ex-wife, Gwendolen. The Old Man of the Sea took pity on her and made her a river goddess.

Sadie
Diminutive of Mercedes or Sarah.

Saffron
Ultimately derived from Arabic *zafaran*, saffron is the name for the substance obtained by crushing the dried stems of the autumn-flowering crocus, used in cooking for colour and flavour. It is the most expensive of all spices. It was adopted as a first name in the 1960s and remains in occasional use.

Sal
Diminutive of Sally or Sarah.

Salena, Salina
Variations of Sally or Selina.

Sally
Diminutive of Sarah, often used in its own right. Diminutive: Sal. Variations: Salena, Salina.

Salma
Arabic, meaning 'peaceful'.

Salome
Greek form of an Aramaic name derived from Hebrew *shalom*, 'peace'. A biblical figure, although not identified by name; she danced for her stepfather, King Herod, and when offered a reward asked, under her mother's influence, for the head of John the Baptist (Matthew 14:1-12). The name Salome derives from Josephus's account of the incident.

Sam, Sammy
Diminutives of Samantha.

Samantha
Origin uncertain, possibly from Hebrew, meaning 'listen', or simply a combination of Sam and the feminine-sounding ending -antha. It spread from the southern states of the US during the 18th century.

Sanchia
Spanish, from Latin *sanctus*, 'holy'. It was a 13th-century introduction to Britain.

Sandie, Sandy
Diminutives of Alexandra or Sandra, sometimes used in their own right.

Sandra
Variation of Alexandra, via the Italian form, Alessandra. It was popularised by George Meredith's 1886 novel *Sandra Belloni*. Variation: Zandra.

Saoirse
(*seer-sha*) Irish Gaelic, meaning 'freedom'.

Sapphire
From Old French *safir*, itself ultimately derived from Greek *sappheiros*, meaning 'lapis lazuli', and denoting a transparent blue precious stone. It was one of the less common of the jewel names that became fashionable in the late 19th century.

Sappho
Greek lyric poet of the 6th century BC, also known as the Tenth Muse, who lived on the island of Lesbos. Despite the lesbian sentiments of her surviving poetry, she is said to have thrown herself into the sea when her advances were refused by the beautiful youth Phaon.

Sara, Sarah
(*sar-a*, *sair-a*) Hebrew, meaning 'princess'. A biblical name; borne by the wife of Abraham and mother of Isaac, whom she conceived when she was 90. Originally called Sarai ('contentious'), she was given the new name Sarah at God's command (Genesis 17:15). The New Testament Greek form Sara was used until the Puritans adopted Sarah. It

has been consistently pooular ever since and was among the most popular names for girls in Britain and the US throughout the late 20th century. Diminutives: Sadie, Sal, Sally. Variations: Saira, Sarina, Sarita, Zara.

Saranna
An 18th-century coinage combining Sarah and Anna.

Sarina, Sarita
Variations of Sarah.

Sasha
Russian diminutive of Alexandra. It is also used for boys, as a diminutive of Alexander. Variation: Sacha.

Saskia
Dutch, of uncertain origin, possibly from German *sachs*, 'Saxon'. It was the name of the wife of the Dutch painter, Rembrandt.

Savanna, Savannah
American coinage, possibly from *savannah*, the Spanish form of a Native American word for a treeless plain, or after the Savannah River.

Scarlet, Scarlett
Adopted surname derived originally from Old French *escarlate*, 'scarlet cloth'. It was first used by Margaret Mitchell for the heroine of *Gone With The Wind* (1936).

Selena, Selina
Origin uncertain, possibly after Selena, Greek goddess of the moon, or a form of the French name Celine. It was first used in Britain in the Middle Ages. Variation: Celina.

Selima
Origin uncertain, possibly from Arabic *selim*, meaning 'peace'.

Selma
Diminutive of Anselma, or possibly a contraction of Selima.

Senga
Scottish, possibly an anagram of Agnes.

Sephronia, Sophronia
From Greek, meaning 'prudent'.

Septima
Feminine form of Septimus, sometimes given to a seventh child, or seventh daughter, in the days of large families.

Seraphina
Hebrew, from *seraphim*, 'fiery', used to describe the highest order of angels. It was borne by two medieval saints.

Seren
Welsh but taken from latin and meaning 'star'.

Serena
From Latin *serenus*, 'calm'. Borne by an early Christian saint, possibly the wife of Emperor Domitian (AD 51-96), it was popularised in Britain in the 18th century.

Shana
(*shar-na*) Modern elaboration and respelling of Sian.

Shane
(*shayn*) Anglicised form of the Irish Gaelic boy's name Seán, reflecting the Northern Irish pronunciation, used in its own right and sometimes for girls.

Shani
Origin uncertain, possibly a feminine variation of Shane.

Shannon
Adopted Irish surname, derived from Ireland's principal river, itself from Irish Gaelic, meaning 'old'. It is also used for boys.

Shari
Anglicised form of Sári, the Hungarian form of Sarah. It is also a diminutive of Sharon.

Sharmaine
Variation of Charmaine.

Sharon, Sharron
From the Plain of Sharon in the Holy Land. A biblical place name, it was adopted by the Puritans, but gradually died out in Britain. It was reintroduced from the US in the early 20th century and became hugely popular in the 1950s and 1960s. Variations: Sharah, Sharun. Diminutive: Shari.

Shauna
Feminine form of Sean.

Sheba
Diminutive of Bathsheba, associated with the magnificent Queen of Sheba who visited Solomon in search of information about his God (1 Kings 10). Balkis, queen of Sheba, also appears in the Koran (ch 27). Sheba was considered by the Romans to be in what is now Yemen. Variation: Shebah.

Sheena, Shena
Anglicised forms of Síne, the Scottish Gaelic form of Jane.

Sheila, Sheilah, Sheelagh, Shelagh
Anglicised forms of the Irish Gaelic name, Síle. Variation: Celia.

Shelley
Adopted surname and place name, from Old English, meaning 'wood on a slope (or ledge)'. Adopted in the 19th century as a boy's name, largely in honour of Percy Bysshe Shelley (1792-1822), it is now almost exclusively used for girls, having become associated with Shirley. Variation: Shelly.

Sherona
Elaborated Latinate form of Sharon.

Sherri, Sherry
From French *cherie*, 'darling'. Variation: Cherie.

Sheryl
Variation of Cheryl.

Shirin
Muslim, of Persian origin, the exact meaning remaining unclear. It is becoming popular in the English-speaking world.

Shirley
Adopted surname and place name, from Old English, meaning 'bright meadow'. It was popularised by Charlotte Brontë's novel *Shirley* (1849) and further boosted by the 1930s child star, Shirley Temple. Diminutive: Shirl. See also: Shelley.

Shona
Gaelic feminine form of John. It is mainly popular in Scotland.

Shula
Jewish, a diminutive of Shulamit, meaning 'peacefulness'. It is also used by non-Jews.

Sian
(*sharn*) Welsh form of Jane. Modern variation: Shân

Sib, Sibbie, Sibby
Diminutives of Sybil.

Sibella, Sibilla
Variations of Sybil.

Sibyl, Sybil
From the Greek name Sibulla, borne by a classical prophetess, and later developing into a generic term for a female prophetess or fortune-teller. The name spread to Britain in the Middle Ages in the form of Sibella, Sibyl and Sybil emerging in the 15th century. The novelist George Eliot was called Sybil by her friends. Diminutives: Sib, Sibbie, Sibby. Variations: Sibella, Sibilla, Sibylla, Sybella, Sybilla.

Sidney
Variation of Sidonie. Its origin is unknown, possibly from Greek *sindon*, 'linen shroud', or from Sidonia, meaning 'woman of Sidon', a city of ancient Phoenicia. Variations: Sidonia, Sidony, Sydney.

Siena
After the Italian town.

Síle
(*shee-la*) Irish Gaelic form of Cecily. It is most common in its anglicised form, Sheila. Variations: Sheila, Sheela, Shelagh.

Silvan
Feminine form of Silvanus.

Silvia, Sylvia
From the Latin name Silvius, from *silva*, 'wood'. In Roman legend Rhea Silvia was the mother of Romulus and Remus. It was used by Shakespeare in *The Two Gentleman of Verona* (1594), and became very popular in the early 20th century. Variation: Sylvie (French).

Simone
French feminine form of Simon.

Sindy
Variation of Cindy.

Síne
(*shee-na*) Irish Gaelic form of Jane, derived from the early French form Jeanne.

Sinéad
(*shin-ayd*) Irish Gaelic form of Janet, derived from the early French form Jeannette.

Siobhán
(*shev-awn, shoo-an*) Irish Gaelic form of Joan, derived from the early French form Jehane.

Siriol
From Welsh 'cheerful'.

Sisley
Variation of Cicely.

Sissie, Sissy
Diminutives of Cecilia or Cicely, in regular use in their own right since the early 20th century, until the association with the word 'sissy' for a cowardly boy made them less popular.

Sky
One of several names derived from nature adopted under the hippy influence of the 1960s. The form Skye is an elaboration reflecting association with the Scottish island. It is also used for boys.

Sonia, Sonja, Sonya
Russian variations of Sophia, popularised by Stephen McKenna's novel *Sonia* of 1917.

Sonnet
Daughter of actor, Forest Whitaker.

Sophia
From Greek, meaning 'wisdom'. Hagia Sophia, meaning 'Holy Wisdom', is the name of the Orthodox cathedral in Istanbul. It was borne by several minor saints, and was introduced to Britain in the 17th century by the granddaughter of James I and mother of George I. Variations: Sonia, Sonja, Sonya, Sophie, Sophy.

Sophie, Sophy
Diminutives of Sophia dating from the 18th century and now widely used in their own right. Sophie is the French form, and the one with which the name achieved immense popularity during the second half of the 20th century.

Sorcha
(*saw-kha*) Irish Gaelic, meaning 'bright'.

Sorrel
After the plant, from Old French *surele*, derived from *sur*, 'sour', referring to the taste of the leaves.

Stacey, Stacie, Stacy
Originally diminutives of Anastasia or Eustacia, now often used in their own right.

Stella
From Latin, meaning 'star'. Stella Maris, 'star of the sea', had long been used as a name for the Virgin Mary when Sir Philip Sidney (1554-86) used it for his collection of sonnets, *Astrophel and Stella*. See also: Estella.

Stephanie
Feminine form of Stephan. Diminutives: Steff, Steffi, Steffie, Steph, Stephie. Variations: Stefanie, Stephany, Stephanie.

Stevie
Originally a diminutive of Steven, sometimes used for girls.

Storm
One of several names derived from nature adopted under the hippy influence of the 1960s.

Su, Sue
Diminutives of Susan, Susannah, Suzanne or Suzette.

Sukey
Diminutive of Susan, Susannah, Suzanne or Suzette, dating from the 18th century.

Summer
One of several names derived from nature adopted under the hippy influence of the 1960s.

Susan
An 18th-century variaiton of Susannah, by the mid-20th century one of the most popular girl's names in the English-speaking world. Diminutives: Su, Sue, Sukey, Susie, Susy, Suzie, Suzy.

Susanna, Susannah, Suzanna
From the Hebrew name Shushannah, meaning 'lily'. The Apocrypha's story of Susanna and the Elders tells of an innocent woman accused of adultery, but finally cleared. Variations: Shushana, Shushanna, Susan, Susanne, Suzanne, Suzette.

Susanne, Suzannc
French variation of Susannah.

Diminutives: Sue, Susie, Susy, Suzie, Suzy.

Susie, Susy, Suzie, Suzy
Diminutives of Susan, Susannah, Suzanne, Suzette.

Suzette
French diminutive form of Susannah.

Sybella
Variation of Sybil.

Sybil, Sibyl
From classical mythology a name borne by a number of prophetesses, ultimately from Greek sibulla.

T

Tabitha
From Aramaic, meaning 'gazelle'. Borne by a New Testament figure, also known as Dorcas, who was restored to life by St Peter (Acts 9:36-41).

Tacey, Tacy
From the imperative form of the Latin verb *tacere*, 'to be silent'. It was considered a suitable name for women from its medieval origins until the 18th century.

Talitha
From Aramaic, meaning 'little girl'. A biblical name; Christ brought a young girl back to life by saying to her: 'Talitha cumi; which is, being interpreted, Damsel, I say unto thee, arise' (Mark 5:41)

Tallulah
North American Indian, meaning 'running water'.

Talulla
From the Irish Gaelic name Tuilelaith, meaning 'abundance'.

Tallulah Belle
Daughter of Demi Moore and Bruce Willis.

Tamar
Hebrew, meaning 'date palm'. A biblical name; borne by the sister of Absalom.

Tamara
Russian form of Tamar, borne by a 12th-century queen of Georgia. Diminutives: Tammie, Tammy.

Tammie, Tammy
Diminutives of Tamara or Tamsin, often used in their own right.

Tamsin
Contracted form of Thomasina, the feminine form of Thomas, dating from the Middle Ages. It was largely confined to Cornwall until a popular revival in the 1950s.

Tania, Tanya
Russian diminutives of Tatiana, now also used in their own right.

Tanith
Phoenician; borne by the chief goddess of Carthage, goddess of love and fertility.

Tansy
From Old French *tanesie*, itself derived from Greek *athanasia*, 'immortal', and denoting an aromatic, bitter-tasting herb. The name was adopted as a first name in the 1960s, probably influenced by Pansy, and remains in occasional use.

Tara
Irish Gaelic, meaning 'hill', and the name

of a place in County Meath, once the seat of the high kings of Ireland. It was popularised in the English-speaking world by the release of the film *Gone with the Wind*, in which Tara is the name of Scarlett O'Hara's family estate. Tara is also an Indian name, from Sanskrit, meaning 'star', and a byname of Durga, the wife of Shiva. In Mahayana Buddhism, Tara is the name of the wife of Buddha.

Taree
Probably from an Aboriginal term for a fig tree, and most common in Australia.

Tasha
Diminutive of Natasha.

Tatiana
Russian, from the feminine form of the Latin name Tatianus, meaning 'of the family of Tatius'. It was also the name of an early Christian martyr of the Eastern Church, who died c. 228.

Taylor
Adopted surname, used for both boys and girls. Variation: Tayler.

Teal
Origin uncertain, but possibly Middle English and related to Low German *telink*, and describing a species of small dabbling duck. The name has been adopted since the 1970s, in line with the trend for taking the names of birds. Variation: Teale.

Tegan
Welsh meaning 'beautiful'.

Tegwen
Welsh, a modern coinage, from *teg*, 'lovely', and *gwen*, 'white, fair, blessed, holy'.

Teresa, Theresa
Origin uncertain, possibly after the Aegean island, Thera. A number of Roman Catholic saints named Teresa have led to its huge popularity throughout the Catholic world and beyond. St Teresa of Avila (1515-82) reformed the Carmelite order of nuns and founded many monasteries. Her feast day is 15th October. St Thérèse of Lisieux (1873-97) was a young Carmelite nun who wrote her autobiography, *L'Histoire d'une âme* (*The Story of a Soul*, 1899) while she lay dying of tuberculosis. Her feast day is 1st October. Diminutives: Terri, Terry, Tess, Tessa, Tessie, Tessy. Variations: Thérèse (French), Theresia, Tracey, Tracy.

Terri, Terry
Diminutives of Teresa, also used in their own right.

Tertia
Feminine form of Tertius, from Latin, meaning 'third'. It was generally given to a third daughter or third child, of a girl

Tesni
From Welsh 'warmth'..

Tess, Tessa, Tessie
Diminutives of Teresa, also used in their own right.

Tettie, Tetty
Diminutives of Elizabeth.

Thalia, Thalya
Greek, from *thallein*, 'to flourish' or 'to bloom'. The name is borne in classical legend by the Muse of comedy and pastoral poetry, represented holding a comic mask and a shepherd's crook; by one of the Three Graces, the daughter of Zeus and Hera; and by one of the Nereids, the

daughter of Nereus and Doris. Variations: Talia, Talya.

Thea
Diminutive of Dorothea.

Thecla, Thekla
Greek, from *theos*, 'god', and *kleia*, 'glory, fame'. Borne by a saint of the Eastern church, the first woman martyr and one of the most famous saints of the 1st century. She was supposed to have been converted by St Paul, and her story is told in the Apocrypha's Book of Paul and Thecla. Her authenticity being in doubt, her cult was supressed in 1969. Variation: Tecla.

Thelma
Invented by Marie Corelli for her novel *Thelma* (1887), possibly drawn from Greek *thelema*, meaning 'wish' or 'will'.

Theodora
Feminine form of Theodore, meaning 'gift of god'. It is an inversion of Dorothea.

Theodosia
Greek, from *theos*, 'god', and *dosis*, 'giving'.

Theophania
Greek, drawn from Epiphany, meaning 'manifestation of God', a Christian festival celebrated on 6th January.

Thérèse
French form of Teresa.

Thirzah, Tirza, Thirsa
From the biblical name Tirzah, possibly Hebrew.

Thomasin
Feminine form of Thomas often now replaced by Tamsin or Tamasine

Thora
Scandinavian, the feminine form of Thor, Norse god of thunder.

Tiane, Tiana
Diminutives of Christiane or Christiana.

Tibbie, Tibby
Diminutives of Isabel.

Ticia
Diminutive of Laeticia or Leticia. Variation: Tisha.

Tiffany
Medieval French corruption of the word theophany, from *theos*, 'god' and *phainein*, 'to show', and referring to manifestations of God, particularly Epiphany (itself a corruption of the word). It also refers to a type of silk-like gauze used to make robes for Epiphany revels (also known as Twelfth Night). The name survived as a surname, and modern use tends to reflect a re-adoption of the surname. See also: Tiphany.

Tilda, Tilly
Diminutives of Matilda.

Tina
Originally a diminutive of Christina, and now used in its own right.

Tiphany
A corruption of Epiphany, supposedly the name of the mother of the Magi, Caspar, Melchior and Balthasar. See also: Tiffany.

Tirion
From Welsh meaning 'gentle' or 'happy'.

Toni, Tonia, Tony, Tonya
Diminutives of Antoinette, Antonia or Antonina, themselves feminine forms of Antony, after the Roman clan name, Antonius.

Topsy
Origin unknown. It was used by Harriet Beecher Stowe for a slave girl in *Uncle Tom's Cabin* (1852).

Tori, Toria, Tory
Diminutives of Victoria.

Tottie, Totty
Diminutives of Charlotte.

Tracie, Tracey, Tracy
Variations of Teresa. The name was popularised by the character of Tracy Lord in the film *The Philadelphia Story* (1940) and its remake *High Society* (1956), played respectively by Katharine Hepburn and Grace Kelly. By the 1970s it was one of the most popular names in the English-speaking world.

Treasa
Irish Gaelic, from *tréan*, 'strength'.

Tricia, Trisha
Diminutives of Patricia.

Trina, Treena
Diminutives of Katrina.

Triona
Diminutive of Catriona.

Trix, Trixi, Trixie
Diminutives of Beatrix.

Troy
Adopted surname, derived from Troyes in France. It is now associated with the ancient city in Asia Minor, and is also used for boys.

Trudi, Trudie, Trudy
German, a common suffix for German female names derived from Old German *prup*, meaning 'strength' (e.g. Gertrude, Hiltrud). It has been adopted as a name in its own right.

Tu
Daughter of Rob Morrow. Full name Tu Morrow, pronounced 'tomorrow'.

U

Ulrica
Feminine form of Ulric. Variation: Ulrika.

Uma
Indian, from Sanskrit, denoting the flax plant or turmeric. Borne by the goddess who mediates between Brahma and the other gods, it is also a byname of Parvati, wife of Shiva.

Una
Anglicised form of the Irish Gaelic name Úna, of uncertain origin, although the most likely contender is from Irish Gaelic *uan*, 'lamb', possibly influenced by Latin *unus*, 'one' or 'unity'. It was borne in Irish legend by the mother of Conn Cétchathach. Variations: Oona, Oonagh.

Undeg
From Welsh 'fair one'.

Unity
Direct adoption from the English vocabulary, from Latin *unitas*. It is also used as an elaboration of Una.

Ursula
Latin, from *ursa*, 'bear'. According to legend St Ursula was a 4th-century British princess who went on pilgrimage to Rome with 11,000 virgins. All were massacred by the Huns at Cologne. Her feast day is 21st October.

V

Val
Diminutive of Valda, Valentina, Valerie, Valetta or Valma.

Valda
From Old German *vald*, 'power'.

Valentina
Feminine form of Valentine, although Valentine itself is sometimes used for girls.

Valeria
From Latin *valere*, 'to be healthy'. Variation: Valerie.

Valerie
French form of the Latin name Valeria. It was borne by a 3rd-century French saint.

Valetta
The name has no connection with the capital of Malta but is a modern coinage combining Val with the Italian diminutive feminine suffix -etta.

Vanda
Variation of Wanda reflecting the German pronunciation.

Vanessa
Invented by the author Jonathan Swift (1667-1745) for his friend Esther Vanhomrigh, combining the first syllable of her Dutch surname with Essa, a nickname derived from Esther.

Vashti
Probably Persian, of uncertain origin but probably meaning 'beautiful'. A biblical name; wife of King Ahasuerus of Persia, she refused to display her beauty before her husband's guests and was thus replaced by Esther (Esther 1 and 2). It was a Puritan adoption.

Velma
Probably a derivative of Wilhelmina, possibly influenced by Selma or Thelma. It emerged in the US at the end of the 19th century.

Venetia
From the Latin name for the city of Venice in northern Italy from Venice. The name is also associated with Venus, Roman goddess of love and fertility.

Venus
Roman goddess of love and fertility.

Vera
Russian, meaning 'faith', but also associated with *vera*, feminine form of Latin *verus*, 'true'.

Verena
Swiss, from the feminine form of Latin *verus*, true. It was used by Henry James in his 1886 novel *The Bostonians*. Variation: Verina.

Verity
From an archaic vocabulary word, itself from the Latin *veritas*, 'truth'. It was adopted by the Puritans.

Verna
Most probably derived from Latin *vernus*, 'of spring', or possibly a feminine

form of Vernon.

Verona
Origin disputed; either after the Italian city, or a contraction of Veronica.

Veronica
Origin disputed; possibly from Latin *vera icon*, meaning 'a true image', and referring to the late-medieval legend in which St Veronica wiped the face of Christ on his way to the cross. A 'true image' of Christ's face was left on the cloth. This story may have been invented to explain the name, which is more likely, in fact, to be a Latin form of Berenice. Diminutives: Ronnie, Vero.

Veronique
French form of Veronica.

Vesta
Roman virgin goddess of the hearth, and custodian of the sacred fire brought by Aeneas from Troy, which was never permitted to go out lest a national calamity should follow. The name is of uncertain origin, but it is the source of the adjective vestal, which described the six virgins who attended the flame with her.

Vi
Diminutive of Viola or Violet.

Vic, Vicki, Vickie, Vicky, Vikki
Diminutives of Victoria.

Victoria
Feminine form of Latin *victorius*, 'victory'. It spread worldwide after the accession of Britain's Queen Victoria (1819-1901), who received the name from her German mother. It has proved enduringly popular, even more so in recent years. Diminutives: Vic, Vicki, Vickie, Vicky, Vikki, Vita, Tori, Toria, Tory.

Victorine
French feminine form of Victor.

Vida
Diminutive of Davida, a Scottish feminine form of David, used in its own right.

Vilma
Derived as a contraction of Wilhelmina, reflecting the German pronunciation.

Vina, Vinia
Diminutives of Davina and Davinia, the Scottish feminine forms of David, used in their own right.

Viola
From Latin, meaning 'violet'. Common in Italy, it was used by Shakespeare in *Twelfth Night* (1602).

Violet
From Latin *viola*, 'violet, and denoting a species of low-growing plant with purple or white flowers. It was popular in Scotland before it spread during the 19th-century fashion for flower names. Variations: Ianthe, Iolanthe, Iole, Ione, Violetta, Violette, Yoland, Yolanda, Yolande.

Violetta, Violette
Variations of Violet.

Virginia
From the feminine form of Verginius, a Roman family name. Virginia, a later spelling, suggests association with *virgo*, 'virgin'; it was for this reason that Sir Walter Raleigh named his new discovery, Virginia, after Elizabeth I, the Virgin Queen.

Vita
From Latin *vita*, 'life'. It is also considered a diminutive of Victoria.

Viv
Diminutive of Vivien and its related names.

Viva
From Latin *vivus*, 'alive'.

Vivia
Variation of Viva.

Vivien
From the Roman family name Vivianus. Its origin is unknown, but it is probably from Latin vivus, 'alive'. Borne in Arthurian legend by the Lady of the Lake, an enchantress and the mistress of Merlin, who stole Lancelot as a child and raised him. The form Vivian is now more commonly used for boys. Variations: Viviana, Vivianne, Vivienne.

Viviana
Variation of Vivien.

Vivianne
Variation of Vivien, reinforcing the association of the second element with Anne.

W

Walburga
From Old German, meaning 'strength' or 'protection'. An 8th-century abbess, St Walburga, gave her name to Walpurgisnacht (1st May), a German festival associated with witchcraft.

Wanda
Origin uncertain, possibly Germanic or Polish. It was popularised by Ouida in her novel *Wanda* (1883). Variation: Wenda.

Wenda
Recent variation of Wanda or Wendy.

Wendy
Invented by J M Barrie for the heroine of *Peter Pan* (1904). It was supposedly derived from 'Friendy Wendy', a nickname given him by a friend's daughter, Margaret Henley.

Whitney
Adopted surname and English place name from Old English *whiten ey*, meaning '(at the) white island'. It is mainly confined to the US, and is probably associated there with Mount Whitney in South Carolina, highest mountain of the Rockies, discovered by Josah Dwight Whitney (1819-96).

Wilhelmina
Feminine form of William formed by adding the feminine suffix -ina to the Germanic form. Diminutives: Iman, Mina, Minna, Minnie. Variations: Velma, Vilma, Willa, Wilma.

Willa
Variation (and diminutive) of Wilhelmina, sometimes used in its own right.

Willow
From the species of tree, noted for its grace.

Wilma
Variation (and diminutive) of Wilhelmina. It is particularly popular in the US.

Winifred, Winifrid
Anglicised form of the Old Welsh name Gwenfrewi, from *gwen*, 'fair, blessed, holy, white', and *frewi*, 'reconciliation', influenced by the Old English masculine name Winfrid, from *wyn*, 'joy', and *frith*, 'peace'. Winifrid, a 7th-century Welsh virgin saint, was decapitated for resisting

the unwelcome advances of King Caradoc, but miraculously restored to life. The healing spring at Holywell, Clwyd, was said to have gushed from where her head came to rest. She is regarded as the patron saint of north Wales. Diminutives: Freda, Win, Winnie.

Winnie
Diminutive of Winifred or Winifrid.

Winona, Wynona
Sioux, meaning 'eldest daughter'. Borne, in the form Wenonah, by the mother of Hiawatha in Longfellow's poem of that name (1855).

X

Xanthe
From Greek *xanthos*, meaning 'yellow'.

Xene
From Greek *xenos*, meaning 'stranger', hence possibly 'a woman guest'.

Xenia
Greek, meaning 'hospitable'. Variation: Zena.

Y

Yasmin, Yasmine
Persian, from *yasmin*, from which 'jasmine' is drawn, and hence a variation of Jasmine.

Yolande
Variation of the French name Iolanthe, in turn influenced by the Italian name Violanta. Variation: Iolanthe, Yolanda.

Yseult
Early French form of Isolde.

Yvette
Feminine form of the French name Yves, itself derived from Ivo.

Yvonne
Feminine form of the French name Yves, itself derived from Ivo. Variation: Evonne.

Z

Zandra
Diminutive of Alexandra, and a variation of Sandra.

Zara
Origin uncertain; possibly Arabic, from *zahr*, meaning 'flower', or from Hebrew, meaning 'bright as the dawn'. Also a diminutive of Sarah.

Zaynab
Arabic, possibly derived from the name of a fragrant plant. It was borne by the Prophet Muhammad's daughter, and by two of his wives. His granddaughter, also Zaynab, is said to have introduced Islam to Egypt. Variations: Zainab, Zeinab.

Zelda
Diminutive of Griselda.

Zelma
Possibly a diminutive of Anselma, a feminine form of Anselm. Variations: Selma, Salma.

Zena
Origin unclear; possibly a variation of Xenia.

Zenobia
Possibly Greek, meaning 'life from Zeus', or a Semitic name in Greek guise.

Zephyrine
From French *zéphyrine*, drawn from the Greek name Zephyros, meaning 'west wind'. It is popular in France.

Zilla, Zillah
Hebrew, meaning 'shade'. A biblical name; borne by one of the wives of Lamech in the Old Testament. It is a very popular Romany name.

Zinnia
Derived from J G Zinn (1727-59), a German physician who identified this species of Mexican daisy-like flower. First adopted as a name in the early 20th century, it has been in occasional use ever since.

Zipporah
Jewish, the feminine form of Zippor, meaning 'bird'. A biblical name borne by the wife of Moses.

Zita
From the Italian dialect word *zitta*, meaning 'little girl'. It was borne by a 13th-century Tuscan saint who led a dull life of domestic service and is considered the patroness of domestic servants. The name was later borne by the last Empress of Austria. It is especially popular in Australia.

Zoe, Zoë
Greek Jewish translation of Eve, a Hebrew name meaning 'life'. It was borne by a 3rd-century Roman martyr, and adopted in Britain in the 19th century.

Zola
Possibly a variation of Zoe, or from the Italian surname, it was adopted as a first name in the late 20th century.

Zora
Origin unclear; possibly Arabic, meaning 'dawn'. Variation: Zorah

Zula
Predominantly a Black African name, drawn from the powerful Zulu people of Southern Africa.

Zuleika
From Persian, meaning 'shining beauty'. A biblical name, it was traditionally ascribed to Potiphar's wife. It is a common name in Persian poetry, and was popularised in the English-speaking world by Lord Byron's poem *The Bride of Abydos* (1813) and later by Max Beerbohm's satirical novel *Zuleika Dobson* (1911).

A to Z
BOYS' NAMES

A

Aaron

Of uncertain origin; most likely Egyptian or Hebrew, possibly from Hebrew *haron*, meaning 'mountain' or 'strong mountain', or from Arabic *haroun*, 'mountaineer'. A biblical name; borne in the Old Testament by the brother of Moses and first High Priest of the Israelites (Exodus 4).

Abdul
Short form of Abdullah.

Abdullah
From the Arabic name Abd-Allah, from *abd*, 'servant', and *Allah*, 'God', and meaning 'servant of Allah'. Borne by the father of the Prophet, who died shortly before Muhammad was born.

Abe
Diminutive of Abraham, Abram or Abel.

Abel
Hebrew, probably from *hevel*, meaning 'breath'. Biblical; borne in the Old Testament by the second son of Adam and Eve, killed by his jealous brother, Cain. He is regarded as a pre-Christian martyr, and his feast day is 2nd January. Diminutive: Abe.

Abner
Hebrew, meaning 'father of light'. Biblical; borne in the Old Testament by the cousin of Saul, whose armies he commanded. A Puritan adoption of the 16th century, it is particularly popular in the US. Li'l Abner was the name of a hillbilly cartoon character created by Al Capp in 1934.

Abraham
From the Hebrew *av haomon goyim*, meaning 'father of a multitude'; Biblical; borne in the Old Testament by the first of the great Jewish patriarchs, who received God's promise that his people would possess the land of Canaan (Genesis 12). His name was amplified from Abram when he was 90 (Genesis 17:5).

Abram
From Hebrew, meaning 'high father', the original name of Abraham.

Absalom
From the Hebrew *avshalom*, from *av*, 'father', and *shalom*, 'peace', meaning 'father of peace'. A Biblical name; borne in the Old Testament by the third son of King David, who rebelled against his father. He was killed while in flight after his defeat, and deeply mourned by his father. Variation: Axel.

Achilles
From Greek, meaning 'with beautiful lips'. Borne in Greek legend by the hero of the *Iliad*, who fought in the Trojan War. Achilles's great friend Patroclus, when Achilles refused to fight, led the Myrmidons and was killed by Hector; in revenge Achilles attacked the Trojans and killed Hector. He was later killed by Paris. It is in occasional use as a first name.

Adam
Hebrew, possibly from *adom*, meaning 'red', or from *adama*, meaning 'earth'. A Biblical name; borne in the Old Testament by the father of the human race created by God from the earth (Genesis 2:7). Variation: Edom.

Adair
Scottish name which could come from Gaelic meaning 'old ford' or possibly a variant of Edgar.

Addison
From Old English 'Adam's son'.

Aden
Variation of Aidan.

Adil
Arabic, meaning 'just', 'honest' or 'fair'.

Adlai
Hebrew, meaning 'ornament'. It is a minor biblical name.

Adolfus
Old German, from *athal*, 'noble', and *wolfa*, 'wolf'. Used by the German royal family in the late 17th century and early 18th century. Variations: Adolf, Adolph(e), Adolphus.

Adrian
Latin, from the Roman family name Hadrianus, (of Adria). It was popularised by the great Emperor Hadrian (AD117-38). Nicholas Breakspear took the name Adrian when he became the first (and only) British pope, in 1154.

Aeneas
(*e-nee-as*) Greek, probably from *ainos*, 'praise', and meaning 'worthy of praise'. Borne in Greek mythology by the son of Anchises and Aphrodite. According to Homer he fought in the Trojan War and afterwards withdrew to Mount Ida. Virgil's epic poem, the *Aeneid*, tells how Aeneas fled Troy and eventually settled in Italy. It is in occasional use as a first name in the English-speaking world, and sometimes used in Scotland as a translation of the Gaelic name Aonghas. See also: Angus.

Ahmad, Ahmed
Arabic, meaning 'highly commendable', or 'praiseworthy'. One of the names applied to the Prophet Muhammad. Borne by a central character of the *Tales of the Arabian Nights*, first introduced to Britain in 1704.

Aidan
Irish Gaelic, anglicised form of Áedán, from *aod*, meaning 'fire'. Borne by several early Irish saints, one of whom founded the famous monastery on Lindisfarne island, off the coast of Northumberland, as well as many churches and schools on the mainland. He died at Bamburgh in Northumberland in 651. Variations: Aiden, Aden. The Welsh names Hayden, Haydn and Haydon are probably drawn from Aidan.

Ainslie, Ainsley
Adopted surname, itself originally from the same source as the place name Annesley, or Ansley, probably from Old English *leah*, meaning 'clearing'.

Aisling
(*ash-ling*) Irish Gaelic, meaning 'vision' or 'dream'. Variation: Aislinn. It is also in use as a girl's name.

Akash
Sanskrit, meaning 'sky'.

Al
Diminutive of several male names beginning Al-, particularly Alan.

Alan, Allan, Allen
Celtic, but origin obscure; 'rock', 'noble' and 'harmony' have been suggested. Borne by a Welsh and a Breton saint. Variations: Alain (French form), Alun (Welsh form). Diminutive: Al.

Alasdair
Scottish Gaelic form of Alexander. More recent variations: Alastair, Alistair, Allaster.

Alban
From either Latin Albanus, meaning 'person from Alba', or from the Celtic word *alp*, meaning 'rock'. St Alban was the first British martyr, who was beheaded at Verulamium (modern St Albans), probably during the Diocletian persecution, in around 305. St Albans Abbey stands near the site of his execution. His feast day is 20th June.

Albert
Norman French name of Old German origin, from *adal*, 'noble', and *berht*, 'bright'. It replaced Ethelbert, an Old English name derived from comparable roots. Borne by Albert the Great, also known as Albert of Cologne (c. 1206-80), a Dominican scholar sometimes referred to as 'Doctor Universalis'. Diminutives: Al, Bert, Bertie.

Aldo
Old German, from *ald*, 'old'. It is popular in Italy, and in the US with families of Italian descent. Variations: Aldis, Aldous, Aldus.

Aldous
From Aldus, the Latinized form of Aldo.

Aldwyn, Aldwin
Old English, from *eald*, 'old', and *wine*, 'friend'. Variation: Alvin

Alec
Diminutive of Alexander.

Aled
Welsh, meaning 'offspring', or, possibly, after a river in Clywd.

Alex
Diminutive of Alexander.

Alexander
Latin, from Greek *alexein*, 'to defend', and *aner*, 'man'. It has a venerable history, being most commonly associated with Alexander the Great (356-23 BC). It was also borne by three Scottish kings, hence the Scottish forms, Alasdair, Alastair, Alistair and Allaster. Diminutives: Al, Alec, Alex, Alick, Lex, Sandy.

Alfred
Old English, from *aelf*, 'elf', and *raed*, 'counsel'. Borne in English history by Alfred the Great (849-899), king of Wessex, noted for his resistance of Danish invaders. He is also famous, in folk legend, for allowing some cakes, or probably bread, to burn when he took refuge in a cowherd's hut while hiding from the Danes. Diminutives: Alf, Alfie, Fred. Variations: Alured, Avery.

Algar, Alger
Old English, from *aelf*, 'elf', and *gar*, 'spear'. Popular in the US.

Algernon
From Old French *grenon*, 'moustache'. Moustaches were rare on Norman soldiers, and worthy of comment. William de Percy, a soldier with William the Conqueror, was so nicknamed, and the name was adopted by succeeding generations of Percys, later Dukes of Northumberland. Diminutives: Algie, Algy.

Algie, Algy
Diminutives of Algernon.

Ali
Arabic, meaning 'sublime'. Borne by a cousin of the Prophet Muhammad, who

married his daughter Fatima. His sons Hasan and Husayn are regarded by Shiites as Muhammad's true successors.

Alick
Diminutive of Alexander.

Alistair
Variation of Alastair.

Allan
Variation of Alan.

Alaric
Old German meaning 'noble ruler'.

Albin
From Latin name Albinus derived from albus 'white'. Also a variant of Alban

Allaster
Variation of Alastair.

Allen
Variation of Alan.

Aloysius
(*al-oo-ish-us*) Latin form of Louis. St Aloysius of Gonzaga (1568-91) is honoured by regular use of the name in Italy and in Roman Catholic families elsewhere.

Alphonso
Old German from athal 'noble' and funsa 'ready'.

Alun
Welsh form of Alan.

Alvar
Old English, from *aelf*, 'elf', and *here*, 'army'.

Alvin
Old English, from *eald*, 'old', and *wine*, 'friend'. For reasons that are unclear the name is particularly popular in the US. Diminutive: Alvie. Variations: Aldwin, Aldwyn, Alwyn, Aylwin, Elvin, Elwyn.

Ambrose
Latin form of Greek *ambrosios*, 'immortal'. St Ambrose (c. 340-397), Bishop of Milan and one of the fathers of the early church, was responsible for introducing music to the liturgy. His feast day is 7th December. The Welsh name Emrys is an alternative form.

Amos
Probably from Hebrew *amos*, 'to carry'. A biblical name; borne in the Old Testament by a minor prophet who foretold the downfall of Israel. He was the first to have his own book in the Bible. Popular with the Puritans, the name survived until the 19th century but is rare in modern times.

Andreas
From Greek 'manly'.

Andrew
Greek, from the root *andr-*, 'man', giving the meaning 'strong' or 'manly'. A biblical name; borne by one of the first of Jesus's disciples, a fisherman and brother of Peter, who was later adopted as a patron saint in Scotland, Russia and Greece. His feast day is 30th November. It is one of the most popular names in the English-speaking world. Diminutives: Andy, Drew. Variations: André, Andreas.

André
French form of Andrew.

Aneirin, Aneurin
Welsh, origin obscure; possibly from *eur*, Welsh for 'gold', or from the Irish

Gaelic *nar*, meaning 'noble'. Borne by the earliest known Welsh poet, from the 6th century, whose work is said to have been preserved in the *Book of Aneirin*. Aneurin is a more modern form. Diminutive: Nye.

Angel
From Greek *angelos*, 'messenger'. Popular in Catholic countries and families.

Angus
Scottish, from the Gaelic name Aonghas or Aonghus (*een-yis*), meaning 'one choice'. Aeneas (*e-nee-as*), from the Greek, meaning 'worthy of praise', is used in Scotland as a variation. Diminutive: Gus.

Anil
Indian, from Sanskrit, meaning 'air' or 'wind'. One of the names, in Vindu epics, of the wind god Vayu. Anil is the charioteer of Indra's golden chariot, pulled by a thousand horses.

Ansel, Ansell
Variation of Anselm.

Anselm
Old German, from *ansi*, 'god', and *helma*, 'helmet'. St Anselm became Archbishop of Canterbury in 1093. After a 19th-century revival the name has become very rare.

Anthony, Antony
Latin, adapted from Antonius, a Roman family name. The 'h' was introduced in the 17th century, when the name was mistakenly taken to derive from the Greek *anthos*, 'flower'. An early bearer was Marcus Antonius, one of the ruling triumvirate of Rome and the lover of Cleopatra. The name was popularised in the Middle Ages by two saints: St Antony the Hermit, a 3rd-century Egyptian monk, and St Antony of Padua (1195-1231), one of the most popular saints of the Christian church. It has been in regular use ever since. Diminutives: Ant, Tony. Variations: Antoine (French), Anton (German, Russian), Antonio (Italian, Spanish).

Antoine
French form of Anthony.

Anton
German and Russian form of Anthony, used in its own right in the English-speaking world.

Antonio
Italian and Spanish form of Anthony, used in its own right in the English-speaking world.

Anwar
Arabic, meaning 'clear' or 'bright'.

Aodh
(*ee*) Irish and Scottish Gaelic, from *aod*, 'fire'. It was the name of the Celtic god of sun and fire, anglicised as Hugh and Eugene. See also: Aidan.

Aonghas, Aonghus
(*een-yis*) Gaelic, meaning 'one choice'. The ancient name from which Angus derives.

Aquila
From Latin meaning 'eagle'. Used from Roman times.

Archer
Adopted surname, originally an occupational name for a skilled archer, from the Latin *arcus*, 'bow'. It has been in occasional use as a first name since the 19th century, and is particularly popular in

Australia where it was first given in honour of the seven Archer brothers, 19th-century explorers of Queensland.

Archibald
Old German from ercan 'true' and bald 'bold'. Particularly popular in Scotland.

Archie/Archy
Diminutives of Archibald sometimes used as names in their own right

Ariel
From Hebrew, meaning 'lion of God' or 'hearth of God'. A biblical place name; used in Isaiah 29 to refer to Jerusalem. In astronomy Ariel is a satellite of Uranus, while the name is used in literature to identify various spirits, the best known of which is the 'airy spirit' of Shakespeare's *The Tempest* (1611). The name is also used for girls.

Arjun
Indian, from Sanskrit, meaning 'white' or 'bright'. Borne by the son of the god Indra, most illustrious of the five Pandava princes in the *Mahabharata*, who received Krishna's divine oration, the *Bhagavad Gita*.

Armand
French form of Herman.

Arnold
Anglicised form of the French name Arnaud, from Old German *arn*, 'eagle, and *wald*, 'ruler'. A Puritan adoption, it was borne by an early saint, said to have been a musician at the court of Charlemagne. The name died out in the Middle Ages, but was revived in the late 19th century. Diminutives: Arn, Arnie.

Art
Diminutive of Arthur.

Artemas, Artemus
Greek in origin, probably related to Artemis, the Greek equivalent of Diana the huntress, goddess of the moon. A biblical name; borne by a minor New Testament figure.

Arthur
Origin obscure; contenders are the Roman clan name Artorious; *art*, an Irish word meaning 'stone'; or *artos*, Celtic for 'bear'. It is most associated with the legend of the 6th-century King Arthur, instigator of the Order of the Round Table. He is first mentioned under the Latin name Artorius in the late 7th century Historia Britonum. Diminutive: Art.

Asa
(*ay-za, ay-sa*) Hebrew, meaning 'physician'. A biblical name; Old Testament king of Judah.

Asher
One of the sons of Jacob in the Old Testament. From Hebrew meaning 'happy'

Ashley
Adopted surname, itself drawn from Old English *aesc*, 'ash', and *leah*, 'wood' or 'clearing'. Initially used as a boy's name, it is now more commonly given to girls. Diminutive: Ash.

Ashok
Indian, from Sanskrit meaning 'not causing sorrow'. Borne, in the form Ashoka, by an Indian emperor of the 2nd century BC who converted to Buddhism and then erected hundreds of commemorative inscribed pillars.

Atticus
The name of a Roman scholar and master of Greek, publisher and patron of the arts (110-32 BC), so highly regarded as

a man of taste and judgement during his lifetime that even Cicero submitted treatises to him. Harper Lee used the name for Atticus Finch, lawyer father of Scout and Jem in her novel *To Kill a Mockingbird* (1960).

Athelstan
Old English, from *aethel*, 'noble', and *stan*, 'stone'.

Athol
From Scottish place name and used as a first name since the 19th century.

Auberon
Origin uncertain, probably Old French; either from the Germanic *adal*, 'noble', and *ber*, 'bear', or a variation of Aubrey. In medieval romance Auberon was the king of the fairies. Variation: Oberon.

Aubrey
Old French, a form of the German name Alberic, itself from *alb*, 'elf', and *ric*, 'power'. In Scandinavian legend Alberic was king of the elves. There is doubtless a connection between Alberic and Auberon, king of the fairies in medieval English romance.

Augustine
(*<u>aw</u>-gus-tin*, UK, *aw-gus-<u>teen</u>*, US) Latin, from *augustus*, 'venerable'. Borne by perhaps the greatest of the fathers of the early church and the first Archbishop of Canterbury, St Augustine of Hippo (354-430). Diminutive: Gus. Variations: Austen, Austin.

Augustus
Latin, meaning 'venerable'. It was given by the senate to the Roman emperor Octavian in 27 BC and used subsequently by his successors. Diminutive: Gus.

Aulay
Scottish Gaelic, the Scottish form of Olav.

Aurelian, Aurelius
Latin, adapted from Aurelius, a Roman family name, itself drawn from *aurum*, 'gold'.

Austen, Austin
Most popular medieval forms of Augustine.

Avery
Adopted surname, itself originally derived from a French variation of Alfred.

Axel
Scandinavian form of Absalom, introduced to the US by Scandinavian immigrants.

Aylmer
Old English, from *aethel*, 'noble', and *maer*, 'famous'. Variation: Elmer.

Aylwin
Variation of Alvin.

Azariah
Hebrew, meaning 'God has helped'. A biblical name; borne by several Old Testament characters.

Aziz
Arabic, meaning 'invincible' or 'cherished'.

B

Bailey
Adopted surname, from various sources; the most common is as an occupational

name for a bailiff, but alternatives include someone living near a bailey, a form of fortification from Old French *baille*, meaning 'enclosed court', or from the English place name, from Old English *beg*, 'berry', and *leah*, 'wood' or 'clearing'. It is more commonly used for girls than boys in the US.

Baldie
Diminutive of Archibald.

Baldric
From the Old German name Baldarick, from *balda*, 'bold', and *ricja*, 'rule'. It was a Norman introduction to Britain. Variations: Baldri, Baudri, Baudrey.

Baldwin
From the Old German name Baldavin, from *bald*, 'bold', and *wine*, 'friend'. From Flanders. Borne in the Charlemagne romances by a nephew of Roland. Also borne by the first king of Jerusalem, from 1100-18. Use in modern times tends to be as an adopted surname.

Balthasar, Balthazar
Corrupt form of the Aramaic name Belshazzar, from the Babylonian *Belu-sharu-usur*, meaning 'Bel protect the king'. Borne, in the 4th-century Latin version of the Bible, the Vulgate, by the third of the Magi, the Three Wise Men of the East. Balthasar presented the infant Christ with myrrh, a prophetic allusion to the persecution unto death that awaited him. More recently, it was used by the English novelist Lawrence Durrell for the main character in *Balthazar* (1958), the second novel of his Alexandria Quartet.

Banjo
Name for the son of Patrick and Rachel Griffiths (based on a character in *The Man Who Came to Dinner*).

Baptist, Baptiste
Popular in Catholic Europe, often used with John (i.e. Jean-Baptiste) in honour of John the Baptist. It stems from Old French *baptiste*, from the Greek for 'one who baptises', derived from the verb *baptein*, 'to dip'.

Barnabas
Hebrew, meaning 'son of consolation'. A biblical name; borne in the New Testament by an apostle who accompanied St Paul on his missionary journeys. His feast day is 11th June, his symbol a rake. Diminutive: Barney. Variations: Barnaby, Barn(e)y.

Barnaby
Medieval vernacular form of Barnabas. Popularised in the mid-19th century by Charles Dickens's novel *Barnaby Rudge* (1841). Diminutive: Barney.

Barney
Diminutive, a contraction of Barnabas, Barnaby or Barnard. The name was common among Irish settlers in the 19th century, who had the reputation for being argumentative. 'Barney' has hence come to mean a dispute, or argument.

Baron, Barron
Adopted surname, first used during the post-Conquest period to mean a vassal of a noble, derived from the Old German *baro*, meaning 'freeman'. By the 13th century this had developed grades, and become a title of status, with some barons being more powerful than others. It is now the lowest order of nobility in Britain.

Barrett
Adopted surname, probably Old German from *bera*, 'bear', and *wald*, 'rule', or possibly from Middle English *baret*, meaning 'dispute'. It was a Norman introduction to Britain.

Barry
From the Old Irish name, Bairre, a diminutive of Fionnbharr (Finbar). It has been in regular and widespread use throughout the English-speaking world in the second half of the 20th century. Diminutives: Bal, Baz, Bazza (especially in Australia).

Bartholomew
Hebrew, from Aramaic *bar-talmay*, meaning 'son of Talmai', Talmai being another name for Nathaniel, the apostle. His feast day is 24th August, and his symbol a knife, a reference to the one with which he was flayed alive, c. 44 AD. Diminutives: Bart, Bat

Basil
Greek, from *basileios*, 'royal, kingly'. St Basil the Great (c. 330-79), brother of Gregory the Great, is considered father of the Eastern church. His feast day is celebrated on 1st January in the Eastern church, on 14th June in the Western church.

Bastian, Bastien
Diminutives of Sebastian. Bastien is the form in which the name survived in France and Spain from the Middle Ages until the present day.

Ben
Diminutive for Benedick, Benedict, Benjamin, and a name in its own right.

Benny
Diminutives of any boy's name beginning Ben-, such as Benedick or Benjamin.

Benedick
Variation of Benedict; the name of the main character in Shakespeare's *Much Ado About Nothing* (1598).

Benedict
Latin, from *benedictus*, 'blessed'. St Benedict (c. 480-c. 547) founded the Benedictine religious order, the first monastic order. Variations: Benedick, Benet, Benito, Bennet(t), Dick.

Benito
Variation of Benedict and originally a diminutive of that name

Benjamin
From the Hebrew name Benyamin, meaning 'son of my right hand'. A biblical name; borne by the youngest son of Jacob and Rachel, who died giving birth to him. Diminutives: Ben, Benjie, Benjy, Benny.

Bennet
Medieval variation of Benedick, from an Old French form of the name. Use in modern times tends to be as an adopted surname.

Berkeley
Adopted surname, originally derived from the English place name, from Old English *bearch*, 'birch', and *leah*, 'wood'.

Bernard
Anglicised form of an Old French name, itself derived from Old German *berin*, 'bear', and *hard*, 'hardy' or 'brave', meaning 'brave as a bear'. An 11th- century St Bernard of Menthon is revered as the patron saint of mountaineers, and a

breed of dog is named after him. A second St Bernard, of Clairvaux (1090-1153) was famously wise and nicknamed the Mellifluous Doctor. It was a Norman introduction to Britain. Diminutive: Bernie. Variations: Barnard, Barnet.

Bernie
Diminutive of Bernard.

Bert
Diminutive of any masculine name incorporating the element 'bert', such as Albert, Bertrand, Robert.

Berthold
From Old German meaning 'bright' and 'power'.

Bertram
From Old German *berht*, 'bright', and *hraben*, 'raven'. A Norman introduction. Used by Shakespeare for the Count of Roussillon, hero of *All's Well that Ends Well* (1602). Diminutives: Bert, Bertie. Variation: Bertrand.

Bertrand
French form of Bertram. Diminutives: Bert, Bertie.

Bevis
Origin uncertain, possibly Old French meaning 'bow' or 'handsome son', or from the French place name, Beauvais. It was a Norman introduction to Britain.

Bharat
Indian name, from Sanskrit, meaning 'being maintained'. Borne by several heroes of the Hindu epics, it was an epithet of Agni, the god of fire, and also the name of the younger brother of Ramachandra, the seventh incarnation of Vishnu. Bharat became the official name of India when it became independent.

Bhaskar
Hindu name derived from Sanskrit, meaning 'bright (like the sun)'. Borne by a 12th-century Indian astronomer, teacher and mathematician.

Bill, Billie, Billy
Diminutives of William, dating from the 19th century, sometimes used in their own right.

Björn
Scandinavian name, meaning 'bear'. Popularised throughout the English-speaking world in the 1970s by the Swedish tennis player Björn Borg, it is occasionally used as a first name.

Blair
Initially used as a surname taken from the Gaelic 'a plain' and popular particularly in Canada.

Blaise
French, either from Latin *blaesus*, 'stammering' or 'lisping'; or referring to an inhabitant of the French town of Blois. St Blaise, a 4th-century Armenian bishop, is regarded as the patron of those suffering from sore throats. Variations: Blase, Blaze.

Blake
Adopted surname, originally from Old English *blaek*, 'black', or *blac*, 'pale'.

Blase, Blaze
Variations of Blaise.

Bleddyn
From Welsh blaidd 'wolf' and diminutive suffix yn giving 'wolfcub'

Bob, Bobbie, Bobby, Bobs
Diminutives of Robert, sometimes used in their own right.

Bonar
Old French meaning 'courteous'.

Boris
Russian, of uncertain origin. Contenders are: from Old Slavonic, meaning 'fight' or 'battle'; a contracted form of the Russian name Borislav, meaning 'glory of battle'; or from a Tartar word, meaning 'small'. Borne by a 9th-century Bulgarian king, a 10th-century Russian saint (also known as Romanus) and by Boris Gudenov, Tzar of Russia (1598-1605).

Boyd
Scottish Gaelic, from *buidhe*, meaning 'yellow (haired)'. A common Scottish surname, it has been in regular use as a first name since the early 20th century.

Bradley
Adopted surname and common English place name, from Old English *brad*, 'broad', and *leah*, 'wood' or 'clearing'. Diminutive: Brad (now often used in its own right).

Bram
A diminutive of Abraham, of Dutch origin.

Brandon
Adopted surname and English place name, from Old English *brom*, 'broom', and *dun*, 'hill'. Some scholars dispute this, claiming it to be a variation of Brendan.

Brayden
From Old English 'brave, broad'.

Breandén
Irish Gaelic form of Brendan.

Brendan
Anglicised form of an old Irish Gaelic name Bréanainn, of uncertain origin. Contenders include: from a Welsh word, meaning 'prince', or from a traditional Irish Gaelic name meaning 'stinking hair'. Borne by a semi-legendary Irish abbot and saint, said to have been born in Tralee in 484 and to have died in 577. Known as St Brendan the Navigator, he founded a monastery at Clonfert, and embarked on a seven-year voyage in search of the Land of the Saints, the Isle of St Brendan. It is said that he may have visited America.

Brent
Adopted surname and English place name, probably, like Brian, derived from the Celtic world for 'hill'. Originally used as a first name in the US in the early 20th century, it has become widespread in both the US and Britain, possibly influenced by the popularity of Brett.

Brett
Adopted surname originally derived from an Old English name for a native of Brittany in Northern France. Originally used as a first name in the late 19th century it has enjoyed great popularity since, particularly in the US, Australia and South Africa.

Brian
Celtic, of uncertain origin, but probably meaning 'hill', or possibly 'high' or 'noble'. The name was probably introduced to England by Norman invaders but was in fact borne by a great Irish chieftain, Brian Bóroimhe, or Boro, who defeated a Viking invasion in the 11th century. Pronunciation in Ireland is *bree-on*, but elsewhere generally *bry-an*. Variation: Bryan.

Brice
Old French, borne by a 5th-century bishop of Tours. Variation: Bryce (the most common form in the US).

Brooke
Adopted surname, derived from Old English *bróc*, meaning 'stream'. Also, and increasingly, used for girls.

Brooklyn
Victoria and David Beckham's first son.

Bruce
Adopted Scottish surname, originally derived from a French place name, Brus, of uncertain origin, introduced to Britain during the Norman Conquest. Robert the Bruce, King Robert I of Scotland (1274-1329), successfully led Scottish forces against the English forces of Edward I at Bannockburn (1314). It is used throughout the English-speaking world but is particularly common in Scotland and Australia.

Bruno
From Old German *brun*, 'brown'. St Bruno was a 10th-century German saint who founded an order of Carthusian monks, and after whom the German town of Brunswick is named.

Bryan
Variation of Brian.

Bryce
Variation of Brice.

Bryn
Welsh, a modern coinage from the Welsh *bryn*, 'hill'. Also used as a diminutive of Brynmor.

Brynmor
Adopted Welsh place name, from Brynmor, Gwynedd, derived from *bryn*, 'hill', and *mawr*, 'large'. Like Bryn, a modern coinage. Diminutive: Bryn.

Bud, Buddy
Originally a nickname derived from buddy, meaning 'friend', but now occasionally used in its own right, particularly in the US.

Burgess
Adopted surname, from Old French *burgeis*, meaning 'freeman of a town'.

Burt
Various sources: in some cases a diminutive of Burton, as is the case with the American actor Burt Lancaster; sometimes a variation of Bert; or from Old English *beorht*, 'bright'.

Byron
Adopted surname and English place name derived from *byre*, 'barn' or 'cowshed'. It was popular in the 19th century, probably in honour of the romantic figure of George Gordon, 6th Lord Byron (1784-1824), the great English poet who died at Missolonghi, serving the cause of Greek Independence.

C

Cadell
Welsh, from *cad*, 'battle'.

Cadfael
Welsh, from *cad*, 'battle', meaning 'battle metal'.

Cadwallader
Welsh, from *cad*, 'battle', meaning 'battle leader', and dating back to the 7th century.

Cadogan
Anglicised form of Cadwgan, from *cad*, 'battle', and *gwogann*, 'glory'. Borne by two characters in the *Mabinogian*, the collection of Welsh legends. A 19th-century revival was partly an adoption of the surname derived from the first name.

Caesar
From the family name of the legendary Roman emperor Gaius Julius Caesar, which was traditionally said to be derived from *caesus*, 'cut', as Caesar was cut from his dead mother's womb, the first Caesarean section. Pliny related the name to the Latin *caesaries*, 'hair', as Caesar is supposed to have been born with a full head of hair. However, the name probably has some other source, possibly Etruscan. The royal titles Kaiser and Tzar are derived from the name, as is the Italian name Cesare, and the French name César.

Cai
Diminutive of Caius, used in Wales in its own right. Variation: Kay.

Caius
(*kai-us*) Variation of Gaius. (Caius College, Cambridge, named after its founder John Caius, is anomalously pronounced '*keez*'.) Diminutive: Cai.

Caleb
Hebrew, from *kalebh*, 'dog'. A biblical name; borne by one of only two people to complete the journey from Egypt to the Promised Land (Numbers 26). A 16th-century adoption, currently very popular in the US.

Calloway
Adopted surname, possibly derived from Old English *calu*, from the Latin *calvus*, 'bald', meaning 'downy' or 'hairless', in the sense of inexperienced. Or it may be a corruption of Galloway, an area of south-west Scotland. It is particularly popular in the US.

Calum, Callum
Scottish Gaelic, derived from the Latin first name Columba, meaning 'dove'. Borne by an early Celtic saint (521-597) martyred on the island of Iona.

Calvin
Adopted French surname, from Old French *chauve*, 'bald', itself derived from the Latin *calvus*. Given at first in honour of the French theologian Jean Calvin (1509-64), it may today be more associated with the designer Calvin Klein.

Cameron
Adopted Scottish surname, from Gaelic *cam sròn*, 'crooked nose', borne by a prominent Highland clan. Rarely used outside Scotland before the 1950s, it is now particularly popular in the US, Canada and Australia, and also used for girls.

Campbell
Adopted Scottish surname, from *cam beul*, 'crooked mouth'. A family name of the Dukes of Argyll, it has been in occasional use as a first name since the mid-20th century.

Caoimhínn
Irish Gaelic, meaning 'handsome'. Borne by a 7th-century Irish saint, it is more commonly anglicised as Kevin.

Caradoc
Anglicised form of the Welsh name Caradog, from *car*, 'love', meaning 'lovable'. The Latin form is Caractacus and both refer to a 1st-century English

ruler famed for his dignity of bearing when taken as a captive to Rome in AD 51. Caradoc was also the name of a knight of the Round Table whose wife was the only one of Guinevere's ladies to be faithful to her husband.

Carey, Cary
Adopted surname and place names in Devon and Somerset. It was boosted in popularity by the actor Cary Grant (1904-89). It is also used for girls.

Carl
Old-fashioned variation of Karl, the German form of Charles. It is popular in the US, having been introduced by Scandinavian and German immigrants, and also very popular in Wales, but why exactly is unclear.

Carlo, Carlos
Respectively the Italian and Spanish forms of Charles.

Carlton
Adopted surname and common English place name, from Old English *carl*, meaning 'peasant', and *tun*, 'settlement'.

Carlyle
Adopted surname and English place name (Carlisle, Cumbria), meaning 'fort of Luguvalium'. It is also used as an expanded form of Carl.

Carol
Eastern European form of Charles, derived from the Latin form *Carolus*.

Carson
Adopted Scottish surname, of uncertain origin but possibly from a medieval name de Carsan.

Carter
Adopted surname, originally an occupational name for a cart driver or maker.

Caryl
Variation of Carol, also used for girls.

Casey, Casy
Exact origin uncertain; possibly a diminutive of Casimir or an adopted Irish surname meaning 'vigilant in war'. However, use in the US is generally after engine driver Casey Jones (1863-1900) who became a folk hero when he gave his life saving passengers on his train. It is also used for girls.

Caspar
German form of an old Persian name, meaning 'master of the treasure'. Early Christian tradition assigns this name to one of the Magi. It is anglicised as Jasper.

Cassidy
Adopted Irish Gaelic surname, Ó Caiside. It is particularly popular in the US.

Cathal
(*<u>ca</u>-hal*) Irish Gaelic, from the Celtic elements *cath*, 'battle', and *val*, 'rule'. A 7th century St Cathal became Bishop of Taranto, Italy. It is sometimes anglicised as Carl.

Cecil
Adopted aristocratic surname, from the Roman family name Caecilius, derived from Latin *caecus*, 'blind'. It was popular in the late 19th century, partly in honour of the explorer Cecil Rhodes, founder of Rhodesia.

Cedric
Origin uncertain, possibly an altered

form of Cerdic, a 6th-century king of Wessex. It was invented by Sir Walter Scott for a character in *Ivanhoe* (1819).

Ceri
Welsh, meaning 'beloved'. It is also used for girls.

Chad
Form of the Old English name Ceadda, borne by a 7th-century Northumbrian saint (d 672), pupil of St Aidan, later bishop of Mercia at Lichfield and Archbishop of York. He is considered the patron saint of springs. In modern times, the Reverend Chad Varah founded the Samaritans.

Chandler
Adopted surname, originally an occupational name for a candlemaker, from Old French *chandele*, 'candle'. It has become widespread in the US as a first name since it was first adopted in the mid-20th century.

Chandra
Indian name, from Sanskrit, meaning 'moon'. It is also used for girls, although the moon is generally considered a male deity.

Chandrakant
Indian, from Sanskrit, literally meaning 'beloved by the moon' and referring to a semi-precious moonstone that features in Hindu texts.

Charles
French form of Old German name Carl, derived from the Old English *ceorl*, 'man'. Charles the Great (742-814), also known as Charlemagne, became king of the Franks in 771 and first Holy Roman Emperor in 800. He is buried at Aix-la-Chapelle; he was said to be eight feet (2.4m) tall and hugely strong, and to have married nine times. It was a Norman introduction to Britain. Diminutives: Charley, Charlie, Chas, Chay, Chuck. Variations: Carl, Carlo, Carlos, Carol, Karl.

Charley, Charlie
Diminutives of Charles.

Charlton
Variation of Carlton.

Chas
Diminutive of Charles.

Chay
Diminutive of Charles.

Chester
Adopted surname and English place name, derived from Latin *castra*, 'camp'. It is particularly popular in the US. Diminutive: Chet.

Chet
Diminutive of Chester, particularly popular in the US.

Chris
Diminutive of any name beginning Chris-, such as Christian or Christopher.

Christian
From the Latin name Christianus, meaning 'follower of Christ'. According to the Bible the term was first used at Antioch: 'And when he had found him, he brought him unto Antioch. And it came to pass, that a whole year they assembled themselves with the church, and taught much people. And the disciples were called Christians first in Antioch' (Acts 11:26). It was used by John Bunyan for the hero of *The Pilgrim's Progress* (1678), who left the City of Destruction to journey to the Celestial City. Diminutives: Chris, Christie, Christy.

Christie, Christy
Scottish and Irish diminutives of any name beginning Chris-, such as Christian or Christopher.

Christopher
From the Greek name Khristophoros, from *Khristos*, 'Christ', and *pherein*, 'to bear'. There is an allegorical legend in which the giant St Christopher, 'the bearer of Christ', carried the Christ child safely across a river. On the other side the child said to him, 'Marvel thou nothing, for thou hast borne all the world upon thee, and its sins likewise.' He is considered the patron saint of travellers and has lent his name to a medallion bearing a picture of the incident, which is worn as a talisman throughout the Christian world. The name has been in regular use since the 15th century, and in the later 20th century has been one of the most popular names in the English-speaking world. Diminutives: Chris, Christie, Christy, Kester, Kit, Kris.

Chuck
Nickname deriving from Charles. Characteristically American, it was originally an English name.

Ciarán
(*kee-a-ran*) Irish Gaelic, from *ciar*, 'black', meaning 'little dark one'. It was the name of various early Irish saints. Anglicised as Kieran.

Clarence
Adopted aristocratic surname, initially bestowed on a son of Edward III when he married an heiress from Clare, in Suffolk.

Clark
Adopted surname, originally an occupational name for a clerk, or cleric. Popularised in the 20th century by the actor Clark Gable (1901-60) and the fictional Clark Kent, otherwise known as Superman.

Claud, Claude
From the Roman family name Claudius, derived from *claudus*, 'lame'. Claude, the French form, was introduced to Britain in the 16th century, where it became anglicised as Claud.

Clay
Either an adopted surname, from Old English *clæg*, 'clay', originally denoting an inhabitant of an area of clay soil; or, more likely, a diminutive of Clayton.

Clayton
Adopted surname and English place name, from Old English *clæg*, 'clay', and *tun*, 'settlement'. Its use as a first name probably dates back to the beginning of the 19th century, and it is particularly popular in the US.

Cledwyn
Welsh, of uncertain origin; possibly from *caled*, 'hard', and *gwen*, 'white, fair, blessed, holy'.

Clem
Diminutive of Clement.

Clement
From Latin *clemens*, 'merciful'. Borne by several early saints, including Clement of Alexandria (c.150-c. 215), a disciple of St Paul who became the first of thirteen popes bearing the name. Popular in Britain in the Middle Ages, it underwent a brief revival in the 19th century but is unusual today.

Cliff
Diminutive of Clifford or Clifton. It was

popularised throughout the English-speaking world in the 1950s by the British pop singer Cliff Richard (born Harry Webb).

Clifford
Adopted surname and English place name, from Old English *clif*, 'cliff, slope', and *ford*, 'ford'. Diminutive: Cliff.

Clifton
Recently adopted surname, from Old English *clif*, 'cliff, slope', and *tun*, 'settlement'. Diminutive: Cliff.

Clint
Diminutive of Clinton. It was popularised by Clint Eastwood (b 1930).

Clinton
Adopted surname and English place name meaning 'settlement by the river Glyme'. It is mainly found in the US, where Clinton has long been an important name in politics, from George Clinton (1739-1812), governor of New York, to William 'Bill' Clinton, President of the US from 1992.

Clive
Adopted surname and place name, from Old English *clif*, 'cliff'. It was popularised as a first name in honour of the British statesman Robert Clive (1725-74), known as Clive of India.

Clovis
Old French form of the Old German name Chlodowig, meaning 'famous warrior', the same root from which Lewis stems. Borne by the first king of the Franks (c.466-511), founder of the French monarchy. A great fighter, he overcame several tribes, including the Burgundians and Visigoths, to establish control over much of Gaul. He converted to Christianity and established Paris as the predominant town of Gaul. The name later altered to become Louis and was borne by a further eighteen French kings. It is in occasional use in the English-speaking world. See also: Lewis, Ludovic.

Clyde
Adopted surname and Scottish river name, possibly derived from the name of an ancient local goddess. It is particularly popular in the US.

Cody
Adopted Irish surname, of uncertain origin. Probably first given in honour of the Wild West hero William Frederick Cody (1847-1917), otherwise known as Buffalo Bill, it has become common for both boys and girls in the US and Australia.

Cole
Adopted surname, itself derived from a medieval name of uncertain origin, possibly from *col*, 'charcoal', meaning 'swarthy'. The nursery-rhyme figure Old King Cole is said to have been the father of St Helena, and hence the grandfather of Emperor Constantine.

Colin
Diminutive of Coll, a medieval short form of Nicholas.

Colm, Colum
Irish Gaelic form of the Latin first name Columba, meaning 'dove'. Variations: Calum, Callum. See also: Malcolm.

Conal, Conall
Irish and Scottish Gaelic, from *con*, 'high'. Borne by several warriors in Celtic legend.

Conan
Irish and Scottish Gaelic, from *con*, 'high'. Borne in Irish legend by a warrior who fought under Finn mac Cumhaill (Finn McCool), and who features in James Macpherson's Ossian poems.

Conn
Irish and Scottish Gaelic, from *con*, 'high'.

Connor, Conor
Anglicised form of the Irish Gaelic name Conchobhar, from *con*, 'high', meaning 'high desire'. Borne in Irish legend by the son of Nessa, who became king of Ulster. He was uncle and guardian of Cuchulain and, as an old man, lusted after the young Deirdre, forcing her to marry him.

Conrad
From the Old German name Konrad, from *conja*, 'bold', and *rad*, 'counsel'. The name of a 10th-century bishop of Constance, it was reintroduced to the English-speaking world in the 19th century. Variations: Curt, Kurt.

Constantine
From Latin *constans*, 'constant'. Constantine the Great (c. 288-337), the first Christian emperor, left Rome to found Constantinople (modern Istanbul). Borne by three medieval Scottish kings, and more recently by two 20th-century kings of Greece.

Corbin
Adopted surname, probably derived from an Old French name, Corbinian, itself possibly derived from Latin *corvus*, 'raven'. Borne by an 8th-century Frankish saint.

Corin
Origin uncertain; sometimes taken as a masculine form of Corinna, it more probably derives from a Sabine word meaning 'spear'.

Cormac
Irish Gaelic, of uncertain origin, possibly meaning 'charioteer'. Borne by a legendary Irish king.

Cornelius
Roman family name, possibly derived from *cornu*, 'horn'. A biblical name; borne by a centurion converted by St Peter (Acts 10). It was imported to Britain in the 15th century, where it was sometimes used as an anglicisation of Conchobhar (Connor).

Cosimo
Italian form of Cosmo. Cosimo de Medici (1389-1464) was a great patron of the Italian Renaissance.

Cosmo
From Greek *kosmos*, 'order'. A 4th-century St Cosmos became patron saint of physicians. It was popular in Italy in the Middle Ages, from where it was brought to Britain by the Scottish Gordon family, one of whom married into a Tuscan family.

Courtney
Used as either a boy's or girl's name taken from Old French meaning 'short nose'.

Craig
Adopted Scottish surname, from *creág*, 'rock, crag'. Originally used in the US in the early 20th century, it spread to the rest of the English-speaking world in the 1950s. See also: Glen, Kyle, Ross.

Crichton
Adopted Scottish surname and place name in Midlothian, from Gaelic *crioch*, 'border', and Old English *tun*, 'settlement'.

Crispian
Variation of Crispin.

Crispin
From a Roman family name, Crispinus, from *crispus*, 'curly'. St Crispin and his brother St Crispinian were Roman shoemakers who journeyed to France to spread Christianity. They supported themselves by mending and making shoes. They were martyred c. 286 and are considered the patron saints of shoemakers. St Crispin's feast day is 25th October. A great English victory over the French at the Battle of Agincourt on St Crispin's Day 1415 has contributed to the name's popularity in Britain.

Cruz
(Pronounced 'Cruth'): a girl's name in Spain, chosen by David and Victoria Beckham for their son.

Cuddie, Cuddy
Diminutives of Cuthbert.

Curt
Variation of Kurt (itself a variation of Conrad) or a diminutive of Curtis.

Curtis
Adopted medieval surname, from Old French *curteis*, 'courteous'. Originally taken as a first name in the 19th century, it has now become well established.

Cuthbert
Old English, from *cuth*, 'famous', and *beorht*, 'bright'. Borne by a 7th-century bishop of Lindisfarne and an 8th-century Archbishop of Canterbury. Diminutives: Cuddie, Cuddy.

Cy
Diminutive of Cyrus.

Cynan
Old Celtic kuno meaning 'great' or possibly 'high'.

Cynferth
From Welsh cyn 'chief' and berth 'beautiful'.

Cyprian
From the Roman family name Cyprianus, meaning 'native of Cyprus'. Borne by a 3rd-century bishop of Carthage, a martyr and saint.

Cyril
From the Greek name Kyrillos, from *kyrios*, 'lord'. Borne by several early saints, amongst them a Greek evangelist named Constantine (827-869) who, with his brother, devised the Cyrillic alphabet in order to communicate with Slavonic peoples. Constantine's religious name was Cyril.

Cyrus
From the Greek name Kyras, from *kyrios*, 'lord'. A biblical name; 'Cyrus, king of Persia' (559-529 BC), mentioned in 2 Chronicles 36, was the founder of the Persian empire.

D

Dafydd
(*dav-ith*) Welsh form of David. Taffy, a nickname for a Welshman, derives from Dafydd. Variations: Dai, David, Dewi, Taffy.

Dai
(*dye*) Welsh diminutive of David.

Dáibhí
(*dye-vee*) Irish Gaelic form of David.

Daibhidh
(*dye-vee*) Scottish Gaelic form of David.

Dale
Adopted surname, from the Old English word for 'valley'. It has been used for both boys and girls, particularly in the US, since the mid-20th century.

Damian
Anglicised form of the Greek name Damianos, from *daman*, 'to tame', meaning 'tamer'. St Damian, a 4th-century Greek martyr killed with his brother, Cosmas, at Aegea, is considered the patron saint of doctors. Variation: Damien.

Damon
From Greek *demos*, 'land' or 'people'. Borne by a goatherd in Virgil's *Eclogues* (1st century BC), after which example it became a type for rustic suitors in pastoral poems.

Dan
The majority of modern instances of Dan will be diminutives of Daniel. However, it is also a biblical name in its own right, borne by one of Jacob's twelve sons and hence a founder of one of the twelve tribes of Israel. The name also had currency as an Old English word for 'sir' or 'master'. Edmund Spenser wrote of Geoffrey Chaucer:

'Dan Chaucer, well of English
undefiled,
On Fame's eternal beadroll worthy
to be filed.'

(From *The Faerie Queene*, IV, ii 1596).

Daniel
Hebrew, meaning 'God has judged'. A biblical name; borne in the Old Testament by a prophet whose story is told in the Book of Daniel, and who is probably most known for surviving being cast into a den of lions (Daniel 6:16). The name underwent a popular revival in the 1980s and 1990s. Diminutives: Dan, Dannie, Danny.

Dante
Medieval contracted form of Durante, meaning 'steadfast', the Italian form of Durand. Modern use tends to be in honour of the Italian poet Dante Alighieri (1265-1321).

Darby
Origin uncertain; possibly an adopted surname and English place name, Derby, from *diur*, 'deer', and *byr*, 'settlement', meaning 'deer park'; or an anglicisation or corruption of the Irish name Diarmait (Dermot). It has come to denote one half of Darby and Joan, an ideal elderly, loving couple first introduced by the writer Henry Woodfall in *Gentleman's Magazine* in 1735. Variation: Derby.

Darcy
Adopted Norman baronial surname (D'Arcy). It was a Norman introduction to Britain. It is also used for girls.

Darius
From the Greek name Dareios, itself from Old Persian *darayavaush*, or *darayavush*, from *daraya*, 'possess', and *vahu*, 'well' or 'good', meaning 'I hold fast the good'. Biblical; borne in the Old Testament by Darius the Great, governor of Persia, who became king in 521 BC (Ezra 4:5). A later king, Darius the Mede, outlawed prayer; it was for

contravening this order that Daniel was thrown into a den of lions (Daniel 6).

Darrell
Adopted surname, from a French place name, Airelle, in the northern French region of Calvados. It is also occasionally used for girls. Variations: Darell, Darrel, Darryl, Daryl.

Darren
Origin uncertain; it is a 20th-century coinage, possibly an adopted Irish surname. Probably first used in the 1950s, it had become widespread by the 1960s.

Dave
Diminutive of David, sometimes used in its own right.

David
From Hebrew *dawid*, meaning 'beloved'. A biblical name; borne in the Old Testament by the youngest son of Jesse, who slew the giant Goliath and found favour with Saul by his harp playing. He married Saul's daughter, Michal. Eventually Saul became jealous and David had to flee, with the aid of his wife and Saul's son, Jonathan. He later became the greatest of the kings of Israel (1 Samuel 16-31). A 6th-century saint, St David, or Dewi, is regarded as patron saint of Wales. The Welsh chronicler, Geoffrey of Monmouth, describes St David as uncle of King Arthur. His feast day is 1st March. David has been a consistently popular name in Britain in the past 50 years. Diminutives: Dave, Davey, Davy. Variations: Dafydd, Dai, Dewi.

Davis
Adopted surname, originally a patronymic meaning 'son of Davy (or David)'. Variation: Davies.

Davy
Diminutive of David, sometimes used in its own right. Davy Jones was an 18th-century sailor's term for the evil spirit of the sea. This might refer to a pirate of that name, or be a corruption of the West Indian *duppy*, meaning 'devil', and Jonah, the disobedient prophet who was swallowed by a giant fish (Jonah 1).

Deaglán
Original Irish Gaelic source of Declan.

Dean
Adopted surname, either from the Old English *denu*, meaning 'valley', or from the Latin *decanus*, literally translated as 'a leader of ten', meaning in this case an ecclesiastical dean.

Decimus
From Latin *decimus*, meaning 'tenth'. In the past it was traditionally given to a tenth child, if a boy, a rare occurrence today.

Declan
Anglicised form of the Irish Gaelic name Deaglán, of uncertain origin. Borne by a 5th-century Irish bishop of Ardmore, County Waterford.

Deepak
Variation of Dipak.

Del
English colloquial diminutive of Derek.

Denholm
Adopted surname and place name, from Old English *denu*, 'valley', and *holm*, 'island'.

Denis, Dennis, Denys
Medieval vernacular form of Dionysius, a 3rd-century evangelist missionary to

Gaul and a traditional patron saint of France. He is supposed to have been beheaded in Paris in 272, after which he is said to have walked for two miles carrying his head, then placed it on the site where the Cathedral of Saint Denis now stands. The form Denis is favoured in Ireland. Variation: Dennis. Diminutives: Dennie, Denny.

Dennie, Denny
Diminutives of Denis or Denton.

Denton
Adopted surname and place name, from *denu*, 'valley', and *tun*, 'settlement'. Diminutives: Dennie, Denny.

Denzil
Adopted surname, from Denzell, in Cornwall. It was first adopted by the Holles family when it became connected to the Denzell family by marriage, but its use subsequently became general.

Deon
Variation of Dion.

Derek
Low German form of Theodoric, introduced to Britain by immigrant Flemish weavers and merchants in the late Middle Ages. Variation: Derrick.

Dermot
Anglicisation of the Irish Gaelic name Diarmait.

Derrick
Variation of Derek.

Des
Diminutive of Desmond.

Desmond
Adopted surname and Irish place name, from Irish Gaelic Deas Mumhain, meaning 'South Munster'. First used in Ireland in the mid-19th century, it subsequently spread throughout the English-speaking world. Diminutive: Des.

Devon
Adopted surname and English county name, widely used in the US, where pronunciation tends to stress the second syllable. It is also used for girls.

Dewi
Welsh form of David; borne by the 6th-century saint now regarded as patron saint of Wales.

Dexter
Adopted surname, itself derived from Old English and meaning a female dyer of cloth. Modern use may be influenced by the Latin *dexter*, meaning 'auspicious' or 'to the right-hand side'. It is especially popular in the US.

Diarmait
(*der-mutt*) Irish Gaelic, from *dí*, 'without', and *airmait*, 'envy'. Borne in Irish legend by the lover of Gráinne.

Dick, Dickie, Dicky
Diminutives of Richard.

Dickon
Diminutive of Richard, often used in its own right.

Didier
French, from Latin *desiderium*, 'longing'. Popular in France, the name is occasionally used in the English-speaking world.

Digby
Adopted surname and English place name, from Old Norse elements *diki*,

'ditch' or 'dyke', and *byr*, 'settlement', meaning 'settlement by the dyke'.

Diggory
Corruption of the name of a figure of French medieval romance, Sir Degare, from French *égaré*, meaning 'lost, gone astray'. It is rare in modern times.

Dilip
Indian, of uncertain origin, but most probably Sanskrit, meaning 'protector of Delhi'. It was borne by several legendary Hindu kings. Variation: Duleep.

Dillan
Variation of Dillon or Dylan.

Dillon
Adopted surname, either Irish of German origin, or English of Old French origin. It is also used today as a variation of Dylan.

Dinos
Greek, meaning 'whirl'. Borne in Greek legend by Diomedes's horse.

Dion
Diminutive of Dionysius, and the Greek source of Denis.

Dionysius
Occasionally used in its own right, Dionysius is the source of the more common name, Denis. It is not to be confused with Dionysus, Greek god of wine (See Girls: Dionysia).

Dipak
Indian, of Sanskrit origin, meaning 'little lamp'. An alternative name of Kama, god of love. Variation: Deepak.

Dirk
Variation of Derek, of Flemish and Dutch origin, popularised throughout the English-speaking world by Dirk Bogarde, a Scottish-born actor and writer of Dutch descent, who was born Derek van den Bogaerde in 1921.

Dolphus
Diminutive or variation of Adolphus.

Dom
Diminutive of Dominic.

Dominic, Dominick
From Latin *dominicus*, meaning 'of the Lord'. St Dominic (1170-1221) founded the Dominican order of monks and popularised the name throughout the Christian world. Diminutive: Dom.

Don, Donny
Diminutives of Donald.

Donal
Early Irish Gaelic form of Donald. Diminutive: Don.

Donald
Anglicised form of the Scottish Gaelic name Domhnall (*doe-nall*), from Old Celtic *dubno*, 'world', and *val*, 'rule'. Borne by several early Scottish kings, it is also the source of the name of the powerful MacDonald ('son of Donald') clan. Diminutives: Don, Donny. Variations: Donal

Donnchadh
(*don-ne-ha*) Irish Gaelic, meaning 'brown warrior'. Adopted in Scotland and subsequently elsewhere in the form Duncan, it tends to be translated in Ireland as Denis.

Donovan
Adopted Irish surname, meaning 'dark brown'. Diminutives: Don, Donny.

Doran
Irish name meaning 'stranger' or 'exile'.

Dorian
Greek, borne by an ancient Greek people and meaning 'from Doris' (an area of northern Greece). Popularised throughout the English-speaking world by Oscar Wilde in his novella *The Picture of Dorian Gray* (1891), it is now also used for girls.

Doug
Diminutive of Dougal or Douglas.

Dougal
Anglicisation of the Irish Gaelic name Dubhghall, meaning 'dark stranger', given by the Irish to invading Vikings in the 9th century. It became popular in Scotland and now has strong Scottish associations. Diminutives: Doug, Dougie. Variations: Dugal, Dugald.

Dougie
(*dug-gy, doog-ie*) Diminutive of Dougal or Douglas. Variation: Duggie.

Douglas
Anglicised form of the Scottish Gaelic surname and place name Dubhglas, from *dubh*, 'black', and *glais*, 'stream', meaning 'dark stream'. Initially derived from the River Douglas, south of Larnark, it was adopted by a powerful clan and as a first name in the 16th century. The river name, and hence the surname, is found elsewhere in Scotland, as well as in Ireland and the Isle of Man. Initially used for both sexes, it is now seen as only masculine. Diminutives: Doug, Dougie.

Drew
Either a diminutive of Andrew, sometimes used in its own right, or a variant form of the Old German name Drogo.

Drogo
Old French name of Old German origin, probably from *dragen*, 'to bear' or 'to carry'. It was a Norman introduction to Britain. Variation: Drew.

Duane
(*dwayne*) Adopted Irish Gaelic surname, probably meaning 'dark' or 'black'. Variations: Dwane, Dwayne.

Dubhghall
Irish Gaelic form of Dougal.

Dud
Diminutive of Dudley.

Dudley
Adopted surname and English place name, from Old English, meaning 'Dudda's place'. The family name of the Earls of Leicester in the Tudor era, it was adopted generally in the 19th century as a first name.

Duff
Adopted surname, from Gaelic *dubh*, 'black (haired)', originally a nickname.

Duggie
Variation of Dougie.

Duke
Diminutive of Marmaduke often used in its own right. It is particularly popular in the US, in line with the trend there for taking British aristocratic titles as first names. See also: Earl, Prince.

Duleep
Variation of Dilip.

Duncan
Scottish form of the Irish Gaelic name Donnchadh (*don-ne-ha*), from *donn*, 'brown', and *chadh*, 'chief' or 'warrior'.

Borne by a 7th-century abbot of Iona and two medieval Scottish kings, including Duncan I, murdered in 1040 by Macbeth, whom Shakespeare immortalised in his eponymous play (1606). The original Donnchadh tends to be translated in Ireland as Dennis rather than Duncan.

Dunstan
From Old English *dun*, 'hill', and *stan*, 'stone'. St Dunstan was a renowned 10th-century Archbishop of Canterbury.

Durand
From Latin *durans*, 'enduring'. A Norman introduction to Britain, it was common in the Middle Ages and remains in occasional use today. Variation: Dante.

Dustin
Origin uncertain, possibly from an Old Norse name Thorsteinn, meaning 'Thor's stone'. It was popularised by the American actor Dustin Hoffman (b 1937).

Dwane, Dwayne
Variations of Duane.

Dwight
Adopted English surname, probably from Diot, a medieval diminutive of Dionysia, the feminine form of Dionysius. It is particularly popular in the US where it tends to be given in honour of the American president Dwight D Eisenhower (1890-1969), although he was so named in honour of Thomas Dwight (1752-1817), an early president of Yale University. See also: Denise, Dennis.

Dylan
Welsh, origin uncertain, although possibly meaning 'son of the sea'. Borne in the collection of Welsh legends, the *Mabinogian*, by the son of a sea god. Its popularity outside Wales in recent times can generally be attributed to the Welsh poet Dylan Thomas (1914-53) or the American folk singer Bob Dylan (born Robert Zimmerman in 1941), who himself took the name in honour of Dylan Thomas.

Dylan Jagger
Pamela Anderson and Tommy Lee's son (also a son called Brandon Thomas).

Dylan Thomas
Name of Pierce Brosnan and Keely Shaye Smith's son.

E

Eamon, Eamonn
(*ay-mon*) Irish Gaelic variation of Edmund.

Earl
Probably a direct adoption of the British aristocratic title, it is particularly popular in the US. Variation: Erle. See also: Duke, Prince.

Eben
Hebrew, meaning 'stone'. A name in its own right but generally used as a diminutive of Ebenezer.

Ebenezer
Hebrew, meaning 'stone of help'. A biblical place name; when the Israelites were victorious over the Philistines, Samuel set up a memorial stone inscribed 'Ebenezer' (1 Samuel 7-12). Its popularity has diminished since Charles Dickens used the name for his miserly character, Ebenezer Scrooge, in *A Christmas Carol* (1843). Diminutive: Eben.

Ed, Eddie
Diminutives of Edgar, Edmund, Edward or Edwin.

Edgar
From the Old English name Eadgar, from *ead*, 'rich' or 'prosperous', and *gar*, 'spear'. Borne by a 10th-century king of England. Like Edmund, Edward and Edwin it was one of few early Anglo-Saxon names to survive the Norman Conquest. Shakespeare used it for the virtuous son of the Duke of Gloucester in *King Lear* (1605). Diminutives: Ed, Eddie, Eddy.

Edmund
From the Old English name Eadmund, from *ead*, 'rich' or 'prosperous', and *mund*, 'protection'. Borne by a 9th-century king of East Anglia who was killed by invading Danes, then buried at Bury St Edmunds. Like Edgar, Edward and Edwin it was one of few early Anglo-Saxon names to survive the Norman Conquest. Shakespeare used it for the bastard son of the Duke of Gloucester in *King Lear* (1605). Diminutives: Ed, Eddie, Eddy, Ned, Neddie, Neddy, Ted, Teddie, Teddy. Variations: Eamon, Eamonn

Edom
Scottish variation of Adam and an alternative name for the Old Testament Esau.

Edryd
From Welsh meaning 'restoring'. May also have links to eddryd 'story teller'.

Edward
From the Old English name Eadweard, from *ead*, 'rich' or 'prosperous', and *weard*, 'guardian'. A consistently popular name and, like Edgar, Edmund and Edwin, one of few early Anglo-Saxon names to survive the Norman Conquest. Borne by three Anglo-Saxon kings and a further eight kings of England. One, Edward the Confessor, king of England 1042-1066, was also a saint. Diminutives: Ed, Eddie, Eddy, Ned, Neddie, Neddy, Ted, Teddie, Teddy.

Edwin
From an Old English name Eadwine, from *ead*, 'rich' or 'prosperous', and *wine*, 'friend'. Borne by a 7th-century king of Northumberland who converted to Christianity. Like Edgar, Edmund and Edward, it was one of few Anglo-Saxon names to survive the Norman Conquest. It underwent a popular revival in the 19th century. Diminutives: Ed, Eddie.

Egbert
From an Old English name Ecgbeorht, from *ecg*, 'sword', and *beorht*, 'bright'. Borne by two 8th-century English saints and a 9th-century king of Wessex. A brief 19th-century revival has not been sustained.

Egil
Norwegian, borne in northern mythology by the brother of the Vulcan, Wayland Smith. Egil was a great archer and the *Saga of Thidrik* contains a tale similar to that of William Tell and the apple.

Eldon
From a surname of uncertain origin.

Eldred
Variation of Aldred.

Eli
Hebrew, meaning 'height' or 'elevation'. A biblical name; borne in the Old Testament by a high priest who brought up Samuel (1 Samuel 1-3). It was adopted by the Puritans.

Elias
Biblical; the New Testament Greek form of Elijah.

Elijah
Hebrew, meaning 'Jehovah is God'. A biblical name; borne by one of the great Old Testament prophets (1 and 2 Kings). Elijah heard 'the still, small voice' of God, and preached against the wickedness of Ahab and Jezebel. Upon his death he was taken up to heaven in a chariot of fire. A Puritan adoption, particularly in early American settlements, it is popular today among Black American Muslims.

Elijah Bob Patricius Guggi Q
Name of Bono's fourth son.

Eliot
Adopted surname, itself derived from the French medieval diminutive of Elias.

Elisha
Hebrew, meaning 'God is salvation'. A biblical name; borne in the Old Testament by a prophet, the disciple of Elijah (1 Kings 19, 2 Kings 2-13). He succeeded Elijah, anointed Hazael and Jehu as future kings of Syria and cured Naaman of leprosy. The name was adopted by the Puritans, and remains in occasional use today.

Ellery
Popularised in modern times by Ellery Queen the main character of detective stories and taken from a surname.

Ellis
Revived recently from a medieval variant of Elias.

Elmer
Adopted surname, from an Old English name derived from *aethel*, 'noble', and *mær*, 'famous'.

Elroy
Variation of Leroy, probably influenced by the Spanish *el*, 'the'.

Elton
Adopted surname and English place name, from a combination of the Old English name Ella, and *tun*, 'settlement'. It has been popularised throughout the English-speaking world by the British singer-songwriter Elton John, who adopted the name in honour of the saxophonist Elton Dean.

Elvis
Uncertain origin; probably a variation of Alvis, itself derived from the Irish Gaelic name Ailbhe (*al-va*), borne by a 6th-century Irish saint, patron of Munster. Despite the vast worldwide popularity of the American rock singer Elvis Presley (1935-77) the name has never been common.

Elwin, Elwyn
Welsh and Irish, of uncertain origin. Contenders include: from the Welsh meaning 'fair brow'; from Old English *aethel*, 'noble', and *wine*, 'friend'; or a variation of Alvin, from *eald*, 'old', and *wine*, 'friend'.

Emery
From Old German name Emmerich amal 'labour' and ric 'ruler' and more usual as a surname

Emil
German name derived from the Latin Aemilius, meaning 'eager'.

Emile
French form of the German name Emil, popularised by the French writer Emile Zola (1840-1902).

Emlyn
Welsh, of disputed origin. Either from

the Roman family name Aemilius (source of Emil and Emily), or from a Welsh place name, Newcastle Emlyn.

Emanuel, Emmanuel
Hebrew, meaning 'God is with us'. A biblical name; given in the Old Testament to the child whose birth Isaiah foretold (Isaiah 7: 14). The name was later applied, in the New Testament, to the coming Messiah. Diminutive: Manny. Variation: Manuel.

Emrys
Welsh form of Ambrose.

Enoch
Hebrew, meaning 'dedicated to God'. A biblical name; borne in the Old Testament by the grandson of Adam and Eve and father of Methuselah (Genesis 4-5). It was popularised by Alfred, Lord Tennyson in his poem, *Enoch Arden* (1864).

Eoan
Celtic form of Eugene.

Eóghan
(*yo-wen*) Irish Gaelic, of uncertain origin. It may be derived from iur, 'yew' and meaning 'born of the yew', or it may be a variation of Eugene or of John.

Eoin
Irish Gaelic form of John.

Ephraim
(*ee-frame*, *ee-fram*, *ee-frey-im*) Hebrew, meaning 'fruitful'. A biblical name; borne in the Old Testament by a son of Joseph. It was adopted by the Puritans.

Erasmus
Latinate form of a Greek name derived from Greek *eran*, 'to love', meaning 'beloved'. Borne by a 3rd-century bishop martyred under Diocletian. Considered the patron saint of sailors, he was also known as St Elmo. The name was adopted by the Dutch scholar Gerhard Geets (1466-1536), and now tends to be associated with him.

Eric
Old Norse, from *ei*, 'always', and *ric*, 'ruler'. It was introduced to Britain in the 9th century by Scandinavian settlers, and a 19th-century revival has been attributed to Frederic Farrar's book *Eric, or Little by Little* (1858). Diminutives: Rick, Ricky. Variation: Erik.

Erle
Variation of Earl.

Ernest
From the Old German name Ernst, meaning 'earnestness' or 'seriousness'. It was introduced to Britain by the Hanoverians in the 18th century, and its popularity was boosted by Oscar Wilde's play *The Importance of Being Ernest* (1899). Diminutives: Ern, Ernie.

Ernie
Diminutive of Ernest, sometimes used in its own right.

Errol
Probably an adopted Scottish surname and place name, although it has also been described as a variation of Harold or Earl.

Esau
Hebrew, meaning 'hairy'. A biblical name; borne in the Old Testament by the elder twin son of Isaac and Rebekah, who was born 'all over like an hairy garment'. Esau sold his birthright to his twin brother Jacob, in exchange for 'a

mess of pottage' (Genesis 25:29-34). The name has been in occasional use in English-speaking countries since the 17th century.

Esmé
French, meaning 'esteemed'. Introduced to Scotland in the 16th century as a masculine name, it is now much more commonly used for girls.

Esmond
From an Old English name Eastmund, from *east*, 'grace', and *mund*, 'protection'. However, its use in modern times is more likely to be as an adopted surname, as in Thackeray's *History of Henry Esmond* (1852), after the publication of which the name had a brief revival.

Ethan
Hebrew, meaning 'firmness'. A biblical name; mentioned briefly in the Old Testament as the name of a man to whom Solomon was superior in wisdom (1 Kings 4). It is mainly popular in the US, where the name is associated with Ethan Allen (1738-89), leader of the Green Mountain Boys, who played an important role in the American War of Independence and whose efforts brought into existence the state of Vermont (*verre mont*, Green Mountain).

Ethelbert
From Old English *aethel*, 'noble', and *beorht*, 'bright'. The original Old English form of Albert. Borne by a 6th-century Kentish king who was converted by St Augustine at Canterbury.

Euan
Anglicised form of the Scottish Gaelic name Eóghan. Variations: Eugene, Ewan.

Eugene
(*yoo-jean, yoo-jean*) Old French form of a Greek name, itself derived from *eugenios*, meaning 'noble'. Borne by several early saints, including a 5th-century bishop of Carthage and four popes. It is also considered an anglicisation of Eóghan. Variations: Eoan, Eóghan, Euan, Ewan, Ewen.

Eustace
Old French form of the Greek name Eustakhios, from *eu*, 'good', and *stakhys*, 'grapes'. Borne in the 2nd century by a Roman soldier and martyr. Diminutives: Stacey, Stacy.

Evan
Anglicisation of Ieuan, the Welsh form of John. In Scotland it is also used as an anglicised form of Eóghan.

Evelyn
Anglicised form of the Norman French feminine name Aveline. Adopted as a boy's name in the 17th century it is now more commonly used for girls.

Everard
From an Old English name, from *eofor*, 'boar', and *heard*, 'hardy' or 'strong'. The Norman invaders brought an Old Germanic version of the name from a comparable source.

Ewan, Ewen
Anglicised from of Eóghan, of Scottish origin. See also: Eugene.

Ewart
Scottish form of Everard.

Ezekiel
Hebrew, meaning 'may God strengthen'. A biblical name; borne in the Old Testament by the most quirky of the

prophets, who had visions, went into trances and periods of speechlessness, and occasionally travelled through the air. It was a Puritan adoption. Diminutive: Zeke.

Ezra
Hebrew, meaning 'help'. A biblical name; borne by the author of the fifteenth book of the Bible, and adopted by the Puritans.

F

Fabian
From the Roman family name Fabius, probably derived from the Latin for 'bean'. The socialist Fabian Society, founded in 1884, was named after Fabian (aka Quintus Fabius Maximus), a Roman general who resisted Hannibal's 3rd-century advance on Rome.

Faisal
Arabic, meaning 'he who separates right and wrong', i.e. a judge. The name has been borne in modern times by kings of Saudi Arabia and Iraq. Variations: Faysal, Feisal.

Farquhar
(*far-ker*) Anglicised form of the Scottish Gaelic name Fearchar, meaning 'dear man'. Borne by an early king of Scotland.

Farran
From a surname of uncertain origin, possibly Old French or medieval form of Ferdinand

Faruq
Arabic, meaning 'he who can distinguish truth from untruth'. Faruq was a byname of Umar ibn-al-Khattab, revered in Islam as the second rightly guided caliph (634-44).

Felix
From Felicitas, Roman goddess of good fortune and happiness. The name was popular with early Christians and was borne by several saints.

Fenn
Adopted surname, originally from the Old English *fenn*, denoting a marsh- or fen-dweller. Its use for boys is largely restricted to the US.

Ferdinand
Spanish name of Old German origin, from *fardi*, farth, 'journey', and *nanthi*, *nand*, 'venture'. Borne by several Spanish kings and three Holy Roman Emperors. Variations: Faron, Farran, Ferdinando (Spanish and Italian), Ferrand (French), Hernán (modern Spanish). Diminutive: Ferdie.

Fergal
Irish, anglicised form of the Gaelic name Fearghal, from *fear*, 'man', and *gal*, 'valour'. Fearghal mac Máeldúin was an 8th-century king of Ireland. It is the source of the surname Farrell.

Fergus
Irish, anglicised form of the Gaelic name Fearghas, from *fear*, 'man', and *gus*, 'vigour'. Although historically associated with Scotland, it was borne in Irish legend by Fergus mac Roich, heroic tutor of Cuchulain, who left Conchobar's court after the treacherous murder of the sons of Usnech. It has recently become popular throughout the English-speaking world. Diminutive: Fergie.

Fernando
Spanish form of Ferdinand.

Ffinian
Welsh 6th century saint.

Fidel
From Latin *fidelis*, 'faithful'. Borne by the Cuban revolutionary leader Fidel Castro (b 1926).

Finbar
Irish, anglicised form of the Gaelic name Fionnbharr, from *fionn*, 'white, fair', and *barr*, 'head'. St Finbar was a 6th-century bishop of Cork, said to have crossed the Irish Sea on horseback. Diminutives: Finn, Bairre and Barry (now used in its own right).

Fingal
Scottish, anglicised form of the Gaelic name Fionnghall, from *fionn*, 'white, fair', and *gall*, 'stranger', and used originally by the Irish for Norse settlers in Ireland. Borne in Gaelic legend by the heroic father of Ossian. James Macpherson's epic poem *Fingal* (1762) purports to be written by him. Fingal is known in Irish mythology as Finn mac Cumhaill (Finn McCool). Variation: Fingall.

Finlay
Scottish, anglicised form of the Gaelic name Fionnlagh, from *fionn*, 'white, fair' and *laogh*, 'warrior'. Borne by Macbeth's father. Variation: Finley.

Finn
Irish, anglicised form of *fionn*, 'fair, white'. Finn mac Cumhaill (Finn McCool) is the great hero of Irish mythology, known in Scotland as Fingal. He may have originated as an aspect of the god Lugh; folklore credits him with being a giant and building the Giant's Causeway. His story is told in the Fenian or Ossianic Cycle, as a result of which he is associated in modern times with the Fenians and the Fianna Fáil political party. Finn is also used as a pet form of Finbar.

Finnian
Irish, anglicised form of the Gaelic name Finnén, derived from *fionn*, 'fair, white'.

Fintan
Irish, anglicised form of the Gaelic name Fiontan, derived from *fionn*, 'fair, white', and *tine*, 'fire'.

Fitzroy
Adopted aristocratic surname meaning 'illegitimate son of the king'. It is the family name of the Dukes of Grafton.

Flann
Irish Gaelic, an ancient byname meaning 'red'.

Flannan
Irish, anglicised form of the Gaelic name Flannán, originally a diminutive of Flann, meaning 'red'. Very popular around Killaloe, County Down, of which St Flannan is the patron saint.

Fletcher
Adopted surname, originally an occupational name for an arrowmaker, from Old French *fleche*, 'arrow'. Fletcher Christian was the naval officer who led the notorious mutiny on the Bounty in 1789.

Florian
Derived from Latin *flos*, 'flower', giving the meaning 'flourishing'. St Florian was a 3rd-century Roman soldier.

Floyd
Adopted Welsh surname, itself a derivative of Lloyd, from the Welsh *llwyd*, 'grey'. It is popular in the US.

Forrest
Adopted surname and place name, originally derived from the word forest. It was first used as a given name in the late 19th century, possibly in honour of General Nathan Forrest, a commander of Confederate soldiers in the southern states of the US.

Foster
Adopted surname, originally an occupational name for a forester, a foster-parent or a cutler.

Francesco
Italian form of Francis.

Francis
Anglicised form of the Italian name Francisco, derived from the Latin name Franciscus meaning 'French'. The name was assumed by St Francis of Assisi (1181-1226), who founded the Franciscan order of monks after he was thrown out by his wealthy father in punishment for making generous gifts to the poor of Assisi. He is associated with nature, and his preaching to birds became a favourite subject of artists. He was canonised a mere two years after his death. The name spread to Britain in the 16th century, with Italian Renaissance culture, and it has remained consistently popular. Diminutives: Frank, Frankie.

Francisco
Spanish form of Francis.

Franco
Medieval variation of Frank, and diminutive of Francesco or Francisco.

Frank
The name of a Germanic tribe that migrated to Gaul in the 4th century, giving France its modern name. It was later regarded as a diminutive of Francis and related names, although it is in fact their source!

Frankie
Diminutive of Francis, Frank.

Franklin
Adopted surname from Old English *francoleyn*, meaning 'a freeman', specifically a landowner not of noble birth. Diminutives: Frank, Frankie.

Fraser
Adopted Scottish surname of unknown origin, but probably Norman French. Variations: Frazer, Frazier.

Fred
Diminutive of Alfred or Frederick.

Freddie, Freddy
Diminutives of Alfred or Frederick.

Frederick
The Old English name Freodhoric was superceded by the Old German, Frithuric, derived from *frithu*, 'peace', and *ric*, 'ruler'. The modern version came to Britain from Germany with the Hanoverians in the early 18th century.

Fulbert
Old German from Filibert meaning 'very bright'.

Fulke
From Old German *volk*, meaning 'tribe, people'. A Norman introduction to Britain, it was popular in the 16th and 17th centuries but is rarely found in modern times.

Fulton
Adopted Scottish surname, probably from a place name that no longer exists.

G

Gabriel

Hebrew, meaning 'man of God'. A biblical name; borne by the Archangel Gabriel, who is sometimes regarded as the angel of death or the prince of fire and thunder but more frequently as one of God's chief messengers. Traditionally said to be the only angel who spoke Syriac, he is recgonised by Muslims as the chief of the four favoured angels and the spirit of truth. According to the Koran it was Gabriel who took Mohammad to heaven, and revealed to him his 'prophetic love'. In the Old Testament Gabriel explained several of Daniel's visions, while in the New Testament he brought news to Zacharias of the future birth of John the Baptist (Luke 1:13), and appeared to Mary to tell her that she was to be the mother of Christ (Luke 1:26-38). Diminutive: Gabe.

Gaius

Latin, from *gaudere*, 'to rejoice'. It was the first name of the Roman emperor Gaius Julius Caesar. Variation: Caius.

Galen

Latinised form derived from the Greek *galen*, meaning 'calm'.

Galfrid

Apparently a 19th-century fake-antique version of Geoffrey.

Ganesa

Indian, from Sanskrit, meaning 'lord of the hosts'. Borne in Hindu mythology by the god of wisdom and good luck, lord of the Ganas (lesser deities). Ganesa is a byname for the god Shiva, and also the name of Shiva's son, who has the head of an elephant and the body of a short, fat imp with a huge belly. He is invoked at the outset of a journey or when commencing important work, and on the first pages of books.

Gareth

Assumed to be Welsh, from *gwared*, 'gentle'. The name first appears in *Morte D'Arthur*, Sir Thomas Malory's 15th-century account of the legend of the Round Table. Variation: Garth. Diminutives: Garth, Garry, Gary.

Garfield

Adopted surname, probably from Old English *gar*, 'spear' and *feld*, 'field', and meaning 'field of spears'. Most likely first adopted in honour of J A Garfield (1831-81), twentieth president of the US, it is now well established in the US and Britain.

Garnet

From the name of a semi-precious, red-coloured stone. The name became popular in the 17th century but is little used today.

Garrett

Irish-influenced mutation of Gerard and Gerald, reflecting medieval pronunciation of the former.

Garrick

Adopted surname, possibly drawn from *gar*, 'spear', plus another, obscure, element; or, as in the case of the actor-manager David Garrick (1717-79), after the Garrigue area of the Languedoc region of France.

Garrison

Adopted surname, probably a patronymic from 'son of Gareth', or Garrett.

Garth

Adopted surname, itself drawn from

garth, from Old English *geard*, meaning 'yard'. Alternatively, a recent contraction of Gareth.

Garry, Gary
Diminutive of Gareth. However, the main reason for Gary's huge popularity was the heart-throb Gary Cooper, who actually took the name from his hometown, Gary, Indiana.

Gavin
Most likely a variation of Gawain, although it may be from the Old German name Gawin, meaning 'an area of land'.

Gawain
Welsh, borne by a hero of Arthurian legend. An earlier incarnation - as Gwalchmai, in the *Mabinogian* - shows more clearly the origin of the name from the Celtic *gwalch*, 'falcon', and *Mai*, 'may'. Gawain was the nephew of King Arthur and probably the original hero of the quest for the Holy Grail. The medieval English poem *Sir Gawain and the Green Knight* (c. 1360) tells how Gawain beheads the Green Knight in single combat.

Gaylord
Adopted surname, itself originally from the French *gaillard*, meaning 'dandy'. It has suffered from the altered meaning of 'gay' during the later 20th century.

Gene
Diminutive of Eugene, now used in its own right.

Geoff
Diminutive of Geoffrey. Variation: Jeff.

Geoffrey
Old German. The second element is from *frith*, 'peace'; the first is of uncertain origin, but may mean 'traveller' or 'area'. A Norman introduction, it was a very popular name in the medieval age. Variations: Jeffery, Jeffrey. Diminutives: Geoff, Jeff.

Geordie
Diminutive of George. It is particularly popular in the north of Britain, giving rise to the use of the term to denote a native of Tyneside.

George
From Greek *georgos*, 'farmer', influenced by Latin and Old French. Borne by several early saints, including the man considered from the 14th-century onwards as patron saint of England. If he existed at all, he may have been a 4th century Roman soldier, martyred near Lydda during the Diocletian persecution c. 300. Popular legend has it that he came to the aid of the crusaders at Antioch in 1098. The legend of his slaying the dragon is probably simply an allegorical tale of good triumphing over evil; St Michael, St Margaret and St Martha are all depicted slaying dragons. George was adopted as patron saint of England by the soldiering king, Edward III. He is also the patron saint of Aragon and Portugal. Six kings have ensured the enduring popularity of the name in England, as has George Washington in the US.

George Junior plus **George II, George III, George IV, George V, George VI**
Sons of George Foreman (who also had two daughters, Freeda George and Georgetta Romeo).

Geraint
(*ger-eyent*, *ger-eyent*, the second syllable as in 'pint') Welsh, origin uncertain, but taken to be a Welsh variation of the

Latin name Gerontius, itself from the Greek *geron*, 'old man'. Like Gawain, Geraint appears in the *Mabinogian*, in which he is the son of Erbin, and in the Arthurian legends, in which he was a tributary prince of Devon. Tennyson retold his story in 'Geraint and Enid', published in *Idylls of the King* (1870).

Gerald
Old French name of Old German origin, from *ger*, 'spear', and *vald*, 'rule'. A Norman introduction, it was popular in the medieval era then died out, except in Ireland, until a 19th-century revival. Diminutives: Ged, Ger, Gerry, Jed, Jerry. Related: Jared.

Gerard, Gerrard
Old French name of Old German origin, from *ger*, 'spear', and *hardu*, 'bold'. A Norman introduction, it was popular in the medieval era and revived in the 19th century. Variations: Garrett, Gerrold, Jerald, Jerold. Diminutives: Gerry, Jerry.

Gerry
Diminutive of Gerald or Gerard.

Gervais, Gervaise, Gervase
(jer-vayz) Old French, of Old German origin, from *ger*, 'spear', and an unidentified second element. The remains of the obscure St Gervase were found in Milan in 386, spawning a popularity of cult-like proportions. Variation: Jarvis.

Gerwyn
From Welsh meaning 'fair love'

Gethin
From Welsh cethin meaning 'swarthy', 'dusky' or 'fierce'

Gideon
Hebrew, of uncertain meaning, although 'he with a stump for a hand' has been suggested. A biblical name; borne by the Israelite leader who rescued his people from the Midianites (Judges 6-8).

Gil
Diminutive of Gilbert.

Gilbert
Old German, from *gisil*, 'pledge', and *berht*, 'bright'. It was a Norman introduction to Britain. St Gilbert of Sempringham (c. 1083-1189) founded the only native British religious order. Diminutives: Gib, Gil, Gillie, Gilly.

Giles
Much-altered version of the Latin name Aegidius, from the Greek name Aigidios, itself from Greek *aigidion*, meaning 'young goat'. St Giles, who probably lived in the 6th century, fled his native Athens for France to escape public attention to his miracles and there adopted the life of a hermit. It is said that he was accidentally wounded by Childeric, king of France, after which he lost the use of his leg and refused treatment the more to mortify the flesh. Giles is regarded as patron saint of cripples, beggars and blacksmiths, and churches dedicated to him tend to be sited outside city centres, where cripples were condemed to live. In the past the name was used for children of either sex, although it is now exclusively used for boys.

Gillespie
Adopted Scottish surname, from *gille easbaig*, 'servant of the bishop'.

Gilroy
Adopted surname, from Gaelic *giolla ruadh*, 'red-haired man'.

Glen, Glenn
Adopted surname, originally Scottish, from Gaelic *gleann*, meaning 'valley'. It is distinct from Glyn, its Welsh counterpart. See also: Kyle, Ross.

Glyn, Glynn
Adopted surname, from Welsh *glyn*, meaning 'valley'. It is distinct from Glen, the Gaelic counterpart.

Glyndwr
(*glen-dow-er*) Welsh, from *glyn*, 'valley', and *dwr*, 'water'. A 20th-century adoption in honour of Owen Glyndwr (1359-1416), who fought Henry V of England, it is anglicised as Glendower.

Godfrey
Old French, of Old German origin, from *god*, 'god', and *frith*, 'peace'. A Norman introduction to Britain.

Godwin
From the Old English name Godwine, from *god*, 'god', and *wine*, 'friend'. It was popular in the Middle Ages, and borne by the 11th-century Earl of Wessex.

Goldwin, Goldwyn
From the Old English name Goldwine, from *gold*, 'gold', and *wine*, 'friend'. It is now more common as a surname.

Gomer
Hebrew, meaning 'complete'. A biblical name, borne by the grandson of Noah. Adopted by Puritans, it is still current in the US.

Gordon
Adopted Scottish surname, itself originally derived from a place name, either Scottish or French. It was apparently adopted as a first name in honour of Charles Gordon (1833-85), the British general killed at Khartoum.

Goronwy
Welsh, origin uncertain, although a character of that name appears in the *Mabinogian*,a collection of tales from Welsh myth, he was the lover of Blodeuwedd. He attempted to murder her husband Lleu Llaw Gyffes but was himself killed.

Govind
Indian name, from Sanskrit, meaning 'cow finder'. An epithet of the god Indra, from the 12th century onwards it became associated with Krishna.

Graham
Adopted Scottish surname, originally derived from the Lincolnshire town of Grantham, from Old English *grand*, 'gravel', and *ham*, 'field'. It was taken to Scotland in the 12th century by Sir William de Graham. Variations: Graeme, Grahame.

Grant
Adopted surname, itself derived from French *le grand* and given to tall men. Its popularity as a first name began in the US and Scotland, and has now spread worldwide.

Granville
Adopted French surname, itself derived from *grande ville*, meaning 'large town'.

Greg, Gregg
Diminutives of Gregor or Gregory, now used in their own right.

Gregor
Early form of Gregory, also common in several northern European countries, and in Scotland. Variation: Grigor.

Gregory
Early Christian, from the Greek name Gregorios, itself derived from *gregoros*, 'watchful'. Gregory the Great (c. 540-604) was the first of sixteen popes of that name, and one of the eleven Doctors of the Western Church. He remodelled the church liturgy and continued the work of Ambrose in the field of church music, including the reforming of plainsong that later became known as Gregorian chant.

Greville
Adopted surname, from the French name for one from Gréville.

Griffin, Griffith
Welsh, drawn from two Welsh names, Griffudd, meaning 'strong' and Gruffydd, meaning 'fighter'. Gruffydd ap Llewellyn (d 1063) was a respected Welsh ruler.

Griger
From Greek to be watchful. Also a form of Gregory.

Grover
Adopted surname, originally for one who lives or works in a grove.

Guido
French form of the Old German name Wido. See also: Guy.

Gunnar
Norse form of Gunter.

Gunter, Gunther
Old German, from *gundi*, 'war', and *hardu*, 'bold'. The legends of the *Nibelungenlied*, from which Wagner derived the material for his *Ring* cycle (1876), tell the story of a Burgundian king, the probable model for whom was Gundaharius, who died at the hands of Attila the Hun in 436. Gunther, the brother-in-law of Siegfried, loved Brunhild, who had vowed only to marry the man who could make his way through the flames surrounding her castle. Siegfried achieved the feat disguised as Gunther and won Brunhild. When she realised the trick Brunhild had Siegfried killed and then killed herself. Gunther was later slain by Attila, because he refused to tell where he had hidden the treasure of the Nibelungs. A Norman introduction to the UK, the name is now most common in Germany.

Gus
Diminutive of Augustine, Augustus or Angus.

Gustaf, Gustave
Respectively Swedish and French, from the Old German name Chustaffus. *Staf* is Old German for 'staff'; the rest is obscure, but possibly meaning 'of the gods'.

Guy
From the Old French name Guido, itself drawn from the Old German name Wido, from *witu*, 'wood', or possibly from *wit*, 'wide'. St Guy was the French name of the early Christian martyr St Vitus. A Norman introduction to Britain, it was no doubt boosted in popularity by Guy of Warwick, a figure of medieval romance and a hero of the Crusades. The name remained popular until it became associated with Guy Fawkes, leader of the Gunpowder Plot of 1605, but it has enjoyed a recent revival.

Gwilym, Gwylim
Welsh, forms of William, probably influenced by the French name Guillaume.

Gwydion
Welsh magician who created Blodeuwedd in the Mabinogi.

Gwyn
Welsh, from *gwyn* 'fair, blessed, holy, white'. Variation: Gwynne, Wyn, Wynne.

Gwynedd
Welsh, from the medieval name now restored for an area of North Wales.

Gwynfor
Welsh, from *gwyn*, 'fair, blessed, holy, white', and a form of *mawr*, 'great'.

Gyles
Variation of Giles.

H

Hadrian
Variation of Adrian.

Hadyn
Often erroneously presumed to have arisen in honour of the Austrian composer Joseph Haydn (note the different spelling), Hadyn is of uncertain origin but popular in Wales. It is conjectured to be a Welsh variant of Aidan. Variations: Hayden, Haydon, both popular in the US.

Hal
Diminutive of Harry.

Ham
Hebrew, meaning 'hot'. A biblical name; borne by the son of Noah. It is now used mainly as a diminutive of Abraham.

Hamilton
Scottish surname and place name also used as a first name.

Hamish
Scottish form of James (English) and Seamus (Irish Gaelic).

Hank
Diminutive of Henry, of Dutch origin. It is popular in the US, where it is used independently.

Hannibal
Phoenician, meaning 'the mercy of the supreme being'. It was popularised by the 3rd-century general of Carthage, who famously attacked Rome via the Alps, with hundreds of elephants.

Harald
From Haraldr, an Old Norse form of Harold.

Hardy
From a surname meaning 'bold' or 'hardy'

Hari
Indian name of Sanskrit origin, denoting a yellow-brown colour, used to describe the horses of Indra, and a byname for Vishnu or Krishna.

Harley
Old English meaning 'hare wood' or 'meadow'

Harold
Old English, from *here*, 'army', and *weald*, 'power', and influenced by the Old Norse name Haraldr. Diminutive: Harry.

Harrison
Adopted surname; originally a patronymic meaning 'son of Harry'.

Harry
Diminutive of Henry or Harold, but now often used in its own right.

Hartley
Adopted surname from an Old English place name, itself derived from *heorat*, 'hart' and *leah*, 'wood', or 'place'.

Harvey
Norman French, a variation of Hervé the name of a Breton saint derived from *haer*, 'battle', and *vy*, 'worthy'.

Hasan
Arabic, meaning 'good, beautiful'. Al Hasan was the Prophet's grandson, the son of Fatima and Haidar. Shiites regard Hasan and his brother Husayn as the rightful successors of Muhammad. Variations: Hasin, Hassan.

Hashim
Arabic name, literally meaning 'crusher'. It is an epithet of the grandfather of the Prophet Muhammed. Muslims are occasionally referred to as Hashemites, meaning 'descendents of Hashim'.

Havelock
Considered a Welsh equivalent of Oliver.

Hayden
Variation of Hadyn.

Haydn
Possibly a misspelling of Hadyn, influenced by the German composer Joseph Haydn (1732-1809). The Welsh names Hayden, Haydn and Haydon, though, are probably drawn from Aidan.

Haydon
Variation of Hadyn.

Heath
Adopted surname, from Old English *haeo*, referring to an area of heathland, or one who lives thereon.

Heber
Hebrew, meaning 'fellowship'. A biblical name; Heber the Kenite was the husband of Jael, who struck a tent peg through the forehead of Sisera (Judges 4:21). The name is also seen as an anglicised form of the Gaelic name Éibhear.

Hector
Greek, meaning 'holding fast'. In classical legend borne by the Trojan hero, the eldest son of Priam, who was killed by Achilles by being lashed to his chariot and dragged in triumph three times around the walls of Troy. In 17th-century theatrical dramas, he is represented as an aggressive bully, from where the verb 'to hector', meaning 'to play the bully' or 'to domineer' entered the language. The name is popular in Scotland, where it is erroneously assumed to be related to the Gaelic name Eachan. Diminutives: Hec(k), Heckie.

Hedley
Adopted surname, from an English place name, itself from Old English *haep*, 'heather', and *leah*, 'wood, clearing'.

Hen
Diminutive of Henry.

Henry
Old French name from Old German elements *haim*, 'home', and *ric*, 'ruler'. It was adopted by the Normans and brought to Britain, where it was subsequently borne by eight English kings. Diminutives: Hal, Hank, Harry, Hen.

Herb
Diminutive of Herbert.

Herbert
Adopted aristocratic surname originally from an Old German name, from *harja*, 'army', and *berht*, 'bright'. A Norman introduction to Britain, it had died out by the Middle Ages except as a surname (most notably the family name of the earls of Pembroke), but was revived in the 19th century. Diminutives: Bert, Bertie, Herb, Herbie.

Herbie
Diminutive of Herbert.

Hercules
Latin form of Greek *hera* (Hera was Greek goddess of marriage) and *kleos*, 'glory'. The son of Zeus and Alkmene, his strength was legendary. As punishment for killing his wife and children he was given twelve labours by Apollo, on completion of which he was awarded immortality.

Hereward
Old English, from Old German elements *here*, 'army' and *weard*, 'protection'. Borne most famously by Hereward the Wake, an 11th-century rebel against William the Conqueror.

Herman
From the Old German name Hariman, from *here*, 'army', and *man*, 'man', and meaning 'soldier'. A Norman introduction, it died out in the Middle Ages but was revived in the 19th century. It is now particularly popular in the US. Variation: Armand.

Hervé
Original French form of Harvey.

Hew
Welsh form of Hugh. Variation: Huw.

Hieronymus
Latin form of Jerome, itself from the Greek and meaning 'holy name'.

Hilary
Medieval form of the late Latin name Hilarius, from *hilaris*, 'cheerful'. Variations: Hilaire (French), Hillary (especially in the US). It is used for both boys and girls, although it is increasingly rare for boys.

Hiram
Hebrew, or possibly Phoenician, probably meaning 'brother of the exalted'. A biblical name; borne by a king of Tyre (2 Samuel 5 and 1 Kings 5). It was adopted by the Puritans, and is particularly popular in the US.

Hob
Diminutive of Robert and Robin (from which we get hobgoblin).

Hobart
Adopted surname, itself a variation of Hubert.

Holden
Old English meaning 'hollow valley'.

Homer
English form of Homeros, name of the Greek epic poet, traditionally the author of the *Iliad* and the *Odyssey*. Estimates of his birth date vary from 1159 BC to 685 BC and no fewer than seven places have been claimed as the site of his birth. The name is particularly popular in the US, and has recently come to worldwide attention as the first name of the father in the popular cartoon series, *The Simpsons*.

Horace
Latin, from the Roman family name Horatius. Borne by Quintus Horatius Flaccus (65-8 BC), the Roman lyric poet. It is sometimes erroneously assumed to be a diminutive of Horatio. Diminutive: Horry

Horatio
Latin; from the Roman family name Horatius, influenced by the late Latin name Orazio. A 16th-century introduction to Britain from Italy, it was used by Shakespeare in his 1602 play, *Hamlet*. Diminutive: Horry.

Howard
Adopted aristocratic surname of uncertain origin; contenders are the Scandinavian name Haward, from *ha*, 'high', and *ward*, 'guardian', and the Old German Huguard, from *hugu*, 'heart', and *hardu*, 'bold'. The family name of the Dukes of Norfolk, it was adopted as a first name during the 19th century.

Howell
Anglicised form of the Welsh name Hywel. It is also an adopted surname from the same root.

Hubert
Old German Hugubert, from *hugu*, 'heart', and *berht*, 'bright'. St Hubert, 8th-century bishop of Liége and of Maastricht, is the patron saint of hunters. Reputedly the son of Bertrand, Duke of Guienne, he was converted as a young man by a vision of Christ crucified between the antlers of a stag. Later he so neglected his religious duties in favour of hunting that he was one day threatened by a stag wearing a crucifix, after which he reformed. His feast day is 3rd November. He is usually depicted with a miniature stag, or kneeling to a stag bearing a crucifix. A Norman introduction to Britain, it was revived in the late 19th century.

Huey
Diminutive of Hugh.

Hugh
From the Old French name Hughes, itself derived from Old German *hug*, meaning 'heart, soul, mind, spirit'. It was a Norman introduction, and was further popularised by St Hugh of Lincoln, a 14th-century bishop of Lincoln. It is used in Scotland and Ireland as an anglicised form of Aodh. Diminutives: Hewie, Huey, Hughie, Shug, Shuggie. Variations: Hew, Huw, Hugo.

Hughie
Diminutive of Hugh.

Hugo
Latinate form of Hugh.

Humbert
Old French name of Old German origin, from *hun*, 'warrior', and *berht*, 'bright'. A Norman introduction to Britain.

Humphrey
Old English, from Hunfrith (possibly meaning 'peaceful giant') and influenced by the Old German name Hunfrid, from *hun*, 'warrior', and *fred*, *frid*, 'peace'. Diminutive: Humph.

Hunter
Adopted surname, originally an occupational name of transparent meaning.

Husayn
Arabic, originally a diminutive of *hasan*, meaning 'good' or 'beautiful'. Borne by the son of Fatima and Haidar, who, with his brother Hasan, is regarded by Shiites as the rightful successor to Muhammad, their grandfather.

Huw
Welsh form of Hugh. Variation: Hew.

Hyacinth
From Greek *Hyakinthos*, the name of a dark lily. In Greek legend dark lilies grew where the blood of Hyacinthus spread when he was accidentally killed by Apollo. Originally a boy's name, it is now used almost exclusively for girls.

Hyman
From Hebrew meaning 'life'. Diminutives: Hy, Hymie.

Hywel, Hywell, Howell
Welsh, from *hywel*, 'eminent'. Howell is the anglicised form, which is now more common as a surname.

I

Iago
Variation of Jacob, of Welsh and Spanish origin. It was used by Shakespeare for the villain in *Othello* (1604).

Iain, Ian
Scottish form of John, Iain being the Gaelic spelling, Ian the anglicised.

Ianto
Welsh pet form of Ifan which is the welsh form of John.

Ibrahim
Arabic form of Abraham.

Idris
Welsh, from *ius*, 'lord', and *ris*, 'impulsive'. Borne in Welsh legend by a giant magician, prince and astronomer whose observatory was on Cader Idris (meaning 'the chair of Idris'), a mountainous ridge in North Wales. There is a legend that anyone who spends a night on Cader Idris will, in the morning, be either dead, mad or poetically inspired. Idris is also an Arabic name, borne by a man described in the Koran as 'a true man' and 'a prophet' and by the founder of the first Shiite dynasty (788-974).

Iestyn
Welsh name from Latin Justinius.

Ieuan
(*ef-an*) Welsh form of John, often anglicised as Evan. Variations: Euan, Evan, Iefan.

Ifor
Welsh, origin unknown. It is anglicised as Ivor, but otherwise the names are unrelated.

Ignatius
From a Roman family name, Egnatius, of unknown origin, and probably influenced by Latin *ignis*, 'fire'. Borne by several saints, including a convert of St John the Evangelist, who later became bishop of Antioch, and was supposedly thrown to the lions by the Roman emperor Trajan c. 107. His feast day is 17th October. The Spanish-born St Ignatius Loyola (1491-1556) founded the Society of Jesus (the Jesuits).

Igor
Russian from of the Scandinavian name Ingvarr, meaning 'watchfulness of Ing (the god Frey)'.

Ike
Byname from Isaac.

Indra
Indian name, of uncertain origin, but probably from Sanskrit, meaning 'with

drops of rain', and borne by the Hindu god of sky and rain, who dispatches the demons of darkness with thunderbolts. He is the son of Heaven and Earth, lives on Mount Meru in the centre of the world, and is represented as having four arms riding an elephant. The name is now most common as a compound element of names such as Jaswinder.

Ingram
Adopted surname, from an Old German name Engelram, from *engel*, 'angle', and *hramn*, 'raven'.

Inigo
Medieval Spanish variation of Ignatius. St Ignatius Loyola was born Iñigo López de Recalde, but the name is usually associated with the architect Inigo Jones (1573-1652).

Innes
Adopted Scottish surname, or an anglicised form of Aonghas (Angus). It is also used for girls.

Iolo
Diminutive of Iorwerth.

Iorwerth
(*yor-werth*) Welsh, from *ior*, 'lord', and *gweth*, 'worth'. Diminutive: Iolo.

Ira
From Hebrew, meaning 'watchful'. A biblical name; borne in the Old Testament by one of King David's soldiers. A Puritan adoption, it is still occasionally found in English-speaking countries, especially in the US, for example by the American lyricist Ira Gershwin (1896-1983).

Irvin, Irvine, Irving
Irvin is a variation of Irvine or Irving, and is most common in the US. Irving is an adopted Scottish surname and the name of a town in Dumfriesshire. Irvine, most common in the US, is an adopted Scottish surname and the name of a town in Ayrshire.

Irwin
Adopted surname, from an Old English name Erwin, derived from *eofar*, 'boar', and *wine*, 'friend'.

Isaac
Hebrew, derived from the verb 'to laugh'. A biblical name; borne in the Old Testament by the only son of Abraham and Sarah, the child of their old age, and father of Esau and Jacob. When Isaac was a young boy God tested Abraham's faith by asking him to sacrifice his son. Abraham built a fire and was preparing to kill his son when God relented, providing a ram as a substitute for the sacrifice. It was a Norman introduction to Britain. Diminutives: Ike, Zack, Zak. Variation: Izaak (17th-century form).

Isaiah
Hebrew, meaning 'the Lord is generous' or 'salvation of the Lord'. A biblical name; borne by one of the greatest of the Old Testament prophets, who lived, approximately, in the 8th century BC. He is best known for foretelling the coming of the Messiah. The name was popular with the Puritans in the 17th century, but is, rather suprisingly, only occasionally found outside Jewish families today.

Isidore
English form of the Greek name Isidoros, from Isis, an Egyptian goddess, and *doron*, 'gift'. Variations: Isadore, Isodor.

Ismail
Arabic form of Ishmail, son of Abraham and Hagar, his wife's maid (Genesis 16). Arabs believe they are descended from Ismail, and are sometimes called Ismailites, meaning 'descendents of Ismail'. Jews believe themselves to be descended from Isaac, Abraham's son by his wife Sarah.

Israel
Jewish, from Hebrew meaning 'he who strives with God'. A biblical name; given by God to Jacob after he wrestled with an angel. Jacob's twelve sons, collectively the 'Children of Israel', founded the twelve tribes of Israel. The name was subsequently adopted as the name of the modern Jewish state, formed in 1948.

Ithel
From Welsh meaning 'generous lord'.

Ivan
Russian form of John. Ivan Ivanovitch is a generic name for a Russian man. Ivan IV of Russia, otherwise known as Ivan the Terrible (1533-84), was a highly energetic if cruel king, the first to take the name of Tzar, in 1547.

Ivo, Ivon
Old German, from *yv*, 'yew'. Variation: Yves.

Ivor
Scandinavian, from Old Norse *yr*, 'yew' and *herr*, 'army'. It is also used as an anglicised form of the Scottish Gaelic name Íomhar.

Izzy
Diminutive of Isidore.

J

Jabez
From Hebrew meaning 'pain' or 'sorrow'. A biblical name; given by a mother to her son because of a painful birth (1 Chronicles 4). It was adopted by the Puritans.

Jack
Diminutive of John, via Jankin. So common in the Middle Ages as to have entered the vocabulary as a general word for 'man', it has recently undergone a surge in popularity as a name in its own right. Diminutive: Jackie. Variation: Jock.

Jackie
Diminutive of Jack.

Jackson
Adopted surname, originally a patronymic meaning 'son of Jack'. The name was probably first taken in honour of President Andrew Jackson (1767-1845) or the Confederate general Thomas 'Stonewall' Jackson (1824-63).

Jacob
Anglicised form of the Hebrew name Yaakov. A biblical name; borne by the greatest patriarch of the Old Testament, son of Isaac, and father of the twelve tribes of Israel. As a young man Jacob bought the birthright from his older twin brother, Esau, for 'a mess of pottage' (Genesis 25:29-34). Living in Laban he fell in love with Rachel and worked for seven years to win her, but was tricked and given her sister, Leah, instead. He did eventually marry Rachel, with whom he fathered Joseph and Benjamin. He later wrestled with an angel, after which he was given the name Israel. Diminutive: Jake. Variations: Iago, Jacques, Jago, James. See also: Israel.

Jacques
French form of Jacob. The name has become a generic name for a French peasant, sometimes in the form Jacques Bonhomme.

Jago
Cornish form of Jacob.

Jake
Diminutive of Jacob, influenced by Jacques, and sometimes used in its own right.

Jaimal, Jamal
Arabic; means 'good looks' or 'beauty'.

Jalal
Arabic, meaning 'greatness' or 'glory'.

Jamil
Arabic, meaning 'handsome' or 'graceful'.

James
Variation of Jacob derived from the Latin form, Jacomus. A biblical name; borne in the New Testament by a relative of Jesus, possibly a brother, and by two apostles. The name spread to Britain in the 13th century, where it later became associated with the royal house of Stuart. Diminutives: Jamie, Jem, Jemmy, Jim, Jimmy. Variations: Hamish (Scottish), Seamus (Irish).

Jamie
Diminutive of James, sometimes used in its own right.

Jan
(*yan*) Dutch, Polish and Scandinavian forms of John.

Japheth
Hebrew, meaning 'may he expand'. A biblical name; borne in the Old Testament by one of the sons of Noah. It was adopted by the Puritans.

Jared
Hebrew, possibly meaning 'a rose'. A biblical name; borne in the Old Testament by the father of Enoch. A Puritan adoption, it underwent a revival in the 1960s. Variations: Jareth, Jarrad, Jarrath, Jarred, Jarrod, Jered.

Jarvis
Variation of Gervase.

Jason
Anglicised form of a Greek name, borne in classical mythology by the leader of the Argonauts who sailed his ship the Argos in search of the Golden Fleece, with which he intended to buy back his kingdom from his uncle Pelias. Eventually, after many years and trials and with the help of the chief heroes of Greece and of his wife Medea, he was successful. Also biblical, from a Hebrew name akin to Joshua, meaning 'healer'; borne by four men, including the reputed author of the Old Testament Book of Ecclesiastes. It was a Puritan adoption, although a late 20th century revival probably owed more to the classical hero.

Jasper
English form of Gaspar (French) and Caspar (German). In medieval tradition the name was given to one of the three Magi, probably meaning 'keeper of the treasure'.

Jay
A diminutive of James, or indeed any name beginning with 'J', it is also used in its own right.

Jedidiah
Hebrew, meaning 'beloved of the Lord'. A biblical name; in the Old Testament it is an alternative name for Solomon. It was adopted by the Puritans. Diminutive: Jed.

Jeff
Variation of Geoff.

Jefferson
Adopted surname, originally a patronymic. It is especially popular in the US, after President Thomas Jefferson (1743-1826).

Jeffrey
Variation of Geoffrey.

Jem
Diminutive of James; originally a medieval vernacular form, it is now used in its own right, or as a diminutive of Jeremy. Diminutive: Jemmy.

Jemmy
Diminutive of Jem.

Jeremiah
Hebrew, meaning 'appointed by God'. A biblical name; borne by a 7th-century BC Hebrew prophet and author of the Book of Lamentations, who prophesied the fall of Jerusalem. It was popular among the Puritans. Diminutive: Jerry. Variations: Jeremias, Jeremy.

Jeremy
Variation of Jeremiah, dating from the 13th century and popular in the second half of the 20th century. Diminutive: Jerry.

Jermaine, Jerman
From the French name Germain, meaning 'German'. It is especially popular in the US.

Jerome
From Greek, meaning 'holy name'. St Jerome (c. 342-420), a biblical scholar and one of the fathers of the Western church, translated the Vulgate Bible into Latin. He is usually depicted in art as an old man in cardinal's dress, writing or studying, with a lion beside him. His feast day is 30th September. Diminutive: Jerry. Variation: Hieronymus (Latin form).

Jerry
Diminutive of Gerald, Jeremy or Jerome.

Jesse
Hebrew, meaning 'God exists'. A biblical name; borne in the Old Testament by the father of King David, from whom the ancestry of Christ can be traced. He is sometimes depicted lying down with a vine coming from his loins. It was adopted by the Puritans and has enjoyed a late 20th century revival.

Jesus
Hebrew, meaning 'God is generous'. Borne by the central figure of Christianity, whose other name, Christ, means 'appointed one'. It is used as a first name in Spanish-speaking countries, but elsewhere it is generally considered too sacred for mortal use. Related name: Joshua.

Jethro
Hebrew, meaning 'pre-eminence'. A biblical name; borne in the Old Testament by the father of Moses's wife, Zipporah. It was common among Puritans.

Jim, Jimmie, Jimmy
Diminutives of James. In Central Scotland the name Jimmy is an informal dialect term for a male stranger; this may reflect the fact that James is such a common name in Scotland that the chances are he <u>will</u> be called Jimmy.

Joachim
Hebrew, meaning 'exalted by God'. In medieval legend borne by the father of the Virgin Mary; he is generally represented as an old man carrying two turtle doves in a basket, a reference to the offering made for the purification of his daughter.

Job
Hebrew, meaning 'persecuted'. A biblical name; Job showed great patience in the face of extreme adversity, as related in the Book of Job. It was adopted by the Puritans.

Jocelyn
Old German, meaning 'one of the Goths'. A Norman introduction to Britain, the name is also used for girls. Diminutive: Joss.

Jock
Scottish diminutive of John.

Joe
Diminutive of Joseph. In the US the name developed as a slang term for the man on the street (e.g. Joe Public), which has now spread throughout the English-speaking world.

Joel
Hebrew, from Yah and El, both meaning 'God'; i.e. God is God. A biblical name; borne by a minor prophet of the 8th century BC, the author of the Old Testament Book of Joel, and also by one of King David's men. A Puritan adoption, still widely popular, especially in the US.

Joey
Pet form of Joe.

John
English form of the Latin name Iohannes, derived from the Hebrew name Yohanan, meaning 'God is gracious' or 'God has forgiven'. A biblical name; borne by several figures, including St John the Baptist, the relative and forerunner of Christ who was sent 'to prepare the way of the Lord'. His feast day is 24th June, and he is traditionally represented in a sheepskin coat, holding a crude wooden cross. St John the Evangelist, the 'beloved disciple', was traditionally the author of the fourth gospel and the Book of Revelation. His feast day is 27th December, and he is usually represented bearing a chalice with a snake coming out of it. The name was also borne by numerous saints and as many as 23 popes, all of which has contributed to its status as one of the most popular masculine names in the English-speaking world. Diminutives: Hank, Jack, Jock, Johnnie, Johnny. Variations: Eoin (Irish Gaelic), Evan (Welsh), Giovanni (Italian), Iain (Scottish Gaelic), Ian (Irish Gaelic), Ivan (Russian), Jan (various European countries), Jean (French), Johann (German), Sean (Irish).

Johnathan
Variation of Jonathan.

Johnny
Pet form of John. It has developed into a general word for a man.

Jolyon
Variation of Julian.

Jon
Diminutive of Jonathan.

Jonah, Jonas
Hebrew, meaning 'dove'. A biblical name; borne in the Old Testament by a prophet who refused God's instruction to journey to Nineveh. God's wrath came down upon the ship in which he was sailing, in the form of a bad storm. At his suggestion his fellow travellers

threw him overboard, whereupon he was swallowed by a giant fish and taken to Nineveh. The name has hence come to be used of a person whose presence brings misfortune upon his companions. Jonas is the New Testament Greek form of the name.

Jonathan
Hebrew, meaning 'God has given'. A biblical name; borne in the Old Testament by a son of King Saul, a great friend of King David. In fact, so close were they that the phrase 'David and Jonathan' has come to denote an exceptionally strong friendship. Jonathan was eventually killed in battle, upon which Saul killed himself. It was adopted by the Puritans. Despite sharing the same diminutives, John and Jonathan are different names. Diminutives: Johnnie, Johnny, Jon. Variation: Jonathon.

Jones
Cerys Matthews's son, named after friend and favourite singer, Tom Jones.

Jordan
From the name of the river in the Middle East where Christ was baptised by John the Baptist. The Hebrew name Hayarden means 'to flow down'. First used in the Middle Ages, it has undergone a big popular revival since the 1980s and is increasingly used for girls, particularly in the US. Diminutive: Judd.

José
Spanish form of Joseph. It is popular in the US, probably thanks to the large Hispanic population.

Joseph
From the Hebrew name Yosef, meaning 'God will add'. A biblical name; borne by three major figures. The favourite son of Jacob and Rachel, Joseph was sold into slavery by his jealous brothers. He nevertheless became a valued advisor to the Pharaoh and when, years later, his brothers came to Egypt to seek relief from famine, Joseph welcomed them and the family was reunited. St Joseph was the husband of the Virgin Mary and the lawful father of Jesus. The patron saint of carpenters, he is generally depicted in art as an old man holding a budding staff. His feast day is 19th March. St Joseph of Arimathea, a rich Jew who felt unable to declare his faith publicly, brought Christ down from the cross and buried him in his own tomb. Non-biblical legends tell of how he brought the Holy Grail to Britain and founded the abbey of Glastonbury. His feast day is 17th March. The name has remained consistently in use throughout the English-speaking world since the 17th century. Diminutives: Jo, Joe.

Josh
Diminutive of Joshua.

Joshua
Hebrew, meaning 'God is salvation'. A biblical name; Joshua succeeded Moses as leader of the Israelites to the Promised Land. He is also known for leading the defeat of the city of Jericho by the blowing of trumpets, a story related in the book of the Bible that bears his name. Adopted by the Puritans, it has undergone a huge surge in popularity lately. Diminutive: Josh. Related name: Jesus.

Josiah
Hebrew, meaning 'may God heal'. A biblical name; borne in the Old Testament by a king of Judah (2 Kings 22) who destroyed idols and re-established strict observance of religious laws. It was popular among Puritans.

Joss
Diminutive of Jocelyn.

Jotham
Hebrew meaning 'Jehovah is perfect'. Used in the Old Testament for Gideon's youngest son.

Juan
(jew-an) Manx form of John, not to be confused with the Spanish form of John (*hwan*).

Juan
Spanish form of John.

Judah
Hebrew, meaning 'praise'. A biblical name; the fourth son of Jacob and Leah and founder of one of the twelve tribes of Israel. When the Israelites divided into two kingdoms his tribe dominated the southern one, which took the name Judah. The words 'Jew' and 'Judaism' are derived from the name. Diminutive: Jude.

Judas
New Testament Greek form of Judah, generally associated with Judas Iscariot, who betrayed Jesus for thirty pieces of silver (Matthew 26:15). The name has thus come to mean 'traitor' and is not commonly used.

Junior
From Latin meaning 'younger'. Often used in the USA to distinguish son from father where they share the same name.

Judd
Originally a diminutive of Jordan, it is now used in own right and as an adopted surname.

Jude
Variation of Judas. A biblical name; the apostle St Jude was author of the New Testament epistle of Jude. A carpenter, he is represented in art with a staff and a carpenter's square. He is regarded as the patron saint of hopeless causes, and his feast day is 28th October. A Puritan adoption, the name was used by Thomas Hardy for the unfortunate hero of his 1895 novel *Jude the Obscure*.

Jules
French form of Julius.

Julian
From the Latin name Julianus, from the Roman family name Julius. Borne by several saints, it spread to Britain in the Middle Ages. It was used for both boys and girls until Gillian replaced Julian for girls in the 16th century. Variation: Jolyon.

Julius
Roman family name, the most illustrious member of the family being the emperor Gaius Julius Caesar. It was possibly derived from the Greek, meaning 'hairy'. Variations: Julian, Jules.

Justin
From the Latin name Justinius, itself from *justus*, 'just'. The name was borne by four saints, whose feast days fall on 1st January, 14th April, 1st August and 17th September. It was also borne by two Byzantine emperors. The name has undergone a revival in the late 20th century.

K

Kamal
Arabic, meaning 'perfection'. The name is also found in India, where its origin is from Sanskrit, meaning 'pink', associated with the lotus flower.

Kane
Anglicised form of the Irish Gaelic name Catháin, it is derived from *cath*, 'battle'.

Karal, Karol
Variation of Carol, the eastern European form of Charles, derived from the Latin form Carolus.

Kareem
From Arabic 'noble'.

Karl
German spelling of Carl, the Germanic form of Charles.

Kay
Variation of the Latin first name Gaius, from the Latin *gaudere*, 'to rejoice'. Borne in Arthurian legend by a knight of the Round Table, Arthur's foster brother, who Arthur appoints as his seneschal. It is also the name of a character in Hans Christian Andersen's fairy tale, *The Snow Queen*.

Kean
Irish; anglicised form of the Irish Gaelic name Cian. Variation: Keane.

Keanu
Hawaiian, meaning 'cool breeze from the mountains'.

Keegan
From Celtic 'little fiery one'.

Keir
Adopted Scottish surname of unknown origin. Probably first adopted in honour of the first Labour MP, James Keir Hardie (1856-1915), it has been in regular use ever since.

Keith
Adopted Scottish surname and East Lothian place name, derived from the Gaelic for 'a wood'.

Kelsall
Adopted surname from an English place name, in Cheshire, of uncertain origin. It was first taken as a first name in the mid-20th century.

Kelsey
Adopted surname, from an Old English masculine name, Ceolsige, from *ceol*, 'ship', and *sige*, 'victory'. It is also, and more commonly, used for girls.

Kelvin
From name of a Scottish river.

Ken
Diminutive of Kenneth.

Kendall
Adopted surname, from a Cumbrian place name, Kendal, meaning 'valley of the River Kent'. It is occasionally used for girls.

Kendrick, Kenrick
Adopted Welsh surname, itself derived from an early first name, Cynwrig, possibly from Old Welsh *cyne*, 'royal', and *ric*, 'ruler'.

Kenelm
From Old English *cene*, 'brave', and *helm*, 'helmet'. Kenelm was a 9th-century Mercian prince, son of King Coenwulf, revered as a saint and martyr, because he was murdered (probably on his sister's orders) at the age of only seven. His feast day is 17th July.

Kenneth
Anglicisation of the Gaelic name

Cainnech (which still survives in Scotland), meaning 'handsome'. Kenneth I was a 9th-century king of Scotland. Diminutives: Ken, Kenny.

Kenny
Diminutive of Kenneth.

Kent
Adopted surname, itself derived from the English county.

Kentigern
From a Celtic name, meaning 'chief lord'. St Kentigern (c. 510 - c. 600) is traditionally believed to have founded Glasgow cathedral and to have been the city's first bishop. He is generally depicted holding an episcopal cross and a salmon. His feast day is 13th January. Mungo is a byname. The name was popular around Glasgow until the end of the 18th century but is now only rarely found. See also: Mungo.

Kenton
Adopted surname and English place name of disputed origin, but possibly from the name of an English river, Kenn, plus the Old English *tun*, 'settlement', or from Old English *cyne*, 'royal', and *tun*, 'settlement'. It is in occasional use as a first name, mainly in the US.

Kermit
Irish/Manx name derived from the patronymic Gaelic surname MacDhiarmaid, meaning 'son of Diarmuid'. The name has now become associated worldwide with Kermit the Frog, the central puppet in Jim Henson's *Muppet Show*, who made his first television appearance as early as 1957.

Kester
Medieval diminutive of Christopher.

Kevin
Anglicisation of the Irish Gaelic name Caoimnín, from *caomh,* 'handsome'. Borne by an Irish hermit saint of the 7th century, patron saint of Dublin. He is reputed to have retired to a cave at Glendalough, County Wicklow, near to which a monastery now stands. He vowed to allow no woman near. When a young girl visited him he threw her from a rock, and was haunted by her ghost ever after. The name was rarely found outside Ireland until the mid-20th century, when it became hugely fashionable throughout the English-speaking world. Diminutive: Kev.

Kieran, Kieron
Anglicisation of the Irish Gaelic name Ciarán, meaning 'dark'. Borne by two early Celtic saints of the 5th century and 6th century, it has undergone a popular revival since the mid-20th century. Variation: Kyran.

Kim
Originally a diminutive of Kimball (as in Rudyard Kipling's 1901 novel *Kim*), or Kimberley, it came to be used in its own right. It is also used as a girl's name.

Kincaid
Celtic 'battle chief'.

Kimball
Adopted surname, possibly derived from Old English *cynn*, 'family', and *bald*, 'bold'. It was the full first name of Kim, the hero of Rudyard Kipling's novel of that name (1901), but has never been common.

Kimberley
Adopted surname and English place name. Its source as a name is Kimberley in South Africa, scene of fierce fighting

during the Boer War and itself named after one Lord Kimberley. The name was given initially to boys, and then increasingly to girls. Diminutive: Kim.

Kingsley
Adopted surname and place name, from the Old English name Cyningesleah, meaning 'king's wood'. Its popularity may derive from the author Charles Kingsley (1819-75). Variations: Kingslie, Kingsly.

Kinnard
Gaelic 'from the high mountain'.

Kirk
Adopted surname, from Old Norse *kirkja*, 'church'. A recent revival was probably influenced by the popular American actor Kirk Douglas, born Issur Danielovich Demsky in 1916.

Kirkby
Taken as a first name from a place name but originally from Old Norse meaning 'church farm'. Used as either a boy's or girl's name.

Kit
Diminutive of Christopher.

Konrad
From German rad 'counsel' and conja 'bold'.

Kris
Scandinavian; a diminutive of Christopher.

Krishna
Indian name, from Sanskrit, meaning 'black' or 'dark'. Borne by a legendary hero, later elevated to the level of a god, and considered an incarnation of Vishnu. He was supposed to be the son of Vasudeva and Devaki, and the nephew of King Kamsa, who, having been told that one of his nephews would kill him, gave orders for all Devaki's children to be murdered. Krishna, however, was smuggled out, brought up by cowherds, and lived to kill his uncle.

Kumar
Indian name, from Sanskrit, meaning 'boy', 'son' or 'prince'. It is an epithet applied to Skanda, beautiful son of Shiva.

Kurt
Variation of Conrad, originally the German diminutive.

Kyle
Adopted Scottish place name, from the characteristically Scottish topographical term *kyle*, meaning 'strait' or 'channel', itself derived from the Gaelic *caol*, 'narrow'. Geographical examples include the Kyle of Lochalsh. It is also the name of the central district of Ayrshire, now in western Strathclyde. See also: Glen, Ross.

L

Laban
Hebrew, meaning 'white'. A biblical name; borne in the Old Testament by the brother of Isaac's wife, Rebekah, and father of Leah and Rachel. Laban made Jacob work for seven years to win Rachel for his wife, then tricked him by substituting Leah; he then made Jacob work another seven years for Rebekah. It was adopted by the Puritans.

Lachlan
From the Scottish name Lachlann, the

Gaelic word for Norway, 'the land of lochs', and hence for a Viking. Diminutive: Lochie. Variation: Lochlann.

Lambert
Old German, from *landa*, 'land', and *berht*, 'bright'. St Lambert, a 7th-century bishop of Maastricht, popularised the name in medieval Belgium and Netherlands, and it spread to Britain in the Middle Ages.

Lance
French, from the Old German name Lanzo, from *landa*, 'land'. Probable diminutives: Lancelot, Launcelot. (Lance is sometimes erroneously considered the diminutive form of Lancelot.) Variation: Launce.

Lancelot
Most probably a diminutive of Lance, rather than the other way around. Borne in Arthurian legend by Lancelot du Lac, one of the most famous knights of King Arthur's Round Table. The son of King Ban of Brittany, he was stolen as a child by the Lady of the Lake, who presented him to King Arthur when he was an adult. He became the adulterous lover of Queen Guinevere, which sparked a war that resulted in the death of Arthur and the destruction of the Round Table. Variations: Lance, Launcelot.

Lanty
Irish diminutive of Laurence or Lawrence.

Larry
Diminutive of Laurence or Lawrence used sometimes in its own right.

Lars
Scandinavian form of Laurence or Lawrence.

Launce, Launcelot
Variations, respectively, of Lance and Lancelot.

Lauren
Variation of Laurence, now more common as a girl's name.

Laurence
French form of the Latin name Laurentius, meaning 'of Laurentium', an ancient Italian town of olive groves. Borne by a 3rd-century deacon of Rome whose responsibility it was to look after the poor. He was martyred in 258 by being roasted on a gridiron. Considered the patron saint of curriers, his feast day is 10th August. Diminutives: Lanty, Larry, Laurie, Lawrie. Variations: Lars, Lauren, Lawrence, Loren, Lorenzo, Lorin.

Laurie
Scottish diminutive of Laurence or Lawrence.

Lawrence
Anglicised spelling of Laurence.

Lawrie
Scottish diminutive of Laurence or Lawrence.

Layton
Variation of Leighton.

Lazarus
Greek form of Eleazar. A biblical name; borne in the New Testament by a beggar who was laid daily at a rich man's gate. When both died, Lazarus went to heaven and the rich man to hell (Luke 16: 19-31). Also borne by the brother of Mary and Martha, whom Christ raised from the dead (John 11: 1-44).

Lea, Lee, Leigh
Adopted surname; from Old English *leah*, 'wood, clearing'. Its popularity as a first name originated in the US, in honour of the Confederate general Robert E Lee (1807-70), but it spread worldwide in the later 20th century in various forms, for both boys and girls.

Leander
Latin form of the Greek name, Leandros, from *leon*, 'lion', and *aner*, 'man'. In Greek legend Leander was the lover of Hero, a priestess of Venus, to whom he swam nightly across the Hellespont. One night he drowned and the desolate Hero drowned herself in the same sea. St Leander was a 6th-century Archbishop of Seville.

Leighton
Adopted surname, itself from the place name; from Old English *leac*, 'leek', and *tun*, 'settlement'.

Lemmy
Diminutive of Lemuel.

Lemuel
Hebrew, meaning 'devoted to God'. A biblical name; borne by an Old Testament king. It is also the name given to the hero of *Gulliver's Travels*, Jonathan Swift's novel of 1726.

Len, Lennie, Lenny
Diminutives of Leonard.

Lennon
Name given to son of Liam Gallagher and Patsy Kensit.

Lennox
Adopted Scottish surname, from the Levenach, one-time name of an area north of Glasgow.

Leo
From Latin *leo*, 'lion'. It is the name of a constellation depicting a crouching lion, and the fifth sign of the zodiac. Borne by thirteen popes, including Leo the Great, and four saints.

Leofric
From Old English *leof*, 'deer', and *ric*, 'ruler'. Borne by the husband of the infamous Lady Godiva, it was one of few Old English names to survive the Norman Conquest.

Leoline
Anglicised form of Llewellyn.

Leon
From Greek *leon*, 'lion', although generally regarded as a variation of Leo, like León (Spanish) and Léon (French).

Leonard
From the Old German name, Leonhard, derived from *levon*, 'lion', and *hardu*, 'hardy'. It was popularised in the 6th century by St Leonard, a Frank at the court of Clovis. The king gave him permission to release the prisoners he visited, and he is thus venerated as patron saint of prisoners. He founded a monastery at Noblac, now Saint-Léonard, near Limoges, and is traditionally depicted holding broken fetters. His feast day is 6th November. Diminutives: Len, Lennie, Lenny, Leo. Variations: Lennard, Leonardo (Italian).

Leonardo
Italian form of Leonard, sometimes given in honour of the artist and inventor Leonardo da Vinci.

Leopold
Old German, from *leudi*, 'people', and *balda*, 'bold'. A 12th-century Austrian saint. The name was popularised in

Britain by one of Queen Victoria's sons, named after his great uncle, Leopold I of the Belgians. Diminutive: Poldie.

Leroy
Adopted surname, from Old French *le roy*, 'the king'. It is widespread in the US. Variation: Elroy.

Les
Diminutive of Lesley or Leslie.

Leslie
Adopted Scottish surname, derived from the place name Lesslyn, in Aberdeenshire. It was taken as a first name during the 19th century. Diminutive: Les.

Lester
Adopted surname, possibly a respelling of the name of the English town, Leicester. A 19th-century adoption.

Levi
Hebrew, meaning 'attached'. A biblical name; in the Old Testament it is the name given to the third son of Leah and Jacob, in the New Testament an alternative name for the apostle Matthew.

Lew
Diminutive of Lewis.

Lewis
Anglicised form of Louis, particularly popular in Wales, where it is taken as a variation of Llewellyn. Variation (though rare): Lutwidge, the middle name of Charles Lutwidge Dodson, aka Lewis Carroll (1832-98), author of *Alice's Adventures In Wonderland* (1865).

Lex
Diminutive of Alexander.

Liam
Originally a diminutive of Uilliam, the Irish variation of William, it is now more common in its own right.

Lincoln
Adopted surname, and English place name, originally indicating 'the Roman colony at the lake'. It was popularised as a first name in honour of Abraham Lincoln (1809-65), sixteenth president of the US, during whose presidency the Union won the Civil War and slavery was abolished.

Lindon
Variation of Lyndon.

Lindsay
Adopted Scottish surname, probably meaning 'Lincoln's marsh'. It was first taken to Scotland from Lindsey, Lincolnshire, by Sir Walter de Lindesay. It is used as a boy's name in Scotland, although elsewhere it is generally regarded as a girl's name.

Linford
Adopted surname and English place name, from *lin*, 'flax', and *ford*, 'ford'.

Linus
Latin form of the Greek name Linos, of uncertain origin. In classical mythology borne by Hercules's music tutor. The name was also borne by the second pope (St Peter's successor), who may conceivably have been the Linus whose greetings are conveyed by St Paul to Timothy (II Timothy 4:21).

Lionel
Originally a medieval diminutive of Leon. Borne by a knight of King Arthur's Round Table, and by Edward III's third son, later Duke of Clarence.

Litton
From Anglo Saxon meaning 'farm on hillside'

Llewellyn, Llewelyn
Welsh, originally spelt Llywelyn, from *llyw*, 'leader'. The modern spelling suggests a belief that the name was associated with the word for 'lion'. Borne by two 13th-century Welsh princes, Llywelyn ap Iorwerth and his grandson Llywelyn ap Gruffydd. Diminutives: Lew, Lyn.

Lloyd
Anglicised form of the Welsh name Llwyd, meaning 'grey'. Variations: Floyd (mainly in the US, to avoid problems with pronouncing the Welsh 'll'), Loyd.

Llywelyn
Early spelling of Llewellyn.

Lochie
Diminutive of Lachlan.

Lochlann
Variation of Lachlan.

Logan
From Scottish 'little hollow'.

Lonnie
Diminutive of Alonso popularised by the British singer Lonnie Donegan in the 1950s.

Loren
Variation of Lauren, itself a variation of Laurence.

Lorenzo
Italian and Spanish forms of Laurence or Lawrence.

Lorin
Variation of Lauren, itself a variation of Laurence.

Lorn, Lorne
An early Scottish chieftain, after whom a place in Argyll was named. A later Marquess of Lorne married one of Queen Victoria's daughters, Louise. Sometimes assumed to be a masculine form of Lorna, R D Blackmore's invention, Lorna Doone, was in fact probably derived from the place name.

Lou
Diminutive of Louie or Louis, and a variation of Lew.

Louie
Variation and diminutive of Louis, probably influenced by the French pronunciation.

Louis
From the Old German name Chlodovech, from *hlud*, 'fame', and *wig*, 'warrior'. It was borne by nineteen kings of France. Diminutive: Lou. Variations: Lewis (anglicised), Ludwig (German).

Lovell
Adopted surname, itself derived in the Middle Ages from the Norman French name, Louvel, a diminutive formed from *lou*, 'wolf'.

Lowell
Adopted surname, itself a variation of Lovell. It is most common in the US, probably after the prominent New England Lowell family, of which the poet Robert Lowell (1917-77) was a member.

Lucas
Variation of Loukas, a Greek name meaning 'man of Lucania', in southern Italy. It was introduced to Britain in the 12th century. Variation: Luke.

Lucian
From the Roman clan name Lucianus, of unknown origin. In the 2nd century AD Apuleius gave the name to the main character in his satire *The Golden Ass*, a personification of the follies and vices of the age.

Lucien
French form of Lucian.

Lucius
From Latin *lux*, 'light'. The name was popular in Ancient Rome, and borne by three popes. It was also the name of a mythical king of Britain, the son of Coillus, and fabled to have been the first Christian king of Britain.

Ludo
Diminutive of Ludovic.

Ludovic
Latinate form of Ludwig, from an Old German name Chlodowig, meaning 'famous warrior'. Popular in Scotland.

Ludwig
German, from the Old German name Chlodovech, from *hlud*, 'fame', and *wig*, 'warrior'. Variations: Lewis, Louis.

Luke
Latinate form of the Greek name Lucas, meaning 'man of Lucania', in southern Italy. A biblical name; St Luke the Evangelist, gentile and convert of St Paul, is supposed to have written the third gospel and the Acts of the Apostles. Described in the Bible as a physician (Colossians 4:14) and traditionally believed to have painted a portrait of the Virgin Mary, he is the patron saint of doctors and painters. His feast day is 18th October.

Lundy
From French lundi, 'born on a Monday'.

Luther
Adopted German surname, from *liut*, 'people', and *here*, 'army'. It was initially bestowed in honour of the German religious reformer Martin Luther (1483-1546), but more recently in honour of his namesake, Martin Luther King (1929-68), the assassinated civil rights leader.

Lyall
Adopted Scottish surname, probably from an Old Norse name, Liulfr.

Lyle
Adopted Scottish surname, from Old French *de l'isle*, meaning 'of the island'. It is sometimes erroneously confused with Lyall.

Lyn
Diminutive of Llewellyn often used in its own right

Lyndon
Adopted surname, from the place name, itself from Old English *lind*, 'lime tree', and *dun*, 'hill'. It is especially popular in the US, after Lyndon Baines Johnson (1908-73), 36th president. Variation: Lindon.

Lynn
Welsh meaning 'from the pool' or 'waterfall'.

M

Mackenzie
Adopted Scottish surname, from Gaelic Mac Coinnich, meaning 'son of Coinneach'. It is also used for girls, particularly in the US.

Madoc
Anglicised form of the Old Welsh name Madóg, meaning 'fortunate', or 'good' or the Irish form, Maedóc. Borne in Welsh legend by one Madóg ap Owain Gwynedd, who is said to have sailed to America, arriving at Mobile Bay, Alabama in 1170, long before any other settlers. Also borne in Ireland by several early saints, a 6th-century abbot of Clonmore and the reformer Mael-Maedóc Ó Morgain (1095-1148). Variation: Madog. See also: Marmaduke.

Magnus
Latin byname, meaning 'great', extracted from the Latin name for Charlemagne, Carolus Magnus. Adopted by St Olaf of Norway, an admirer of Charlemagne, it was subsequently borne by seven Norwegian kings and several early Scandinavian saints. One of these visited the Scottish islands of Orkney and Shetland; the main church in Kirkwall, capital town of Orkney, is dedicated to him. Variation: Manus.

Makram
Arabic, meaning 'generous', 'noble' or 'magnanimous'.

Malachi
Hebrew, meaning 'my messenger'. A biblical name; borne by the eponymous author of the last book of the Old Testament, a prophet whose prophesies are mainly concerned with the coming of Judgement Day. His name is thought by some to derive from the text itself: 'Behold , I will send my messenger, and he shall prepare the way before me' (Malachi 3:1). Variation: Malachy.

Malachy
Irish, first adopted in reference to an early Irish king, Maoileachlainn, and further influenced by the name of the Old Testament prophet, Malachi. it was popularised in the 12th century by St Malachy (1095-1148), a bishop of Armagh, born Máel Maedhog Ó Morgair.

Malcolm
Anglicised form of the Old Gaelic name Mael Coluim, meaning 'devotee of St Columba'. (St Columba was largely responsible for the conversion of Scotland.) It was subsequently borne by four medieval Scottish kings. Variations: Callum, Colm.

Malise
Gaelic meaning 'servant of Jesus'

Mallory
Old French meaning 'unfortunate'.

Malvin
Masculine form of Malvina.

Manasseh
Hebrew, meaning 'to forget'. A biblical name; borne in the Old Testament by the elder son of Joseph and the brother of Ephraim (Genesis 41), both progenitors of tribes. First used in the Middle Ages, the name was revived by the Puritans but is rarely found today outside Jewish families.

Manfred
From Old German *man*, 'man', and *fred*, 'peace'. A Norman introduction, it fell

into disuse after the Middle Ages, but was then reintroduced in the 19th century from Germany. Lord Byron used the name for his poetic drama *Manfred* (1817).

Manley
Adopted surname and English place name, from *gemæn*, 'common', and *leah*, 'wood', or 'clearing', meaning 'common lands'. Its adoption as a first name may also be due to an association with the English word manly.

Manny
Diminutive of Emanuel, Manuel.

Manuel
Spanish form of Emanuel. Diminutive: Manny.

Manus
Irish variation of Magnus.

Marc
French form of Mark.

Marcel
French, derived from the Latin name Marcellus, originally a diminutive of Marcus. Borne by a 3rd-century missionary. The name has been in occasional use in the English-speaking world since the 19th century.

Marco
Italian form of Marcus. Borne by the Venetian merchant and traveller Marco Polo (1254-1324) who sailed to China bearing letters from the pope to Kubla Khan. It is in occasional use in the English-speaking world.

Marcus
Original Latin form of Marc, probably derived from Mars, Roman god of war.

Mario
Italian, Portuguese and Spanish form of Marius.

Marius
Probably a direct adoption of the Roman family name Marius, from Mars, Roman god of war. It is in occasional use in this form thoughout the world; the form Mario is particularly popular in Italy, Portugal and Spain.

Mark
Anglicised form of the Latin name, Marcus. A biblical name; borne in the New Testament by St Mark, author of the second gospel who died in prison c. 68. He is sometimes depicted with a lion at his feet, or holding a pen and the gospel. His feast day is 25th April. In medieval Arthurian legend King Mark of Cornwall was the treacherous and cowardly betrothed of Isolde, and uncle of her beloved Tristan. Variations: Marco, Marcus.

Marlon
Origin uncertain, possibly intended as a diminutive of Mark. Marlon appears to have been popularised by the American actor Marlon Brando (b 1924), whose father also bore the name. Marlin, Marlo and Marlon are all found in the US, but seldom elsewhere.

Marmaduke
Anglicised form of the Irish Gaelic name Mael-Maedóc, meaning 'devotee of Madoc'. The name is largely confined to Yorkshire, where the Celtic influence of Norse invaders has persisted. Diminutive: Duke.

Marshall
Adopted surname, originally derived from a Norman French occupational

name for a groom, *marescal*, from Old German *marah*, 'horse', and *scalc*, 'servant'.

Mart, Marty
Diminutives of Martin.

Martin
Anglicised form of the Latin name Martinus, probably, like Mark, derived from Mars, Roman god of war, and possibly meaning 'warlike'. St Martin of Tours (c. 316-97) was responsible for the name's huge popularity in medieval Europe. Born in what is now Hungary, he was converted to Christianity while a soldier in Rome, became bishop of Tours, and is probably best known for cutting his cloak in two to share with a beggar. His feast day is 11th November, which is also the Feast of Bacchus, Roman god of wine, and he has hence become erroneously considered the patron saint of innkeepers and drunkards. Diminutives: Mart, Marty. Variation: Marytn.

Martyn
Variation of Martin.

Marvin
Origin uncertain, possibly a medieval form of Mervyn. It is particularly popular in the US, where recent use is likely to be in honour of the American singer Marvin Gaye (1939-84).

Matt, Mattie
Diminutives of Matthew.

Matthew
From the Hebrew name, Mattathia meaning 'gift of God'. A biblical name; borne in the New Testament by one of Christ's twelve apostles, who was also known as Levi, son of Alphaeus. The first gospel bears his name and is generally thought to have been written by him, although some biblical scholars dispute this. He is represented in art as an evangelist, with an angel close by dictating the Gospel, or as an apostle, holding a purse. His feast day is 21st September. A Norman introduction to Britain, it has remained perennially popular. Diminutives: Matt, Mattie. Variation: Mathew.

Matthias
New Testament Greek form of the Hebrew name Mattathia, meaning 'gift of God'. A biblical name; borne in the New Testament by 'the thirteenth apostle', the man who replaced Judas Iscariot after his death (Acts 1:23-26). Variation: Mathias.

Maurice
From the Latin name Mauricius, or Mauritius, meaning 'Moorish'. Borne by a 3rd-century saint martyred in Switzerland, after whom the Swiss town of St Moritz is named; by a 6th-century Benedictine monk; and by an early Byzantine emperor (c. 539-602). It was a Norman introduction to Britain. Variations: Meurig, Morris. See also: Seymour.

Max
Originally a diminutive of Maximilian or Maxwell, now often used in its own right.

Maxim
Variation of Maximus. It was used by Daphne du Maurier as the first name of Mr de Winter in her novel *Rebecca* (1940).

Maximilian
From the Latin name Maximilianus, from *maximus*, 'greatest'. Borne by a 3rd-century martyr, and later thought to have been 'reinvented' by Emperor Frederick III of

Germany for his son, by combining the names of two Roman generals Quintus Fabius Maximus and Scipio Aemilianus. Diminutives: Max, Maxim.

Maxwell
Adopted Scottish surname and place name, originally meaning 'Mack's (or Magnus') well', the name of a small town on the River Tweed. Used in Scotland since the mid-19th century, it spread elsewhere in the 20th century.

Maynard
Adopted surname, originally from Norman French *magin*, 'strength', and *hard*, 'hardy' or 'brave'. It was a Norman introduction to Britain.

Medwyn
After a Welsh saint who is celebrated on January 1st.

Meical
Welsh form of Michael.

Mel
Diminutive of Melchior, Melville or Melvin.

Melchior
Persian, probably from *melk*, 'king', and *quart*, 'city'. The name was ascribed by medieval legend to one of the Magi, the Three Wise Men.

Melville
Adopted Scottish surname, originally a Norman French baronial name derived from Malleville, or 'poor settlement'. Diminutive: Mel.

Melvin, Melvyn
Origin uncertain, possibly a variation of Melville. Diminutive: Mel.

Mercer
Adopted surname, originally an occupational name for a trader, from Old French *mercier*, 'haberdasher', itself derived from *mercarius*, 'merchandise'. Particularly popular in the US, it was probably first given in honour of General Hugh Mercer, killed at the Battle of Princeton in 1777.

Meredith
Adopted Welsh surname, from Maredudd, probably meaning 'great lord'. It has recently become popular as a girl's name. Diminutive: Merry.

Merfyn
Old Welsh, possibly a form of Myrddin, the source of Merlin; or an independent name possibly derived from *mer*, 'marrow', and *myn*, 'eminent'. Diminutive: Merf. Variation: Mervyn.

Meirion
From Welsh for 'dairyman'.

Merlin
From the Latinate form, Merlinus, of the Old Welsh name Myrddin, meaning 'sea fort'. Borne most famously in Arthurian legend by the magician Merlin Ambrosius, whose story has probably become confused with that of an historical Merlin, a 6th-century Welsh bard who is said to have fought on behalf of King Arthur. It is in occasional use today, although more commonly used for girls.

Merrill
Adopted surname, itself probably of medieval origin and derived from the girl's names Meriel or Muriel.

Merton
Adopted surname and English place

name, from Old English *mere*, 'lake', and *tun*, 'settlement'.

Mervyn
Anglicised form of the Welsh name Merfyn. Diminutive: Merv. Variation: Mervin.

Meurig
Welsh variation of Maurice.

Micah
Hebrew, meaning 'who is like Jehovah?'. A biblical name; borne in the 8th century BC by a prophet notable for having foretold that the promised Messiah would be born in Bethlehem. He is the author of the 33rd book of the Old Testament.

Michael
Anglicised form of the Hebrew name, meaning 'who is like God?', a root comparable to that of Micah. A biblical name; borne by St Michael the Archangel, leader of the seven archangels, great prince of all angels and leader of the celestial armies (Revelation 12: 7-8). He is used as a symbol of the Church Militant, and is also regarded as the patron saint of soldiers. He is generally depicted slaying a dragon, and his feast day is 29th September. The name has been perennially popular thoughout the English-speaking world since the Middle Ages. Diminutives: Mick, Mickey, Micky, Mike, Mikey, Mischa, Misha, Mitch. Variations: Meical, Micah, Miles, Myles.

Mick, Mickey, Micky
Diminutives of Michael.

Mihangel
Old Welsh, probably a variation of Michael and representing a contraction of 'Michael the Archangel'.

Mike, Mikey
Diminutives of Michael.

Milburn
Old English meaning 'mill stream'.

Miles, Myles
Norman French, of uncertain origin. It could be a variation of Michael, influenced with the Latin *miles*, 'soldier', owing to the military associations of St Michael the Archangel. Its use in Ireland tends to be as an anglicised form of names beginning Maol- or Maoil-, such as Maol Mhuire (devotee of Mary), or Maoileas (devotee of Jesus). Variation: Milo.

Milo
Latinate form of Miles, which coincides with an Old German name, possibly meaning 'merciful'. Borne by a celebrated Greek athlete of the late 6th century. First used in the Middle Ages, it was revived in the 19th century.

Milton
Adopted surname and place name, from the Old English *mylentun*, meaning 'settlement with a mill'. Its use as a first name was probably initially in honour of the great English poet John Milton (1608-74), author of *Paradise Lost*. It is particularly popular in the US. Diminutive: Milt.

Mischa, Misha
Russian diminutive forms of Michael.

Mitchell
Derived from Michael. Diminutive Mitch.

Mohamed, Mohammad, Mohammed
Variations of Muhammad.

Mohan
Indian, from Sanskrit, meaning 'attractive' or 'enchanting'. A byname of Shiva, and of one of the five arrows of Kama, the god of love. It is also a byname of Krishna.

Monroe
Adopted Scottish surname, possibly derived from Scottish Gaelic *bun Rothe*, meaning 'from the mouth of the River Roe', the area in County Derry, Ireland, where the family originated. Use of the name in the US is probably attributable to the fifth president, James Monroe (1758-1831). Variations: Monro, Munro, Munroe.

Montague
Adopted aristocratic English surname, itself derived from a Norman baronial name and place name, Montaigu, from Old French *mont*, 'hill', and *aigu*, 'pointed'. Drogo de Montaigu, founder of the family, came to England with William the Conqueror. It was adopted as a first name in the 19th century. Diminutive: Monty.

Montgomery
Adopted surname, originally a Norman baronial name and place name, from Calvados in northern France, from Old French, *mont* 'hill', and Gomeric, an Old German name meaning 'powerful one', thus ultimately meaning 'mountain of the powerful one'. The Welsh county of Montgomeryshire was named after a Norman settler.

Monty
A diminutive of Montague, or of Montgomery.

Mordecai
Biblical, of uncertain origin, but possibly meaning 'follower of Marduk (a Babylonian god)'. Borne in the Old Testament by a cousin and guardian of Esther. Mordecai warned Esther of Haman's plans to massacre all Jews, enabling Esther to plan to save them (Esther 4-7). The name was popular with the Puritans in the 17th century and remained so until the late 18th century, but is now largely confined to Jewish families.

Morgan
Welsh, of uncertain origin. Possibly derived from the Old Welsh name Morcant, from *mor*, 'sea', and *can*, 'bright', or *gan* 'born', meaning 'sea bright' or 'sea born'. The Welsh county of Glamorgan is named after a Morgan who lived there in the 10th century. In modern times the name is also used for girls.

Morley
Adopted surname and English place name, from Old English *mor*, 'moor', and *leah*, 'wood' or 'clearing'.

Morris
Medieval anglicised form of Maurice.

Mortimer
Adopted aristocratic surname, itself derived from a Norman baronial name and place name, Mortemer in Normandy, from *morte*, 'dead', and *mer*, 'sea'. It was adopted as a first name in the 19th century.

Morton
Adopted surname and English place name, from Old English *moor*, 'moor', and *tun*, 'settlement', meaning 'settlement on the moor'. The name is popular

among Jews, where it is taken as an approximate anglicisation of Moses.

Moses
Anglicised form of the apparently Hebrew name Moshe, possibly of Egyptian origin and of uncertain meaning. A biblical name; borne by the Hebrew patriarch who led the Israelites out of Egypt for the Promised Land. As a baby he was found floating in a basket on the Nile by a Pharoah's daughter. 'She called his name Moses: and she said, Because I drew him out of the water' (Exodus 2:10). This is a pun on Moshe, from Hebrew *masho*, 'to pull', but does not reveal the name's true meaning. It is known to have been popular in medieval Britain, and was revived by the Puritans after the Reformation.

Moshe
Original Hebrew form of Moses, possibly of Egyptian origin.

Mostyn
Adopted Welsh surname and place name in Clywdd, North Wales, derived from Old English elements *mos*, 'moss', and *tun*, 'settlement'.

Muhammad
Arabic, meaning 'praiseworthy'. Borne by the Prophet of Islam, Abu al-Qasim Muhammad ibn-'Abd-Allah ibn-'Abd-al-Muttalib al-Hashimiyy, 'father of Al-Qasim Muhammad son of Abdallah son of Abd-al-Muttalib the Hashemite'. He was born at Mecca c. 570 and died at Medina in 632. This is probably the most popular Islamic boy's name. Variations: Mohamed, Mohammad, Mohammed.

Muhsin
Arabic, meaning 'charitable' or 'benevolent'.

Mungo
Scottish byname of St Kentigern, a 6th-century bishop of Glasgow, and now patron saint of the city. A possible root of the byname is from Old Welsh, meaning 'my dear friend' or 'my dear pet'. Largely confined to Scotland, the name was borne by the Scottish explorer Mungo Park (1771-1806), who led expeditions to the River Niger in Africa. See also: Kentigern.

Murchadh
(*moor-ha*) Scottish Gaelic, from *muir*, 'sea', and *cadh*, 'battle'. Borne by several early Scottish kings, it can be anglicised as Murdo.

Murdo
Most probably an anglicised form of the Scottish Gaelic name Murchadh, from *muir*, 'sea', and *cadh*, 'battle', and meaning 'sea battle', although some dispute this, claiming another, albeit similar, source, meaning 'seaman'. It is particularly popular in north-west Scotland and on the Hebridean islands. Its variation, Murdoch, became a common surname.

Murgatroyd
Adopted Yorkshire surname and place name, meaning 'Margaret's clearing', derived from Marga, an old-fashioned form of Margaret, and *royd*, a dialect word meaning 'clearing'. Its use is still largely confined to Yorkshire although it is occasionally found elsewhere.

Murray
Adopted Scottish surname, from Scottish Gaelic *muir*, meaning 'sea'. The area of Scotland called Moray derives its name from the same source, and Moray is an alternative spelling of Murray. It was adopted as a first name in the 19th century.

Myles
Variation of Miles.

Mustafa
Arabic, meaning 'pure' or 'chosen'. Al-Mustafa is one of the names used to describe the Prophet Muhammad. For Arabic-speaking Christians it is an epithet for St Paul. Borne in recent times by Mustafa Kamal (1881-1938), founder of modern Turkey and also known as Ataturk, meaning 'father of the Turks'.

Myron
From the Greek, meaning 'fragrant' or 'scented oil'. Borne by a Greek sculptor of the 5th century BC, noted for his realistic statues of gods, heroes, athletes and animals.

N

Nahum
(*nay-hum*) Hebrew, meaning 'full of comfort'. A biblical name; borne in the Old Testament by a prophet of the 7th century, author of the 34th book of the Bible, in which he foresees the fall of Nineveh. It was adopted by the Puritans.

Naim
Arabic, meaning 'comfortable', 'tranquil' or 'happy'. Variation: Naeem.

Nairn
Celtic dweller by the alder tree.

Naoise
(*nee-sha*) Irish Gaelic, of uncertain origin. Borne in Irish legend by the lover of Deirdre, who was murdered by Conchobhar, king of Ulster.

Napoleon
Uncertain origin possibly from the ancient name for Naples, Neapolis with influence from Italian leone 'lion'.

Nasser
Arabic, meaning 'helper'. Variation: Nasir.

Nat
Diminutive of Nathan or Nathaniel.

Nathan
Hebrew, meaning 'gift'. A biblical name; borne in the Old Testament by a prophet who advised King David to build the temple (2 Samuel 7) and dared to reprimand David for arranging the killing of Uriah, husband of Bathsheba (2 Samuel 12). Diminutives: Nat, Nath.

Nathaniel
Hebrew, meaning 'gift of God'. A biblical name; borne in the New Testament by one of Christ's apostles, better known as Bartholomew. The Authorised Version of the New Testament has the spelling Nathanael. Nathaniel was used by Shakespeare in *Love's Labour's Lost* (1594). The name is particularly popular in the US. Diminutives: Nat, Nath, Nathan.

Neal, Neale
Variations of Neil.

Ned
Diminutive of Edmund or Edward, dating from the Middle Ages. Variations: Neddie, Neddy.

Nehemiah
From Hebrew, meaning 'comfort of the Lord'. A biblical name; borne in the Old Testament by a 5th-century BC governor of Jerusalem, author of the book that bears his name. Adopted by the Puritans in the

17th century, the name is rare in modern times.

Neil
Variation of Niall dating from the Middle Ages, probably introduced to Britain from Continental Europe. Variations: Neal, Neale, Niall, Nigel.

Nelson
Adopted surname, originally a patronymic ('son of Niall') or metronymic ('son of Nell'). It was adopted as a first name in the 19th century, probably in honour of Admiral Lord Horatio Nelson (1758-1805), commanding officer of the victorious English fleet at the Battle of Trafalgar.

Nerville
Adoption of a French town name as a first name

Neville
Adopted aristocratic surname and Old French place name, from Old French *neuve*, 'new', and *ville*, 'town', after several places in northern France. It was a Norman introduction to Britain. The Neville family was influential in 15th-century British politics, Richard Neville (1428-71) becoming Earl of Warwick. He was nicknamed 'Warwick the Kingmaker'. See also: Newton.

Nevin
Anglo Saxon 'nephew'.

Newton
Adopted surname and common English place name, from Old English *neowe*, 'new', and *tun*, 'settlement'. it is particularly popular in the US. Diminutive: Newt. See also: Neville.

Niall
Irish and Scottish, from Irish Gaelic *niadh*, meaning 'champion'. Borne by a 5th-century Irish king, Niall of the Nine Hostages. This, the original spelling of the name, is undergoing a revival among non-Gaelic communities throughout the world. Variations: Neal, Neale, Neil, Nigel.

Nichol, Nicholl, Nicol
Medieval vernacular forms of Nicholas, particularly in Scotland. Currently undergoing a revival.

Nicholas
Anglicised from of the Greek name Nikolaos, from *nike*, 'victory', and *laos*, 'people', and meaning 'victory of the people'. The addition of the 'h' was a learned modification, possibly as early as the 13th century. Borne by a 4th-century bishop of Myra, in Asia Minor, who is now considered patron saint of Greece and Russia, as well as of children, sailors and pawnbrokers. By repute a benevolent, generous figure, St Nicholas, in his Dutch incarnation of Santa Claus, is associated throughout the Christian world with the bringing of Christmas presents. Diminutives: Nick, Nicky, Nico. Variations: Colin, Nichol, Nickolas, Nikolas.

Nick, Nicky, Nico
Diminutives of Nicholas.

Nicodemus
From Greek *nike*, 'victory', and *demos*, 'people'. A biblical name; borne in the New Testament by a Pharisee to whom Jesus explained the meaning of 'born again' (John 3), and who later assisted Joseph of Arimathea with the burial of Christ (John 19: 33-42).

Nigel
Medieval anglicisation of Nigellus, itself a Latinate form of Neil, probably

influenced by the Latin *niger*, 'black'. It was not adopted until the 19th century, when a general fashion for medieval names led to its revival in this form. Variations: Neal, Neale, Neil, Niall.

Ninian
Found in Ireland and Scotland, but of uncertain origin. Possibly derived from Nennius, an early Welsh chronicler. Borne by a 5th-century British saint who acted as missionary to northern Britain and the Picts of Scotland.

Noah
Hebrew, meaning 'rest', or 'repose'. A biblical name; borne in the Old Testament by the man whose family was chosen to be saved from the Great Flood (Genesis 6-8). A Puritan adoption, it has become increasingly popular in modern times.

Noël
An Old French, from *noel*, *nael*, derived from the Latin *dies natalis*, meaning 'birthday' and referring specifically to the birthday of Christ, i.e. Christmas. The name is often given to boys – and sometimes to girls – born at Christmas.

Nolan
Adopted Irish surname, from the Irish Gaelic name Ó Nualláin, meaning 'descendant of Nuallán'.

Norbert
From an Old French name of Old German origin, from *nord*, 'north', and *berht*, 'bright'. It was borne by an 11th-century French saint, founder of the Norbertian order of monks. Diminutives: Bert, Bertie, Norrie.

Norman
Old English, itself derived from Old German *nord*, 'north', and *man*, 'man'. The name was already in use in Britain before the Norman Conquest, when it was reinforced and used to describe the invaders and their descendants, as it still is. Diminutive: Norm.

Norris
Adopted surname, itself originally derived from the Old French *norreis*, meaning 'northerner', derived from Old German *nord*, 'north'.

Norton
Adopted surname and English place name, from Old English *nord*, 'north', and *tun*, 'settlement'.

Nye
Diminutive of Aneurin.

O

Oakley
Old Anglo Saxon 'from the oak tree meadow'.

Oberon
Variation of Auberon. Oberon, king of the fairies, first appeared in a French romance, *Huon de Bordeaux*, as the son of Julius Caesar and Morgan le Fay. The name was more famously used by Shakespeare for the king of the fairies in *A Midsummer Night's Dream* (1595).

Octavius
Latin octavus 'eight' Given to the eighth child of large families.

Odysseus
Original Greek form of the hero of Homer's epic, the *Odyssey*. See also: Ulysses.

Oisín
(*osh-een*) Original Irish Gaelic form of Ossian.

Olaf
From the Old Norse name Anleifr, meaning 'relic of his ancestors'. It was borne by several Scandinavian kings, among them St Olaf, patron saint of Norway. Variations: Olav, Oliver.

Oliver
From the French name Olivier, of uncertain origin. It may be a variation of Olaf, or possibly from Old French *olivier*, 'olive tree', itself derived from Latin *oliva*, 'olive'. The name first appears in Old French romances, borne by the son of Regnier, duke of Genoa. A knight in the armies of Charlemagne, he was the devoted companion of Roland. Charlemagne's knights were generally of Frankish German origin and hence the name is probably an altered Germanic name. The name fell dramatically from favour after the death of Oliver Cromwell (1599-1658), but was restored in the 19th century, partly under the influence of Charles Dickens's novel *Oliver Twist* (1838). Diminutives: Noll, Ol, Ollie, Olly. Variations: Havelock, Olivier.

Olivier
French form of Oliver, occasionally used in its own right in the English-speaking world.

Omar
Variation of Umar, or from Hebrew, meaning 'eloquent'.

Onslow
An old Anglo Saxon name meaning 'hill of the zealous one'

Orlando
Italian form of Roland, used by Shakespeare in *As You Like It* (1600).

Orson
Old French *ourson*, meaning 'little bear'. In medieval legend it was borne by the twin brother of Valentine, the two being the sons of an exiled Byzantine princess. Orson was carried off by a bear as a baby, and reared by bears in the forest. It is rare in modern times, and any instance is likely to have been inspired by the American film director and actor Orson Welles (1915-85).

Orville
An 18th-century invention, coined by Fanny Burney for the hero of her novel *Evelina* (1778).

Osbert
From an Old English name, from *os*, 'god', and *beorht*, 'bright'. Popular during the Middle Ages, it underwent a revival in the 19th century along with many other pre-Conquest names. Diminutives: Oz, Ozzie, Ozzy.

Osborn, Osborne
From an Old English name, from *os*, 'god', and *beorn*, 'man'. Popular during the Middle Ages, it was one of the many pre-Conquest names that underwent a revival in the 19th century.

Oscar
Of disputed origin. Some claim it as Old Irish, from *os*, 'fawn', and *cara*, 'friend', others as Old English, from *os*, 'god', and *gar*, 'spear'. Whatever its true source, the name was used by the Scottish writer James Macpherson (1736-96) for the son of Ossian in his Ossian poems, which Macpherson claimed to have 'discovered' but almost certainly wrote himself.

Napoleon Bonaparte, a great admirer of Macpherson's work, gave the name to his godson, later King Oscar I of Sweden, which accounts for the name's popularity in Scandinavia. It fell into disuse after the infamous trial and imprisonment for homosexuality of the Irish poet and dramatist Oscar Wilde (1854-1900) but has recently undergone a revival. Diminutive: Os

Ossian
(*os-sian*, *osh-een*) Anglicised form of the Irish Gaelic name Oisín, meaning 'fawn'. Borne in Irish legend by the son of the national hero Finn mac Cumhaill (Finn McCool). Niamh fell in love with him and carried him off to the land of eternal youth. The name was revived by the Scottish writer James Macpherson (1736-96) in his Ossian poems. See also: Girls: Niamh.

Oswald
From an Old English name, from *os*, 'god', and *weald*, 'rule'. Borne by a 7th-century saint and king of Northumbria, after whom the Shropshire town of Oswestry is said to have been named, and by a 10th-century Archbishop of York. Popular during the Middle Ages, it underwent a moderate revival in the 19th century, with many other pre-Conquest names. Diminutives: Oz, Ozzie, Ozzy.

Otis
Adopted surname of medieval Germanic origin, at root a patronymic meaning 'son of Odo'. (See also: Otto). The name has been particularly popular in the US, initially in honour of the Revolutionary hero James Otis (1725-83).

Otto
Modification of a common element of Old German names, *od*, meaning 'prosperity'. Borne by four Holy Roman Emperors, including Otto the Great (912-73), who is generally regarded as the founder of the Holy Roman Empire. The name dropped from use in Britain after the Middle Ages, was briefly revived in honour of the German statesman Otto von Bismarck (1815-98), but faded from popularity following two World Wars.

Owen
Welsh, of uncertain origin. It may derive from the Welsh *oen*, 'lamb', or simply be a variation of Eugene, comparable to Ewan. Borne in Welsh legend by several important figures, the most notable being Owen Glyndwr, or Glendower (1359-1416), who fought Henry V of England. The name is hugely popular in Wales.

P

Pablo
Spanish form of Paul.

Paddy
Diminutive of Patrick.

Padgett
From French 'young attendant'.

Pádraig
Irish Gaelic form of Patrick.

Paolo
Italian form of Paul.

Parry
Welsh meaning 'son of Harry'.

Pascal
French, meaning 'pertaining to Easter',

from the ecclesiastical Latin (derived from Hebrew) *paschalis*, meaning 'pertaining to Passover'. Variation (Cornish): Pascoe.

Pascoe
Cornish variation of Pascal.

Pat
Diminutive of Patrick.

Patrick
Possibly from Latin *patricius*, meaning 'patrician', or 'of the ruling class'. St Patrick (c. 389-461) was a Briton, a Christian and a Roman citizen who travelled as a missionary to Ireland, landing at Wicklow in 432, and is credited with converting almost the entire country single-handedly. He is also supposed to have rid Ireland of vermin and snakes. He is the patron saint of Ireland and his feast day is 17th March.

Paul
From the Roman family name Paulus, originally from *paulus*, 'small'. It was given to Saul of Tarsus (acts 13:9), a Roman citizen, Jew and, until his conversion, persecutor of Christians. As St Paul he is considered co-founder, with St Peter, of the Christian church. Author of ten books of the Bible, he was martyred by beheading in Rome in AD 65.

Peadar
Irish Gaelic form of Peter.

Pearce
Variation of Pierce.

Pedro
Spanish form of Peter.

Pelham
From a British place name. Best known use was as the first name of the writer P.G.Woodhouse.

Perce
Diminutive of Perceval or Percy.

Perceval, Percival
From Old French *perce*, 'pierce', and *val*, 'valley'. First mentioned by the medieval poet Chrétien de Troyes in his 12th-century accounts of the Arthurian legend, Perceval was the son of Sir Pellinore and the only knight able to succeed in the search for the Holy Grail. The German version of the story provided the basis of Richard Wagner's opera *Parsifal* (1882).

Percy
Adopted aristocratic surname, borne by the Dukes of Northumberland. Origin is disputed; contenders are the Old French *perce*, 'pierce', and *haie*, 'hedge', or from a baronial name from Perci in Normandy. Another tale, no doubt untrue, tells how when Malcolm III of Scotland attacked the castle of Alnwick, Robert de Mowbray brought him the keys of the castle suspended on his lance. Offering them from the wall, he thrust his lance into the king's eye, and was thereafter known as 'Pierce-eye'. Use of the name spread beyond the Percy family in the 19th century.

Peregrine
From Latin *peregrinus*, meaning 'stranger' or 'traveller', and hence 'pilgrim'. It was borne by several early saints. Diminutive: Perry.

Perry
Diminutive of Peregrine.

Perse
Variation of Pierce.

Pete
Diminutive of Peter.

Peter
From Greek *petra*, 'rock', via *cephas*, Aramaic meaning 'a stone'. The name was given by Jesus to his apostle Simon: "Thou art Peter, and upon this rock I will build my church" (Matthew 16: 18). Peter is considered, with St Paul, co-founder of the Christian church. The first Bishop of Rome, and thus the first pope, he was crucified upside down in that city in AD 65. A fisherman by trade, Peter is considered the patron saint of fishermen, and his feast day is 29th June. The name fell out of favour in Protestant countries after the Reformation, but was revived by J M Barrie's play *Peter Pan* (1904).

Phelan
Gaelic origins suggesting 'brave as a wolf'.

Phil
Diminutive of Philip.

Philemon
From Greek, meaning 'kiss'. A biblical name; the eighteenth book of the New Testament is so named, after the recipient of one of St Paul's letters. According to Ovid's *Metamorphoses* (1st century AD), the name was also borne by a poor cottager who, with his wife, Baucis, entertained the disguised Jupiter and Mercury with such generosity that the gods transformed their house into a temple. When they died Philemon became an oak, Baucis a linden tree. It was popular with the Puritans in the 17th century.

Philip, Phillip
The Greek name Philipos means 'lover of horses', from *philein*, 'lover', and *hippos*, 'horses'. A biblical name; borne by one of Christ's apostles and several early saints. St Philip the Apostle's feast day is 1st May. The name fell out of favour in the 16th century, after England's conflict with King Philip II of Spain, but was later restored and remains in regular use throughout the English-speaking world today.

Phineas, Phinehas
From the Egyptian name Panhsj, meaning 'the Nubian'. A biblical name; borne by two characters, the grandson of Aaron (Numbers 25) and son of Eli (1 Samuel 1 and 4).

Piaras
Irish Gaelic form of Piers.

Pierce
Variation of Piers.

Pierre
Modern French form of Peter.

Piers
French medieval vernacular form of Peter, introduced to Britain in the Middle Ages. It was borne by the hero of *The Vision of Piers Plowman*, a long allegorical poem written in Middle English by William Langland (c. 1332-c. 1400). In the poem the character of Piers represents the honest and hard-working English labourer. The name underwent a revival in the mid-20th century.

Pilot Inspektor
The son of Scott Lee and Beth Riesgrat.

Pip
Diminutive of Philip.

Placido
Spanish, from *placidus*, meaning 'untroubled'. It has been popularised

throughout the world by the popular Spanish tenor, Placido Domingo.

Plantagenet
Commonly given to the English royal line from Henry II to Richard III. In truth only a byname, it derives from the family symbol of Henry II's father, a sprig of broom, or *planta genesta*. It is in only very occasional use as a first name, usually in the case of a distant family connection.

Porter
From French 'gatekeeper'.

Preston
Old English meaning 'priest's settlement'.

Prince
Probably a direct adoption of the British royal title, it is mainly popular in the US. See also: Duke, Earl.

Prince Jackson
Son of Michael Jackson (also sons Prince Michael and Prince Michael II).

Prospero
Borne in Shakespeare's last play, *The Tempest*, by the Duke of Milan, who becomes a magician when marooned on an island. He uses his magic to control the island and its inhabitants, and to bring the ship of his usurping brother Antonio to the island for a reconciliation. It is in occasional use as a first name in the English-speaking world.

Pryderi
(*prid-er-ee*) Welsh, meaning 'caring for'. Borne by a figure in the *Mabinogian*.

Q

Quentin
Old French form of the Latin name Quintius, from *quintus*, 'fifth'. It was the name of a 3rd-century saint and missionary to Gaul. It is occasionally also given to girls.

Quincey, Quincy
Adopted surname, originally a baronial name from Cuinchy in northern France. Use in the US is after a prominent New England family after which Quincy, Massachusetts is named. It is also used for girls.

Quinn
Adopted Irish surname, from the Gaelic name Ó Cuinn, meaning 'descendent of Conn'.

Quintin, Quinton
Adopted surname and place name, from Old English *cwen*, 'queen', and *tun*, 'settlement'. It was a Norman introduction to Britain.

Quintus
Roman name, meaning 'fifth'. It was often given to the fifth-born son, in the days of large families.

R

Rab, Rabbie
Scottish diminutives of Robert.

Rafael, Raphael
Hebrew, meaning 'God heals'. A biblical name; borne in the Apocrypha's Book of Tobit by the Archangel Raphael, who accompanied Tobias on

his travels to Media and back, and healed his eyesight. He is regarded as the patron of doctors and travellers. Confined mainly to Jewish families until the 16th century, the name then became more widely used but has never been common.

Rafe
Variant (phonetic) spelling of Ralph, reflecting the medieval pronunciation.

Raghnall
(*ran-nal*) Irish Gaelic, from the Old Norse name Rognvaldr, itself derived from *regin*, 'counsel', and *valdr*, 'ruler'. It is anglicised as Ranald.

Rainer
Variation of Rayner, from Old German *ragan*, 'counsel', and *harja*, 'army'. It was a Norman introduction to Britain.

Ralph
(*rafe*, *ralf*) From the Norman French name Raulf, itself from *rad*, 'counsel', and *wulf*, 'wolf'. The replacing of 'f' with 'ph' represents the classicising influence of the 18th century.

Rama
Indian, from Sanskrit, meaning 'pleasing'. Ramachandra was the seventh incarnation of Vishnu, whose wife Sita was abducted by the demon king of Ceylon, Ravana. After many trials Rama rescued her; the story is told in the *Ramayana*. The name was also borne by Parasurama, 'Rama of the axe', the sixth incarnation of Vishnu, and Balarama, 'the strong Rama', the eighth incarnation.

Ramon
Spanish form of Raymond, popular in the US.

Ramsay, Ramsey
Adopted Scottish surname, originally derived from the Huntingdonshire town of Ramsey; from Old English *hramsa*, 'wild garlic', and *eg*, 'island'. It was taken to Scotland in the 12th century by David, Earl of Huntingdon and Northampton, who succeeded his brother Alexander as king of Scotland.

Ran
Diminutive of Raghnall, Ranald, Randall, Randolf or Ranulf.

Ranald
Scottish, anglicised form of Raghnall.

Randall
Medieval form of Randolf. Variations: Randal, Randell, Randle. Diminutives: Ran, Randy.

Randolf
From the Old Norse name Rannulfr, from *rand*, 'shield', and *ulfr*, 'wolf'. Variation: Randolph. Diminutives: Ran, Randy.

Randy
Diminutive of Raghnall, Ranald, Randall, Randolf or Ranulf.

Ranulf
Scottish form of the Old Norse name Reginulfr, from *regin*, 'advice', 'decision', and *ulfr*, 'wolf'.

Raoul
French form of Ralph. This was a common form in medieval Britain.

Rasmus, Rastus
Variations of Erasmus, meaning 'beloved', from the Greek *eran*, 'to love'.

Raven
Vocabulary word, from Old English *hræfn*.

Ravi
Indian, from Sanskrit, meaning 'sun'. It was the name of the sun god.

Ray
Diminutive of Raymond, now used independently, associated with Old French *roi*, 'king'. See also: Elroy, Leroy, Roy.

Raymond
From the Old French name Raimund, from Old German *ragan*, 'counsel', and *mund*, 'protector'. It was a Norman introduction to Britain. Diminutive: Ray. Variations: Ramon, Raymund.

Rayner, Raynor
From Old German *ragan*, 'counsel', and *harja*, 'army'. It was a Norman introduction to Britain. Variation: Rainer.

Redmond
Irish, an anglicised form of Réamann. A variation of Raymond, it was a Norman introduction to Ireland.

Redvers
Adopted aristocratic surname, originally derived from Reviers in Normandy.

Rees
Anglicised form of Rhys. Variation: Reece.

Reg, Reggie
Diminutives of Reginald.

Reginald
Latin form (Reginaldus) of the Old English name Regenweald (Reynold), from *regen*, 'counsel', and *weald*, 'power'. It was a 15th-century introduction. Diminutives: Reg, Reggie, Rex. Related: Ranald, Reynold, Ronald.

René
French, meaning 'reborn', ultimately from Latin *renatus*.

Reuben, Ruben
Hebrew, meaning 'behold, a son'. A biblical name; borne by the eldest son of Jacob.

Rex
Latin, meaning 'king'. A late 19th century introduction. It is also considered a diminutive of Reginald.

Reynard
From Old German *ragan*, 'counsel', and *hardu*, 'hard'. It was a Norman introduction to Britain.

Reynold
From the Old French name Reinald, of Frankish German origin, from *ragin*, 'counsel', and *wald*, 'ruler'. It was a Norman introduction to Britain.

Rhett
Adopted surname, the anglicised form of the Dutch name de Raedt, taken to the US by William Rhett (1666-1723). It was famously used by Margaret Mitchell for the hero of her 1936 novel *Gone With the Wind*.

Rhodri, Rhodrhi
Welsh, from *rhod*, 'wheel, circle', and *rhi*, 'ruler'. The name was given to a 9th-century king of Wales.

Rhydian
Early Welsh saint.

Rhys
Welsh, meaning 'ardour'. Borne by two medieval Welsh lords, Rhys ap Tewdur (d 1093) and Rhys ap Gruffudd (1132-97). The Welsh surname Price derives from a contraction of the patronymic 'ap Rhys'.

Rian
Irish Gaelic, probably derived from *ri*, 'king', and meaning 'little king'. Variation: Ryan.

Ricardo
Spanish form of Richard.

Rich, Richie
Diminutives of Richard.

Richard
From an Old German name Ricohard, from *ric*, 'ruler', and *hardu*, 'hard'. Diminutives: Dick, Dickie, Dickon, Dicky, Rich, Richie, Rick, Ricky.

Rick, Ricky
Diminutives of Richard.

Ridley
Adopted surname and place name, from Old English elements *hreod*, 'reeds', and *leah*, 'wood, clearing'.

River
One of several vocabulary words adopted under the hippy influence of the 1960s.

River Jude
A son of Demi Moore and Bruce Willis.

Roald
Scandinavian, meaning 'famed power'.

Rob, Robbie, Robby
Diminutives of Robert.

Robert
From the Old German name Hrodebert, from *hrod*, 'fame', and *berht*, 'bright'. A Norman introduction, it was popularised particularly in Scotland by Robert the Bruce (1274-1329). Diminutives: Bob, Bobbie, Bobby, Hob, Rab, Rabbie, Rob, Robbie, Robby. Variation: Robin. Related: Rupert.

Robin
Originally a diminutive of Robert, it has long been used in its own right.

Rocco
A son of Madonna and Guy Ritchie.

Rod
Diminutive of Roderick or Rodney.

Roderick
From Old German *hrod*, 'fame', and *ric*, 'power'. In the form Rodrigo it was borne by the last of the Visigoth kings, a Spanish hero, who was probably killed by the Moors c. 711. After raping Florinda of Ceuta, he spent the rest of his life in repentance. First introduced to Britain by Norman invaders, the name died out but was later reintroduced by Sir Walter Scott in his poem *The Vision of Don Roderigo* (1811). Diminutives: Rod, Roddy.

Rodge, Rog
Diminutives of Rodger or Roger.

Rodger
Variation of Roger.

Rodney
Adopted surname and place name. It was adopted in honour of Admiral Lord Rodney (1719-92), who led the defeat of the French navy in 1759. Diminutives: Rod, Roddy.

Rodrigo
Spanish form of Roderick.

Roger
From the Old French name Rogier, derived from Old German *hrod*, 'fame', and *gar*, 'spear'. The name was a Norman introduction to Britain. Diminutives: Rodge, Rog.

Rolan
Name for son of Gloria Jones and Marc Bolan.

Roland
Old French, of Old German origin, from *hrod*, 'fame', and *land*, 'land'. Borne by the most famous of Charlemagne's soldiers, who died c. 778. The son of Duke Milo of Aigland and his wife Bertha (Charlemagne's sister) Roland is also known as the Christian Theseus and the Achilles of the West. His story is told in the 12th-century French epic poem, *Chanson de Roland*. The name is anglicised as Rowland. It was adopted and introduced by the Normans. Variation: Orlando. Diminutive: Roly.

Rolf, Rolph
From the Old German name Hrodulf, derived from *hrod*, 'fame', and *wulf*, 'wolf'. A Norman introduction, the name has been reinforced in modern times by its popularity in northern Europe.

Rollo
Latinised form of Roul, an Old French version of Rolf. Borne by a Norman pirate (c. 860-932), an ancester of William the Conqueror, who became a vassal of Charles III of France.

Roly
Diminutive of Roland or Rowley.

Roman
Anglicised form of Romeo, in that its literal meaning is 'a citizen of Rome'.

Romeo
Italian, meaning 'a citizen of Rome'. Although common in Italy (where it is pronounced Rom-ay-oh, rather then the crude anglicised pronunciation Roam-ee-oh), it is rare in the English-speaking world, despite Shakespeare's Romeo and Juliet (1595). Romeo has been used as the name for one of the sons of David and Victoria Beckham.

Ron, Ronnie
Diminutives of Ronald.

Ronald
From Rognvaldr, the Old Norse form of Reginald. It was revived in the late 19th century. Diminutives: Ron, Ronnie. Variations: Ranald, Reynald. Related: Reginald.

Ronan
Irish, from the Gaelic name Rónán, originally a diminutive of *rón*, 'seal'.

Rory
Anglicised form of the Irish Gaelic names Ruaidhri, Ruari, and the Scottish Gaelic Ruairidh and Ruaraidh.

Roscoe
Adopted surname and place name, derived from *rá*, 'roe deer', and *skógr*, 'wood'.

Roshan
Muslim, from Persian, meaning 'shining' or 'splendid', although it also corresponds to an Urdu word meaning 'famous'.

Ross
Adopted surname and place name, originally derived from Scottish Gaelic ros, 'headland'.

Rowan
Adopted Irish surname, the anglicised form of the Gaelic name Ruadhan, meaning 'little red-haired one'. Borne by a 6th-century Irish saint who founded a monastery at Lothra.

Rowland
Anglicised form of Roland.

Roy
From Scottish Gaelic *ruadh*, 'red', later influenced by Old French *roi*, 'king'.

Ruaidhri, Ruari, Ruairidh, Ruaraidh
From Scottish Gaelic *ruadh*, 'red', meaning 'red-haired'. Ruaidhri and Ruari are Irish Gaelic, Ruairidh and Ruaraidh Scottish Gaelic.

Ruben
Variation of Reuben.

Rudi, Rudy
Diminutives of Rudolf or Rudolph.

Rudolf, Rudolph
From Rudolphus, the Latinate form of Hrodwulf, from *hrod*, 'fame', and *wulf*, 'wolf' (see Rolf). A family name of the Hapsburgs, Holy Roman Emperors and rulers of Austria-Hungary, it was popularised by Anthony Hope in his 1894 novel *The Prisoner of Zenda*. Diminutives: Rudi, Rudy.

Rufus
Latinate byname, meaning 'red-haired'. The epithet was attached to William II of England (c. 1056-1100), Otto II of German (955-83) and Gilbert de Clare, Earl of Gloucester (1243-95). It began to be used as a first name in the 19th century and is now fairly popular.

Rupert
From Rupprecht, a Low German form of Robert. It was popularised in Britain by Prince Rupert of the Rhine (1618-92), nephew of Charles I. In modern times it has become associated with a cartoon bear who first appeared in the *Daily Express* in 1920.

Russ
Diminutive of Russell, sometimes used in its own right.

Russell
Adopted surname from Old French *roux*, 'red', first used in the late 19th century. Diminutive: Russ.

Rusty
Originally a nickname for someone with red hair.

Ryan
From the Irish Gaelic surname O'Riain, meaning 'a descendant of Rian', Rian being the archaic form of the name. It is a mid-20th century adoption, especially popular in the US.

S

Sacheverell

(*sash-ev-er-al*) Adopted surname, of uncertain origin, possibly a French place name. Never common, it was brought to public attention in the early 20th century by the writer Sacheverell Sitwell (1897-1985), who was probably named in honour of Henry Sacheverell, an 18th-century politician.

Sage Moon Blood
Name for son of Sylvester Stallone.

Salvador
Spanish, derived from Latin *salvator*, 'saviour'. See also: Salvatore.

Salvatore
Italian, from Latin *salvator*, 'saviour'. See also: Salvador.

Sam, Sammie, Sammy
Diminutives of Samson or Samuel.

Sampson
A variation of Samson, probably an adopted surname derived from the original Hebrew form.

Samson
From the Hebrew name Shimshon, from *shemesh*, 'sun', and meaning 'sun child'. A biblical name; borne in the Old Testament by the leader of the Israelites who used his extraordinary strength in the fight against the Philistines (Judges 13-16). Samson's mistress, Delilah, betrayed him by cutting off his hair, source of his strength, as he slept. The name was later borne by a 6th-century Welsh bishop and saint. Diminutives: Sam, Sammie, Sammy. Variation: Sampson.

Samuel
From the Hebrew name Shemuel, meaning 'God has heard'. A biblical name; borne in the Old Testament by the last of the judges of Israel and the prophet second only to Moses, who was brought up in the temple by Eli and went on to choose and anoint Saul and David as the first two kings of Israel (1 and 2 Samuel). A Puritan revival, it remained popular throughout the 17th, 18th and 19th centuries. It has recently undergone a resurgence, its diminutive, Sam, becoming one of the most popular boy's names in the English-speaking world. Diminutives: Sam, Sammie, Sammy.

Sandy
Diminutive of Alexander often used in its own right.

Sasha
Russian diminutive of Alexander. It is also used for girls, as a diminutive of Alexandra. Variation: Sacha.

Saul
Hebrew, meaning 'asked for' or 'prayed for'. A biblical name; borne in the Old Testament by the first king of Israel, the father-in-law of David (1 Samuel 9-31), and in the New Testament by Saul of Tarsus, a Pharisee who was converted to Christianity while on the road to Damascus, whereupon he changed his name to Paul (Acts 9). A Puritan adoption of the 17th century, in modern times the name is largely regarded as a Jewish name.

Scott
Adopted Scottish surname, meaning 'Scottish', in regular use since the early 20th century when it was popularised by the American writer F Scott Fitzgerald (1896-1940).

Seamas, Seamus
(*shay-mus*) Modern forms of the Irish Gaelic name Seumas, the Irish form of James.

Sean
(*shawn*) Irish form of John, derived from the French form, Jean. Shaun and Shawn are variations that reflect the name's pronunciation. Variation: Shane.

Seb
Diminutive of Sebastian.

Sebastian
From the Latin name Sebastianus, meaning 'man of Sebastia', a town in Asia Minor, itself derived from Greek *sebastos*, 'venerable'. Borne by an early Roman soldier who converted to Christianity, and whose fellow officers attempted to kill him with arrows. He became a hugely popular subject with Renaissance artists, and was generally depicted pierced by many arrows. However, it seems that he in fact survived the arrows, only to be beaten to death later by his assailants. The name fell from favour after the Middle Ages except in Spain and France, where it was shortened to Bastien, but was revived in the early 20th century. Evelyn Waugh used the name for the aristocratic Lord Sebastian Flyte in his novel *Brideshead Revisited* (1945). Diminutives: Bastian, Bastien, Seb.

Selwin
Variation of Selwyn.

Selwyn
Adopted surname, of disputed origin. It may be derived from the medieval name Selewyn, from Old English *sele*, 'house' or 'hall', and *wine*, 'friend', or from the Latin name Silvanus, from *silva*, 'wood'. It may also be Welsh, from elements meaning 'ardour' and 'fair'. Its adoption as a first name in the mid-19th century was probably in honour of George Selwyn (1809-78), bishop of New Zealand. Selwyn College, Cambridge, was founded by Selwyn's son, John, in memory of his father, in 1881. Variation: Selwin.

Septimus
From Latin *septimus*, meaning 'seventh'. In the past it was generally given to a seventh child, or seventh son, a rare occurrence today.

Serge
French form of Sergius.

Sergei
Russian form of Sergius.

Sergio
Italian form of Sergius.

Sergius
Latin, of uncertain origin. Borne by four popes, including St Sergius (d 701) who made several liturgical innovations and whose feast day is 8th September. It was also borne by a medieval Russian abbot and saint (1314-92) who was influential in Russian history. His feast day is 25th September. The name is now probably obsolete, but survives in its French, Russian and Italian forms. Variations: Serge, Sergei, Sergio.

Seth
Hebrew, meaning 'appointed'. A biblical name; borne in the Old Testament by the third son of Adam, born after the death of Abel and considered by Eve as a replacement for her dead son. It was popular with the Puritans of the 17th century, who took the name to America,

where it remains in greater use than in Britain.

Seumas
Original Irish Gaelic form of James.

Seward
Anglo Saxon meaning 'guard of the sea'.

Sextus
From Latin *sextus*, meaning 'sixth'. In the past it was generally given to a sixth child, or sixth son, an unusual occurrence today.

Seymour
Adopted aristocratic surname and French place name, from St Maur in France. St Maur is the French form of St Maurice, derived from the Latin name Mauricius, meaning 'Moorish'. The name has been in occasional use as a first name since the mid-19th century.

Shamus
Alternative modern spelling of the Irish Gaelic name Seamus, reflecting the name's pronunciation.

Shane
(*shayn, shawn*) A variation of Sean, popularised throughout the world in its own right by the classic western *Shane* (1953), which established *shayn* as the standard pronunciation. The name is especially popular in Australia.

Shannon
Adopted Irish surname, derived from Ireland's principal river, itself from Irish Gaelic meaning 'old'. It is also used for girls.

Shaw
Adopted surname, from Old English *sceaga*, meaning 'copse' or 'wood'. The name has been in occasional use as a first name since the mid-19th century.

Shawn
Anglicised form of the Irish Gaelic name Sean, representing the pronunciation of the name.

Sheldon
Adopted surname, derived from various English place names of differing origins, including 'flat-topped hill' or 'steep-sided valley'.

Shem
Hebrew, meaning 'renown'. A biblical name; borne by one of the sons of Noah, the traditional ancestor of the Hebrews. The modern terms Semite and Semitic both derive from his name. Use has largely been confined to Jewish families, but is occasionally found in English-speaking countries.

Sheridan
Adopted Irish surname, from O Sirideáin, meaning 'descendent of Sirideáin'. Widely popularised by the Irish playwright Richard Brinsley Sheridan (1751-1816), the name is increasingly used for girls, particularly in the US.

Shiva, Siva
Indian, from Sansrit, meaning 'benign' or 'auspicious'. Shiva is one of the most important of the Hindu gods, associated in particular with asceticism, reproductive power and cosmic destruction. His wife, Durga, is the Hindu goddess of death and destruction.

Sholto
From the Scottish Gaelic name Sìoltach, meaning 'sower'.

Sid, Syd
Diminutives of Sidney and Sydney respectively.

Sidney, Sydney
Adopted surname and place name, of disputed origin. It may be derived from Old English *sidan*, 'wide', and *eg*, 'island', meaning 'wide island', or from Saint-Denis in France. The name has been used as a first name since the 17th century, possibly in honour of the British politician Algernon Sidney, and was boosted in popularity when Charles Dickens used the name for the hero of *A Tale Of Two Cities* (1859). The variation Sydney first appeared in the 19th century, probably in honour of Thomas Townshend, Viscount Sydney, after whom the Australian city of Sydney is named. Diminutives: Sid, Syd.

Siegfried
German, from Old German *sig*, 'victory, and *frid*, 'peace'. Borne by the hero of the *Nibelungenlied*, from which Richard Wagner's derived the material for his operas *Siegfried* and *Götterdämerung* (1876).

Sigismund
Variation of Sigmund.

Sigmund
German, from Old German *sig*, 'victory', and *mund*, 'protection'. It has been in occasional use in the English-speaking world since Richard Wagner used it for Siegfried's father in his operas *Siegfried* and *Götterdämerung* (1876). The name was further popularised by the Austrian-born father of psychoanalysis, Sigmund Freud (1856-1939).

Silas
New Testament Greek form of the Latin name Silvanus, from *silva*, 'wood'. A biblical name; borne in the New Testament by a companion of St Paul. A Puritan adoption, it has never been common, despite its use in George Eliot's novel *Silas Marner* (1861).

Silvanus, Sylvanus
Latin, the name of the Roman god of trees and forests, derived from *silva*, 'wood'. Also biblical; borne in the New Testament by a companion of St Paul who is generally referred to as Silas, the New Testament Greek form of the name.

Silvester, Sylvester
From Latin, meaning 'of the woods' or 'in the woods'. Borne by an early Christian martyr and three popes, one of whom is traditionally believed to have baptised Emperor Constantine.

Sim
Medieval diminutive of Simon, and more recently of Simeon.

Simeon
Hebrew, probably meaning 'listening'. A biblical name; borne in the Old Testament by a son of Jacob and Leah and hence a founder of one of the twelve tribes of Israel. It was also borne in the New Testament by an aged man who recognised the infant Christ as the Messiah and then felt ready to die (Luke 2: 25-35. His words 'Lord, now lettest thou thy servant depart in peace, according to thy word' form the Nunc Dimittis, part of the Christian evensong service. His feast day is 18th February. Diminutive: Sim.

Simon
Variation of Simeon. A biblical name; borne in the New Testament by several characters, including Simon Peter and

Simon the Zealot (two of Christ's twelve apostles), a half-brother of Jesus and a man who carried Jesus' cross to the Crucifixion. It was also borne by Simon Magus, a sorcerer who offered the apostles money in return for their powers, giving rise to the term simony. The name has remained consistently popular since the Middle Ages. Diminutives: Si, Sim.

Sinclair
Adopted Scottish surname, probably derived from a French baronial name and place name, Saint Clair. The name has been in occasional use as a first name since the mid-19th century.

Skip
Scandanavian form of skipper 'shipmaster'.

Sky
A 20th-century coinage, ostensibly from the vocabulary word and probably reflecting the hippy trend in the 1960s for taking names from nature. (See also: Leaf, River.) However, the name had been used before; Sky Masterson was a character in the hugely successful film *Guys and Dolls*.

Solomon
From the Hebrew name Shlomo, itself derived from *shalom*, 'peace'. A biblical name; borne in the Old Testament by a king of Israel, the son of David and Bathsheba, who was noted for his wisdom and justice. Solomon was a popular medieval name, and it underwent a revival in the 17th century. Use in modern times is only occasional.

Spencer, Spenser
Adopted aristocratic surname, originally an occupational name for a steward or butler, derived from an Old English word, meaning 'to dispense'. The name has been associated with the Churchill family, Dukes of Marlborough, since the 18th century. It entered more general use in the 19th century, and modern use is probably influenced by the American actor Spencer Tracy (1900-67).

Spike
Originally a nickname, probably for someone with a spike of hair, it is now occasionally used in its own right, partly influenced by the veteran poet, comedian and ex-Goon, Spike Milligan (π1918-2002).

St John
(*sin-jen*) Adopted surname and French place name, Saint Jean. The name has been in occasional use as a first name since the late 19th century.

Stafford
Adopted aristocratic surname and English place name, from Old English *staeo*, 'landing stage', and *ford*, 'ford', and meaning 'ford by a landing stage'. The name has been in occasional use as a first name since the mid-19th century.

Stan
Diminutive of Stanley.

Stanford
Adopted surname and English place name, from Old English *stan*, 'stoney', and *ford*, 'ford'.

Stanislaus
Latin form of the Slavic name Stanislav, probably meaning 'to be glorious'. St Stanislaus of Cracow was an 11th century Polish bishop and martyr. The name has been used occasionally in the English-speaking world.

Stanley
Adopted surname and place name, from Old English *stan*, 'stoney', and *leah*, 'wood' or 'clearing'. The name has been in occasional use as a first name since the late 19th century, when it was probably first used in honour of Sir Henry Morton Stanley (1841-1904), the journalist and explorer who went in search of Dr Livingstone in 1869. Diminutive: Stan.

Stephen, Steven
From Greek *stephanos*, meaning 'crown'. St Stephen, the first person to be martyred for his Christian faith, was accused of blasphemy and stoned to death by the Jews (Acts 6-8). His feast day is 26th December. The name was also borne by several other saints and ten popes. A Norman introduction to Britain, it was popular in the Middle Ages in the form Steven. This was gradually replaced with Stephen, until the revival of Steven in the 20th century. Diminutives: Steve, Stevie.

Steve, Stevie
Diminutives of Stephen and Steven.

Stew
Diminutive of Stewart.

Stewart
Adopted Scottish surname, from Old English *stigweard*, 'steward'. Stewart was the family name of the royal house of Scotland from 1371 to 1714, and of England from 1603. The original spelling Stewart was replaced by the French-influenced spelling Stuart during the reign of Mary Queen of Scots, who had been brought up in France. Diminutives: Stew, Stu. Variation: Stuart.

Stirling
Adopted surname and Scottish place name, of uncertain origin. It may be from Old Welsh *ystre Velyn*, meaning 'the dwelling-place of Melyn'.

Stu
Diminutive of Stuart.

Stuart
French form of Stewart, introduced by Mary Queen of Scots. Diminutives: Stew, Stu. Variation: Stewart.

Sullivan
Irish 'black-eyed.

Swithin
From Old English, meaning 'strong'. Borne by a 9th-century bishop of Winchester and adviser of Egbert of Wessex. When he died, his funeral was delayed by rain for forty days, which led to the superstition that if it rains on St Swithin's Day (15th July) it will rain for forty days thereafter.

Syd
Diminutive of Sydney. Variation: Sid.

T

Tad
Diminutive of Tadhg or Thaddeus, now used in its own right.

Tadhg
(*teeg*) Irish Gaelic, meaning 'poet'. Variations: Tadg, Teague, Teigue (the latter two anglicised). It has been largely replaced in Ireland by Timothy.

Talfryn
Welsh, meaning 'high hill'. A modern coinage.

Taliesin
(*tal-yes-in*) Welsh, from *tâl*, 'brow', and *iesin*, 'shining'. Borne by a 6th-century Welsh poet.

Tam
Scottish diminutive of Thomas.

Tancred
From Old German *thancharat*, from *thanc*, 'think', and *radi*, 'counsel'. Boccaccio's *Decameron* (1349) includes the story of Tancred, prince of Salerno, who killed the lover of his daughter Sigismonda, cut out his heart and sent it to her, whereupon she killed herself. The story appears in other guises, including Robert Wilmot's play *Tancred and Gismund* (1591). The name was also borne by Tancred (d 1112), son of Otho the Good and Emma Guiscard, and one of the heroes of the First Crusade. He appears as one of the leading characters in the Italian Torquato Tasso's epic poem *Jerusalem Delivered* (1581), and provided the inspiration for both Rossini's opera *Tancredi* (1813) and Disraeli's novel *Tancred*. A Norman introduction to Britain, it remains in occasional use today.

Tara
Indian, from Sanskrit, meaning 'carrying', 'saviour' or 'shining'.

Tarquin
Of uncertain origin, probably Etruscan. It was the family name of a legendary line of early Roman kings including Tarquinius Superbus 'the Proud' (534-510 BC), seventh king of Rome, and his son Tarquinius Sextus, whose rape of Lucretia disgraced the family and resulted in their banishment from Rome.

Teague, Teigue
Anglicised forms of Tadhg.

Ted, Teddie, Teddy
Originally diminutives of Theodore, they are now more often regarded and used as diminutives of Edward.

Tel
Diminutive of Terry.

Terence, Terrence
Latin, from the Roman family name Terentius; or an anglicised form of an Irish Gaelic name meaning 'one who initiates an idea'. Diminutives: Tel, Terry (Terence is sometimes used as an expanded form of Terry, although Terry is in fact from a different root).

Terry
From an Old French form of the Germanic name Theodoric. A Norman import, it is today more often used as a diminutive of Terence. Diminutive: Tel.

Tertius
Latin, meaning 'third'. It has traditionally been given to a third-born son.

Tex
Shortened form of the US state, Texas, now adopted as a first name, although largely confined to the US.

Thaddeus
Latin form of Jude or Judas. In the New Testament Thaddeus was an apostle also known as Judas, brother of James, who as St Jude is the patron saint of lost causes. Its origin is uncertain. Diminutive: Thad.

Theo
Diminutive of Theobald or Theodore, now often used in its own right.

Theobald
Old French, of Germanic origin, from

peud, 'race', and *bald*, 'bold'. The first element was later influenced by *theos*, the Greek word for 'god'). Diminutive: Theo. Variation: Tybalt.

Theodore
Greek, from *theos*, 'god', and *doron*, 'gift'. Its popularity was boosted after a stuffed toy bear was named Teddy in honour of the US president Theodore Roosevelt (1858-1919). Diminutives: Ted, Teddie, Teddy, Theo.

Theodoric
Old German, meaning 'leader of the people', from *theuda*, 'race, people', and *ric*, 'ruler'. The name was borne by a king of the Ostrogoths (c. 454-526) who invaded Italy. He appears in the *Nibelungenlied*, source of Richard Wagner's *Ring* cycle. Diminutives (most common modern use): Derek, Derrick, Theo.

Thomas
Biblical, of Aramaic origin; the apostle Thomas (sometimes called Doubting Thomas) was originally Didymus, a Greek name meaning 'twin'. The Apocrypha's Acts of Thomas tells of the apostle's missionary work in India. His feast day is 3rd July. St Thomas Aquinas (c. 1225-74) was a Dominican scholar of outstanding intellectual distinction who became the fifth Doctor of the Church. His feast day is 28th January. Thomas has become one of the most popular names for boys in Britain. Variations: Tomas (Scottish), Tomás (Irish). Diminutives: Tom, Tommie, Tommy, Tam (Scottish).

Thorley
Old English meaning 'thorn wood'.

Thurston
Old Norse meaning 'Thor's stone'. Variation: Thurstan.

Tierney
Adopted surname, from the Irish Gaelic name Ó Tíghearnaigh, meaning 'descendent of Tíghearnach'. It is popular in the US as a girl's name.

Timothy
Biblical; from the Greek name Timotheos, from *time*, 'honour', and *theos*, 'god', meaning 'honouring God'. Diminutives: Tim, Timmie, Timmy.

Titus
Roman, of uncertain origin, though possibly Etruscan. The Roman emperor Titus destroyed the temple at Jerusalem in AD 70.

Tobias
Biblical; the Greek form of the Hebrew name Tobiah, meaning 'God is good'. In a popular story from the Old Testament Apocrypha's Book of Tobit, Tobias was accompanied on a journey to Ecbatana by the Archangel Raphael, from which he returned prosperous.

Toby
English vernacular form of Tobias. Variation: Thoby.

Todd
Adopted surname, from the English dialect word for a fox. The name was probably first used to indicate colouring, or cunning.

Tom, Tommie, Tommy
Diminutives of Thomas.

Tony
Diminutive of Anthony.

Torcal, Torcul
Variations of Torquil.

Torquil
Scottish Gaelic, from *porketil, por* being a contraction of Thor (the Norse god of thunder) and *ketil*, meaning 'kettle' or 'cauldron'. Thor's cauldron was a sacrificial instrument. It was a Viking introduction.

Traherne
Traherne Anglicized form of Welsh Trahaearn 'greatly akin to iron'.

Travers, Travis
Adopted surname; from Old French *travers*, meaning 'crossing'.

Trefor, Trevor
Adopted Welsh surname; Trefor is a frequently occurring Welsh place name, from *tre*, 'settlement, homestead', and *fôr*, 'large'. Diminutive: Trev.

Trelawney
Cornish adaptation of the town name

Tremain(e)
Adopted Cornish surname, from *tre*, 'homestead', and *men*, 'stone'.

Tristan, Trystan
Celtic, from the name Drostan, meaning 'din', but subsequently (and erroneously) influenced by Old French *triste* - from Latin *tristis* - meaning sad. Tristan was a hero of Celtic legend and medieval romance, the tragic lover of the Irish princess Isolde.

Tristram, Trystram
Variations of Tristan and Trystan respectively.

Troy
Adopted surname, derived from Troyes in Frances. It is now associated with the ancient city in Asia Minor, and is also used for girls.

Truman
Adopted surname, from Old English *treowe*, 'true', and *mann*, 'man', mainly found in the US.

Tudur
Old Welsh, related to the Germanic name Theodoric (not Theodore, as is commonly believed). Variations: Tudor (anglicised), Tudyr.

Tybalt
Medieval English form of Theobald.

Tyler
Adopted surname, itself occupational, from Old English *tigele*, 'tile'. It is encountered particularly in the US.

Tyrone
Adopted surname, itself after the Northern Ireland county. It is popular in Northern Ireland and the US. Diminutive: Ty.

U

Ulick
Anglicised form of the Irish Gaelic name Uilleac, or Uilleag, from Old Norse *hugr*, 'heart', 'mind' or 'spirit', and *leikr*, 'game'. It is also used as a diminutive of Uillean, a Gaelic form of William.

Ulric
From the Old English name Ulfric, from *wulf*, 'wolf', and *ric*, 'ruler'. St Ulric was a 10th-century bishop of Augsburg. The name more or less died out in Britain after the Middle Ages but remained consistently popular in Germany, from where it was reintroduced to Britain in the mid-20th century. Variation: Ulrich.

Ulysses
Latin form of the Greek name Odysseus, of uncertain origin. Ulysses was the hero of Homer's epic *Odyssey*. Modern use is possibly associated with James Joyce's mammoth work, *Ulysses* (1922), or as a classicised form of Ulick.

Umar
Arabic, meaning 'flourishing'. Borne by the lifelong companion of the Prophet Muhammad.

Umberto
Italian, of Old German origin, from *hun*, 'warrior', and *berht*, 'bright', and hence a form of Humbert.

Upton
Adopted surname and place name, from Old English *up*, 'higher', and *tun*, 'settlement'.

Urban
From Latin *urbanus*, meaning 'citizen'. A biblical name; borne by a character in the New Testament, and by seven popes.

Uri
From Hebrew 'light'.

Uriah
Like Uriel, derived from Hebrew *uri*, 'light', and *el*, 'god'. A biblical name; borne in the Old Testament by the husband of Bathsheba who was sent to certain death in battle by David, in order that he might marry Bathsheba (2 Samuel 11).

Uriel
Hebrew, from *uri*, 'light', and *el*, 'god'. A biblical name; borne in the Apocrypha by one of the seven archangels. The name also occurs twice in biblical genealogies.

Urien
Welsh, after Urien of Rheged, a character in the *Mabinogian*. It is possibly an Old Welsh form of the Latin *urbigenus*, 'born in a town', effectively the same root as Urban.

V

Vail
Anglo Saxon 'from the valley'.

Val
Diminutive of Perceval or Valentine.

Valentine
From Latin *valens*, meaning 'strong' or 'healthy'. Borne by a 3rd-century Roman priest and martyr. The pagan associations are incidental; St Valentine was martyred on 14th February, the day before an established pagan festival of fertility associated with Juno, wife of Jupiter. It is occasionally used for girls.

Valmai
A 20th-century Australian coinage, probably a modification of Val, although some claim that it has Welsh roots.

Van
Diminutive of Ewan and Ivan, sometimes used in its own right, as in the case of the Irish singer Van Morrison (b 1945).

Vaughan
Adopted Welsh surname, from *fychan*, meaning 'small'. Variation: Vaughn.

Vere
Adopted surname and French baronial name, derived from Old French *vern*, 'alder', and probably meaning 'alder grove'. See also: Vernon.

Vergil
Variation of Virgil.

Vernon
Adopted surname and French baronial name, derived from Old French *vern*, 'alder', and probably meaning 'alder grove'. Richard de Vernon came to Britain with William the Conqueror in 1066. It was adopted as a first name in the 19th century, since when it has become widespread throughout the English-speaking world. See also: Vere.

Vic
Diminutive of Victor.

Victor
From Latin, meaning 'conqueror', and taken as a reference to Christ's victory over death. Borne by two saints; one was pope from 189-198, the other a 6th-century bishop of Capua. Their feast days are celebrated on 28th July and 17th October, respectively.

Vikram
Indian name, from Sanskrit, meaning 'stride' or 'pace'. A byname of Vishnu, it probably derived from an early myth in which he strides around the world in just three steps.

Vin, Vinnie, Vinny
Diminutives of Vincent.

Vince
Diminutive of Vincent.

Vincent
Old French form of Latin *vincens*, meaning 'conquering'. Borne by several early saints, among them the 5th-century St Vincent of Lérins, France; the 4th-century Spanish martyr St Vincent of Saragossa; and the 17th-century St Vincent de Paul. Popular during the Middle Ages, it was revived in the 19th century and remains in regular use

throughout the English-speaking world. Diminutives: Vin, Vince, Vinnie, Vinny.

Virgil
Anglicised form of the name of the Roman poet Publius Vergilius Maro (c. 79-19 BC), associated with the Latin *virgo*, 'virgin'. Regarded as the greatest poet of ancient Rome, he was reponsible for the *Aeneid*, the *Eclogues* and the *Georgics*. From early on he was considered to have had magic powers and many medieval romances and poems tell of his magical exploits. As a first name it is particularly popular in the US. Variation: Vergil.

Vishnu
Indian, from Sanskrit, meaning 'he who works everywhere'. Borne by the secondary god in the *Rig-Veda*, although he is regarded by many Hindus as the supreme god. The personificaion of the sun, he is reputed to have been reincarnated ten times, of which only Rama and Krishna are fully recognised. He is depicted with four arms holding a mace, a disc, a lotus and a conch-shell, and often riding the eagle Garuda. His wife is Lakshmi.

Vitus
Borne by a Sicilian-born Christian martyr, killed under Diocletian in c. 303. He is regarded as the patron saint of dancers, and is invoked against sudden death and a convulsive disorder, chorea, which has come to be alternatively known as St Vitus's dance. His feast day is 15th June. Guy is the French form of the name. See also: Guy.

Viv
Diminutive of Vivian, Vivien, Vivyan or Vyvyan.

Vivian
Old French form of the Latin name Vivianus, from *vivus*, 'alive', and meaning 'lively'. Variations: Vivien (now more commonly used for girls), Vivyan, Vyvyan. Diminutives: Vi, Viv, Vivi.

Vivyan, Vyvyan
Modern variations of Vivian.

W

Waldo
Derived from a Latinised form of Old German *wald*, meaning 'to rule'.

Wallace
Adopted surname, originally from Old German *waleis*, meaning 'foreign', and used by the Norman conquerors to describe Britain's Celts, most notably in Wales. Use as a first name probably began in honour of the Scottish hero William Wallace (executed 1305). Variation: Wallis.

Wally
Diminutive of Wallace or Walter.

Walter
From Old German *wald*, 'power', and *harja*, 'people'. It was introduced to Britain by the Normans. Diminutives: Wal, Wally, Walt, Wat.

Ward
Adopted surname, from the Old English word for 'guardian'.

Warner
Adopted surname, from Old German *warin*, 'guard', and *harja*, 'people'. Variation: Warren.

Warren
From Old German *warin*, meaning 'to guard'. It was a Norman introduction to Britain. Variation: Warner.

Warwick
Adopted surname and Old English place name in the English Midlands.

Washington
Adopted surname of the first president of the US, George Washington (1732-99). It was originally derived from the Old English name Wassingtun, meaning 'place of Wassa's people'.

Wasim
Arabic, meaning 'handsome'.

Wat
Medieval English diminutive of Walter.

Wayne
Adopted surname, originally given to cart makers or drivers (from Old English *waegen*, meaning 'cart'). It was popularised by the American actor John Wayne (1907-82), whose true name was in fact Marion Michael Morrison.

Webster
Adopted surname, derived from Old English *webbestre*, meaning 'weaver'.

Wendell
Germanic, meaning 'wanderer'. It is found mainly in the US.

Wentworth
Adopted surname and English place name, from Old English *winter*, 'winter', and *word*, 'enclosure', a reference to settlements used only during the cold winter months. It is popular in Australia, probably after 'the Australian patriot', William Wentworth (1790-1872).

Wesley
Adopted surname, after John Wesley (1703-91), founder of the Methodist Church.

Weston
Adopted surname and English place name, from Old English *west*, 'west', and *tun*, 'settlement'. It was taken as a first name in the mid-20th century, particularly in the US.

Wilberforce
Adopted surname and English place name, from the Old English name Wilburg (source of Wilbur) and *fosse*, 'ditch'. Initially it was probably given in honour of William Wilberforce (1759-1833), the anti-slavery campaigner.

Wilbur
Adopted surname, from Old English *will*, 'desire', and *burh*, 'fortress'. It is most popular in the US.

Wilfred, Wilfrid
Old English, from *will*, 'deserve', and *frid*, 'peace'. The Northumbrian St Wilfrid (c. 634-709), educated at Lindisfarne and later bishop of York and of Hexham, was largely responsible for the adoption of the Roman liturgy at the Synod of Whitby (664). His feast day is 12th October. Diminutive: Wilf.

Will
Diminutive of William and other boy's names beginning Wil-.

Willard
Adopted surname, from *will*, 'deserve', and *heard*, 'hardy' or 'brave'.

William
Old French, of Germanic origin, from *will*, 'desir', and *helm*, 'helmet' or 'pro-

tection', and meaning 'desiring of protection'. Introduced to Britain by the Norman invader William the Conqueror, it was probably the first name to enjoy popularity on a massive scale; within a century of the Norman Conquest it was the most popular name in Britain. An indication of its popularity is that no less than four prominent saints of that name lived within the next hundred years: St William of Maleval was a French saint who died in Tuscany in 1157; St William of Montevergine was a 12th-century Italian hermit who died in 1142; St William of Norwich (1132-44) was supposedly crucified by the Jews; and St William of York, chaplain to King Stephen and Archbishop of York, died in 1154. The name was also borne by four kings of England. Diminutives: Bill, Billie, Billy, Will, Willie, Willy. Variations: Gwilim, Gwilym, Gwyllim, Liam, Uilleam, Uilliam.

Willoughby
Adopted surname and English place name, from Old English *welig*, 'willow', and Old Norse *byr*, 'settlement'.

Wilmer
Old English, from the Old German *will*, 'desire', and *mær*, 'famous'. Modern use is probably also as a masculine form of Wilma.

Windsor
Adopted surname from Old English name Windels-ora, meaning 'landing place with a winch'. Its use as a first name pre-dates its adoption by the British royal family by some 60 years.

Winston
Adopted surname and English place name, from the Old English name Wynn, and *tun*, 'settlement', meaning 'Wynn's place'. The British statesman Winston Spencer Churchill (1874-1965) was given his mother's maiden name, and most subsequent use of the name has been in honour of him. It is particularly popular in the West Indies.

Woodrow
Adopted surname and place name, meaning 'living in the row of houses by the wood'. It was initially given in honour of the 28th President of the US, Thomas Woodrow Wilson (1856-1924). Diminutive: Woody.

Woody
Diminutive of Woodrow, or possibly a nickname for a bearer of any surname beginning Wood-, such as Woodhead, Woodford or Woods.

Wyatt
Adopted surname, from Old English *wig*, 'war', and *heard*, 'hardy' or 'brave'.

Wyn, Wynne
Welsh, from *gwen*, 'fair, holy, blessed, white'. It is also a variation of Gwynne.

Wyndham
Adopted surname, a contracted form of the Norfolk town Wymondham.

Wystan
From the Old English name Wigstan, from *wig*, 'battle', and *stan*, 'stone'. It was the name of a 9th-century king of Mercia murdered in 849 by his nephew, Bertulf.

X

Xavier
After St Francis Xavier, a Spanish Jesuit missionary (1506-52). The name is especially popular in Roman Catholic families. Variation: Javier (Spanish).

Xerxes
Persian, meaning 'king'.

Y

Yasser
Arabic, meaning 'wealthy'. Variation: Yasir.

Yehudi
Hebrew, meaning 'Judah'.

Yorick
Variation of Jorck, a Danish form of George. Shakespeare used the name for the court jester in *Hamlet* (1601).

Yves
French variation of Ivo, possibly drawn from Old German *yv*, meaning 'yew'.

Z

Zacchaeus
Biblical, possibly of Aramaic origin; borne by a figure in the New Testament who climbed a sycamore tree to catch sight of Jesus (Luke 19).

Zachariah, Zacharias, Zachary
Greek, meaning 'God has remembered'. Biblical; Zachariah was an Old Testament king of Israel; Zacharias was the father of John the Baptist. Zachary is an anglicized vernacular form. Variations: Zecharia(h), Zecharias. Diminutives: Zac, Zack.

Zack
Diminutive of the several forms of Zachariah and Isaac. It is also used independently. Variation: Zac.

Zane
Adopted surname, of uncertain origin. It was brought to public attention by the American novelist Zane Grey (1875-1939), who was named after an ancestor, Ebenezer Zane, founder of Zanesville, Ohio.

Zebedee
Biblical; borne by the father of the apostles James and John. It was adapted from the Greek form of the Hebrew Old Testatment name Zebadiah, meaning 'gift of Jehovah'.

Zebulun
Hebrew, from *zabal*, 'to dwell'. Biblical; borne by the sixth son of Jacob and Leah. Leah chose the name in the belief that Jacob would certainly stay with her and their six sons. Variation: Zebulon.

Zechariah
Hebrew form of the Greek New Testament name Zachariah. Variations: Zachariah, Zacharias, Zachary.

Zedekiah
Hebrew, meaning 'God is righteous'. In the Old Testament it was the name of the last king of Judah. Diminutive: Zed.

Zeke
Diminutive of Ezekiel.

Zephaniah

Hebrew, meaning 'hidden by God'. Biblical; borne by a minor Old Testament prophet. Diminutive: Zeph.

Zowie Bowie

Name for son of David Bowie (singer) and former wife, Angela.

BIBLIOGRAPHY

Brown, Lesley
The New Shorter Oxford English Dictionary
Oxford University Press, 1993

Cresswell, Julia
Bloomsbury Dictionary of First Names
Bloomsbury, London, 1992

Cross. F L and Livingstone E A, ed
Oxford Dictionary of the Christian Church
Oxford University Press, 1997

Drabble, Margaret, ed
Oxford Companion to English Literature
Oxford University Press, 1985

Dunkling, Leslie
First names first
J M Dent & Sons Ltd, London, 1977

Fergusson, Rosalind
Choose Your Baby's Name
Penguin, London, 1987

Glennon, James
4001 Babies' Names and their meanings
Robert Hale, London,1968

Hall, James
Dictionary of Subjects and Symbols in Art
John Murray, 1992

Hanks, Patrick and Flavia Hodges
A Concise Dictionary of First Names
Oxford University Press, Oxford, 1997

Harewood, The Earl of and Antony Peatti
The New Kobbé's Opera Book
Ebury Press, 1997

HMSO, First names
HMSO, 1995

Holy Bible
Cambridge University Press

Jameson, Mrs
Sacred and Legendary Art
Longmans & Co, 1900

Macleod, Iseabail and Terry Freedman
The Wordsworth Dictionary of First Names
Wordsworth Editions Limted, London, 1995

Room, Adrian
Brewer's Names
Cassell, London, 1992

Room, Adrian, ed
Brewer's Dictionary of Phrase and Fable
Cassell, 1997

Strong, James
Strong's Concordance of the Bible
Thomas Nelson, 1980

Withycombe, E G
Oxford Dictionary of English Christian Names
Oxford University Press, Oxford, 1977